Understanding MS-DOS®

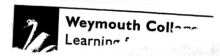
Weymouth Coll___
Learning ___

Written by: Kate O'Day

Revised by: John Angermeyer

HOWARD W. SAMS & COMPANY

A Division of Macmillan, Inc.
4300 West 62nd Street
Indianapolis, Indiana 46268 USA

Dedication:

To Seamus Matthew Mercer Hursh—who, waiting patiently for his trip to
the beach or to see the latest movie, has no choice but to be part of the
"computer generation." This book is for you!

FIRST EDITION
FOURTH PRINTING — 1988

International Standard Book Number: 0-672-27067-6
Library of Congress Catalog Card Number: 86-82255

Acquisitions Editor: James S. Hill
Editor: Madelaine Cooke
Waite Group Editor: James Stockford
Cartoonist: Bob Johnson
Illustrator: T. R. Emrick
Production Art: Creative Design Services
Cover Art: Diebold Glascock Advertising, Inc.
Photography: Cassell Productions, Inc.
Components: Courtesy of CPT of Indianapolis,
              and Muncie Business Machines
Compositor: Shepard Poorman Communications Corp.

Acknowledgments:
Kim House started me off on the right path and helped develop the concept for this
revision. Special thanks to Mary Johnson, not only for her sensitive editing but also
for her patience and understanding throughout the writing of this book. Finally, my
thanks to Bob Johnson for his cartoons, which help illustrate that learning computer
concepts can be entertaining.

Printed in the United States of America

All terms mentioned in this book that are known to be trademarks or service marks
are listed below. In addition, terms suspected of being trademarks or service marks
have been appropriately capitalized. Howard W. Sams & Co. cannot attest to the
accuracy of this information. Use of a term in this book should not be regarded as
affecting the validity of any trademark or service mark.

EasyWriter is a registered trademark of Computer Associates International, Inc.
Framework is a trademark of Ashton-Tate.
LOTUS 1-2-3 is a trademark of Lotus Development Corporation.
MS-DOS is a registered trademark of Microsoft Corporation.
WordStar is a registered trademark of Micropro International Corporation.

Table of Contents

Preface

MS-DOS is the powerful disk operating system developed by Microsoft for use in today's microcomputers. It provides the instructions that enable microcomputers to manipulate files, handle interactions between the computer and the user, and manage peripherals.

This book is different from many books on MS-DOS and other operating systems in several ways. First, you don't need a computer background to read it. Second, it is written with the belief that computer concepts don't have to be complicated or boring. Third, when you have finished this book, you will find that in addition to having had fun reading it and working the examples, you will have learned how to utilize the power of MS-DOS.

Understanding MS-DOS begins with a description of what a computer is and why it needs an operating system. You then learn how to start your system, how to handle diskettes, and how to get information into and out of your system. You are shown how to maximize the editing capabilities of MS-DOS's line editor, EDLIN, and how to shape up your files. Then you move into high gear and learn about the power of the keyboard—function keys and keystroke combinations that can make everyday tasks easier. In a clear and entertaining style, ways are shown to develop routines so that repetitive tasks are automated. The real power of MS-DOS is revealed in the tree-structured directories and pathnames of Version 2.0 (and higher) and in the advanced features of redirection, piping, and filtering. For the hard-disk user, the BACKUP and RESTORE commands are explained clearly and concisely. An appendix explains the most common error messages in MS-DOS and possible solutions.

Like other books in this series, this book builds understanding through the subject in a step-by-step manner. Knowledge and confidence are gained as each subject is completed. A quiz is included at the end of each chapter for self-evaluation of what has been learned. Answers to the questions are found in the back of the book.

J.A.

Introducing MS-DOS

ABOUT THIS CHAPTER

In this chapter, we will explore how this book will help you discover the power of MS-DOS. We will also take a look at the parts of your computer system, both inside and out, and get you started on the road to building a computer vocabulary.

WHAT'S IT ALL ABOUT?

MS-DOS is one of the most popular operating systems available for microcomputers.

This book is about using your computer system. It is especially for new computer owners. To read, use, and enjoy *Understanding MS-DOS* you don't have to know a thing about MS-DOS, operating systems, or computer terminology. The only thing you need to know right now is that MS-DOS is the operating system that comes with your computer.

There are several implementations of MS-DOS; the IBM PC is one of them. The differences between the implementations, however, are slight.

This book is particularly about MS-DOS, one of the most popular operating systems used in microcomputers today. It is available for a wide variety of computers, from self-contained portables to the many IBM PC compatibles. The IBM PC itself uses a special version of MS-DOS.

Understanding MS-DOS employs a well-known educational technique—"learning by doing." Computer folks have translated this into the "hands-on" approach. Whichever term you prefer, this book is not only descriptive, it presents examples and exercises for each part of MS-DOS. You will get your "hands wet" typing information into the computer and seeing the results of your labor. These projects are designed to help you understand the information being discussed.

WHAT'S AHEAD?

If this is your first experience with computers, the layout of this book is for you. Just start with this chapter and don't look back. In this chapter, you will get an introduction to computer systems. Then in Chapter 2, "Your Operating System," you will gain some knowledge about operating systems in general. You will begin using your operating system in Chapter 3, "Getting Started with MS-DOS." If you are already familiar with the components of a computer system and understand what an operating system is and does, you can go directly to Chapter 3.

Chapter 4, "System Insurance," shows you how to protect your investment in MS-DOS by explaining how to care for and make copies of your diskettes. Chapter 5, "EDLIN," explains the operation of the EDLIN line-editing program that comes with MS-DOS. With this program you can write letters, memos, and other long documents and make changes and corrections as you go along. All of the EDLIN commands are explained here for you. Chapter 6, "Getting the Files in Shape," expands your understanding of MS-DOS by leading you step-by-step through file creation, naming, and command use. You will learn how to look at a file, to copy a file, to rename files, and to erase files. In Chapter 7, "Special Keys and Key Combinations," the power of the keyboard and function keys is described. You will learn techniques to speed up entering and changing data and how certain key combinations can enhance your use of your system. In Chapter 8, "Batch Processing," you will learn what batch files are and how they can make your job easier. You will see how to program your system to perform many functions automatically. After you learn all the interesting things that your MS-DOS–equipped system can do for you, Chapter 9, "Tree-Structured Directories," will show you how to organize your information files into easy-to-use directories, as well as show you how to rapidly access the data that you have so carefully arranged. For those of you without hard-disk-drive systems, Chapter 10, "Data Management Commands," will bring you to the end of your studies. You will learn how to make your system direct, sort, and find data and files in such a way that you will wonder why you waited so long to acquire your computer. Chapter 11, "For Hard-Disk Users," will be of interest to non-hard-disk users as well because it explains the advantages and disadvantages of both types of systems (floppy and hard disk). It also shows the hard-disk user how to perform two critical hard-disk operations: backing up and restoring information on the disk system. By moving through the chapters, you will gradually build on your growing knowledge of MS-DOS. The chapters are best read in order. Of course, once you have finished this book, it will be a valuable reference tool.

What You Need to Use This Book

To learn about MS-DOS you'll need a personal computer equipped with one of several versions of MS-DOS.

To use this book you need a personal computer equipped with a keyboard, monitor, and the MS-DOS operating system. You also need at least one disk drive (two are preferable). Much of the material presented is applicable to MS-DOS Versions 1.0 and 1.1. However, *Understanding MS-DOS* is aimed principally at users of MS-DOS Version 2.0 or higher. If you have MS-DOS Version 3.0, this book provides information on fundamentals that you need to make full use of your system.

If you have the above equipment, an MS-DOS diskette, and a willing mind, you're ready to begin.

WHAT IS A COMPUTER SYSTEM?

Microcomputer systems can range from single, self-contained units such as portables to desktop machines with several external components attached.

A microcomputer system can range from a small portable machine that you can store under an airplane seat to a desktop machine with fancy graphics capabilities and three printers. Most likely, your machine falls somewhere in between. MS-DOS is available for almost all of these machines and many more that fall inside the broad definition of "computer system."

Check your computer or component manuals for specific information on names, displays, keys, or messages

This book will help make your learning experience more enjoyable. But you may sometimes be confused when our discussion or illustrations do not match your specific computer layout, as shown in *Figure 1-1*. Because MS-DOS is available for many types of computers, our discussion will deal with general definitions and components of computer systems, and generic elements of MS-DOS. If at times you are confused about specific names, displays, keys, or messages, check the manual that the manufacturer packages with your system.

Figure 1-1.
Hardware and Software

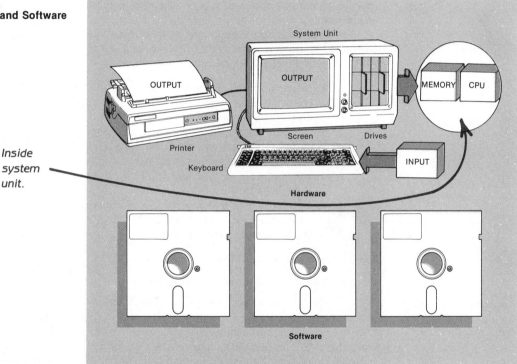

The hardware includes the main system unit, keyboard, disk drives, monitor, and other optional equipment called peripherals.

Your computer system is made up of many different components, as shown in *Figure 1-1*. The machine parts are called hardware. This includes your keyboard, disk drives, and monitor. You can connect peripherals (additional hardware) to your machine through specialized ports, or connectors (the places where they plug into your machine). One typical peripheral is a printer.

The part of your computer system that makes this hardware perform is called *software*—the programs that control the operation of your machine. You are already acquainted somewhat with one type of software, your MS-DOS operating system. Other types of software include application programs (e.g., word processors, games, accounting packages) and utility programs (e.g., sorting programs and printing routines). Software also includes programming languages, such as BASIC, and assembly language programs that communicate directly with your computer in the machine's native language.

HARDWARE

MS-DOS is used to control how the computer does its work.

One of the advantages of MS-DOS is the ability of many machines to operate with this system. This simply means that MS-DOS is the operating system that controls how the computer performs its work. Many types of computer systems run MS-DOS; this allows you to choose the specific system you want and still use the most popular operating system on the market.

Your computer system may be an on-the-plane portable or a specialized workstation that is part of a large office networking system. Still, every system has several common features:

- Information that is fed into the computer is called input. Most often this input comes from you. You will use a keyboard to type in your entries.
- The information that comes from the computer to you is called output. Messages and results are displayed on a monitor, or screen.
- When the computer is not actually using some information, the information is put into storage. Computers use floppy diskettes or hard disks to store data.
- Inside every microcomputer is a microprocessor chip. This chip is what makes your computer do the things it does so well. Also inside the machine is some memory.

Let's explore the inside of the machine first.

Central Processing Unit (Microprocessor)

Computers containing a microprocessor chip are called microcomputers.

The "brain" of your computer is contained in the central processing unit (CPU). CPUs vary in size, speed, and the amount of work they are capable of performing. The CPU is the workhorse of your computer. MS-DOS makes the most of the common CPUs used in today's personal computers. But the design and technology of CPUs is growing at a rapid rate and, as more and better CPUs are developed, there will be enhanced versions of MS-DOS to take advantage of the latest advances in technology.

Memory

Computers have two types of memory: random-access memory (RAM) and read-only memory (ROM).

The computer has two types of memory (depicted in *Figure 1-2*), each with very specific characteristics.

Random-Access Memory

Random-Access Memory (RAM) is memory that is used by the computer to hold the information it is currently working on. Information in RAM changes as you edit and enter data. It is very important to remember that RAM is transient: things stored in RAM are only temporary; when you turn off the machine, RAM is wiped clean.

You must transfer any data or programs in RAM to storage (on a diskette or hard disk) before you turn off your machine. Application programs, which come on their own diskettes, or information that you do not alter and already have on a diskette do not need to be returned to storage at the end of a working session.

**Figure 1-2.
ROM and RAM**

Instruction to machine. Always available when machine is on.

Stores files you are using. Contents must be stored to be saved.

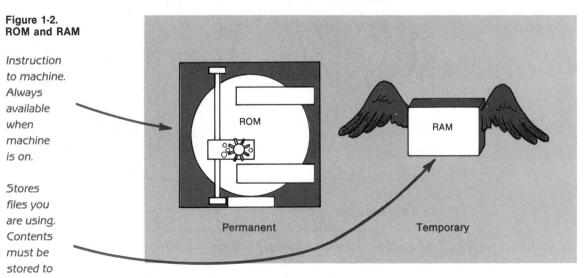

Read-Only Memory

Read-Only Memory (ROM) is permanent. It is actually contained in hardware on your CPU. ROM contents are determined by your computer manufacturer.

Measurement

The amount of memory in your computer is measured in bytes. Each byte contains 8 bits. A byte can be thought of as one character. As text is entered on a word processor, it takes 6 bytes to store "MS-DOS" (actually 8, if you count the quotation marks).

Computer memory is often described in terms of K, as in "I know where I can get some additional K real cheap!" K is shorthand for "kilobytes," which means 1024 bytes. You may have seen the claim "expandable to 640K." This means the total computer memory of that system would be 640 × 1024, or 655,360 bytes.

The relationship between bits, bytes, and K is shown in *Figure 1-3*.

Computer memory is usually measured in bytes (8 bits) or kilobytes (1024 bytes). For example, 640K of memory actually means 655,360 bytes (640 × 1024) or 5,242,880 bits (640 × 1024 × 8).

**Figure 1-3.
Bits, Bytes, and K**

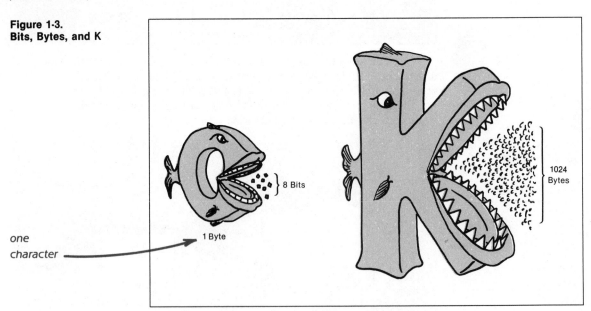

Storage Devices

The two most common storage devices used to store information in a permanent manner are floppy-diskette drives and hard-disk drives.

Many computer systems use disk drives to read and write information to storage. There are two kinds of drives, floppy-diskette drives and hard-disk drives.

Floppy diskettes are small magnetic disks that are coated to contain information. You insert these diskettes into disk drives. Your system may have one, two, or several disk drives. Although many types of computers use the same size diskettes, you may not (generally) interchange diskettes between different types of machines. This is because computers place information on diskettes in various ways.

Hard-disk drives can be built into your machine, or they can be peripherals. The hard disk inside one of these drives is not removable. The advantages of hard disks are that they can store much more information than floppy disks and they are faster than floppies. However, they are also more expensive. The various kinds of disk drives and disks are shown in *Figure 1-4.*

**Figure 1-4.
Storage Devices**

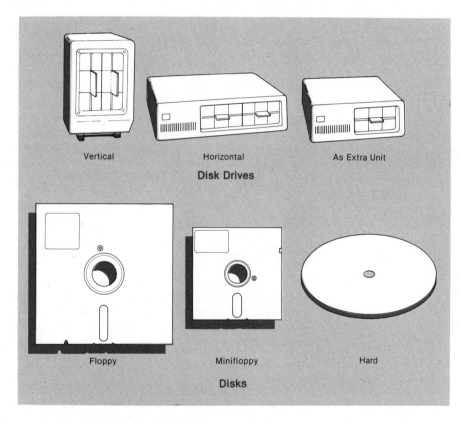

Vertical   Horizontal   As Extra Unit

Disk Drives

Floppy   Minifloppy   Hard

Disks

Storage disks are used together with your system's RAM. As the computer requires information, it reads it from the disk, stores it in the RAM, and manipulates it as necessary. When instructed to, the computer copies information from RAM and stores it on the disk.

As mentioned earlier, disks store programs and data that you are not actively using. Information is read from the disk into the computer's RAM (temporary memory). As you need more information, the drive retrieves it from your diskette. When you are finished working, the information is sent to the diskette for storage.

Your understanding of these few terms that apply to software may clear up the confusion you experience whenever you venture inside your friendly computer store. Knowledge of these terms will boost your computer confidence considerably.

SOFTWARE

Software is another name for "computer programs." According to
buying experts, when you choose a computer system, you should first find
the software you want and then buy the computer to fit the software's
specifications. That's how important the software is in a computer system.
Although you want convenience and ease of use in the system hardware, if
the software does not do what you want, you really have nothing but an
easy-to-use white elephant. The interaction of software with your computer
hardware is depicted in *Figure 1-5.*

**Figure 1-5.
Software**

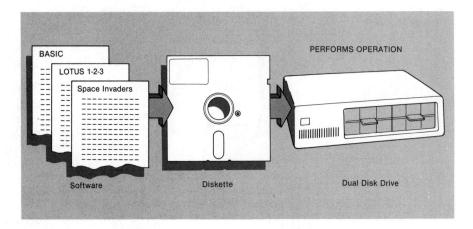

Application Programs

A program that does something for you is an application program.
Some of the most common types of application programs are word
processors (e.g., WordStar or EasyWriter) and *integrated* (multiple use)
packages (e.g., Lotus 1-2-3 or Framework). Games are also considered
application programs.

Programming Languages

Another type of software lets you write instructions, in the form
of programs, for your computer. This software is known as a programming
language. You use languages to design your own application programs.
Your computer probably uses the BASIC programming language. BASIC
may be contained inside ROM, or you may have it on your operating-
system diskette. Other programming languages include Pascal, Logo, and
COBOL.

Operating Systems

Your operating system is a type of specialized software. The
operating system manages all the disk input and output operations of your
computer. You are an important part of the input and output system
because you are the originator and receiver of this input and output. How

well you, the information, and the machine all work together is the secret of an effective operating system. In Chapter 2 you will learn about your operating system.

SUMMARY

This first chapter has served several purposes. For those of you unfamiliar with computers, it defined some useful computer terms: hardware, software, memory, storage, input, and output. Along the way it introduced most of the parts of your computer system that are used in the operation of MS-DOS.

WHAT HAVE WE LEARNED?

1. Your microcomputer system is composed of hardware and software.
2. The brain of your microcomputer is the central processing unit (CPU).
3. Random-Access Memory (RAM) is a temporary storage place to hold data that the CPU is currently working on. Be sure to transfer data from RAM to a storage device, such as a floppy diskette or hard disk, before you turn off the system.
4. Read-Only Memory (ROM) is permanently contained in the hardware; its contents are determined by the manufacturer.
5. Floppy-disk drives are built to read and write on removable diskettes coated with magnetic material. Each type of computer writes data on floppy diskettes in its own characteristic way.
6. Hard-disk drives contain built-in disks; they are faster, hold more information, and are more expensive than floppy drives.
7. Application programs are those that let you do a useful, specific kind of work.
8. Programming languages let you write programs of instructions for your computer.
9. Operating systems help your computer system manage the input and output of the data.

Quiz for Chapter 1

1. MS-DOS is:
   a. a microcomputer operating system.
   b. a minicomputer operating system.
   c. a mainframe operating system.
   d. an operating system for any computer.

2. MS-DOS's popularity is due to:
   a. its capabilities.
   b. its availability for a wide variety of computer systems.
   c. the large number of application software programs compatible with it.
   d. all of the above.

3. The most basic and important parts of a computer are:
   a. the keyboard and screen.
   b. the hardware and software.
   c. any of the above.
   d. none of the above.

4. Almost all microcomputers consist of a:
   a. system unit.
   b. keyboard.
   c. screen, or monitor.
   d. floppy-diskette drive.
   e. all of the above.

5. Input to your computer is accomplished by using the:
   a. screen.
   b. keyboard.
   c. memory.
   d. carrying handle.

6. Output from your computer can be seen on the:
   a. screen, or monitor.
   b. printer.
   c. either of the above.
   d. none of the above.

7. The central processing unit (CPU), or microprocessor, is:
   a. the "brain" of the computer.
   b. a type of memory.
   c. a type of disk drive.
   d. none of the above.

8. The types of memory almost all microcomputers contain are:
   a. random-access memory (RAM).
   b. read-only memory (ROM).
   c. both of the above.
   d. none of the above.

9. Your computer's random-access memory (RAM) is used for:
   a. temporarily holding information that is currently being worked on by the computer.
   b. permanently storing information.
   c. discarding unwanted information.
   d. storing only random numbers.

10. When your computer's power is turned off, information stored in RAM will:
    a. always remain intact.
    b. remain intact for a predetermined period of time.
    d. immediately be erased.

11. Your computer's read only memory (ROM) is used to contain:
    a. permanent information.
    b. manufacturer-specific software.
    c. software that can only be read.
    d. all of the above.

12. Computer memory is usually measured in:
    a. bits.
    b. bytes.
    c. kilobytes (1024 bytes).

d. either a or b.

e. either b or c.

f. either a, b, or c.

g. none of the above.

13. A byte equals:

    a. 8 bits.

    b. 16 bits.

    c. 1 character (sometimes).

    d. 1 character (always).

    e. a and c

    f. b and d

    g. none of the above.

14. A kilobyte, also referred to as K, always equals:

    a. 1000 bytes.

    b. 1024 bytes.

    c. 1500 bytes

    d. none of the above.

15. Storage devices usually used in microcomputers are:

    a. floppy diskette drives.

    b. hard-disk drives.

    c. compact cassette tape recorders.

    d. card punches.

    e. paper punches.

16. Disk-storage devices can be:

    a. part of the system unit.

    b. a peripheral to the system unit.

    c. removable or fixed.

    d. any of the above.

17. Floppy diskettes cannot always be interchanged between different computers because:

    a. computers put information on disks in various ways.

    b. not all computers use the same size diskettes.

    c. they are not easily removable.

    d. they are too fragile.

18. Examples of application software are:

    a. word-processing programs.

    b. data management, or integrated, programs.

    c. game programs.

    d. all of the above.

Your Operating System

ABOUT THIS CHAPTER

This chapter explains what an operating system is, what it does for the computer, and what it can do for you. It also takes a brief look at the evolution of operating systems, the history of MS-DOS, and the unique position of MS-DOS in the operating system world of today.

WHAT IS AN OPERATING SYSTEM?

When you first encountered the term "operating system", it was probably in the small print of an advertisement or part of an eager salesperson's technobabble. Among all those other incomprehensible terms, such as RAM, ROM, modem expandability, peripherals, RS232, and CPU, its significance may have escaped you. But operating system is not a complex or confusing concept. Let's start with definitions from the *Random House Dictionary of the English Language:*

Operate (1) to work or perform a function, like a machine does; (2) to work or use a machine.

That's clear. Operate has to do with performing machine-like actions.

System (1) A complex or unitary whole; (2) a coordinated body of methods or a complex scheme or plan of procedure.

MS-DOS, like other operating systems, runs the computer by organizing information going into and coming out of the computer.

So, an operating system is a coordinated body of methods or a plan of procedure for controlling machines. MS-DOS, the operating system in your computer, organizes the information that goes into and comes out of the machine, and it controls how the parts of your computer system interact. The operating system runs the computer.

WHAT DOES AN OPERATING SYSTEM DO?

As you read in Chapter 1, a computer system is a collection of hardware—the machine parts—and software—the instructions that tell the computer how to perform the actual computing operations.

The computer's software, particularly the operating system, gives instructions to the computer about what to do, when to do it, and with what data.

You use the hardware, such as they keyboard, disk drives, monitor, and printer, to coordinate data. Hardware provides the tools to type in data, feed data to or from a diskette, receive data from other machines, or copy it to the printer.

Software, usually in the form of programs, gives instructions to the computer. Software tells the computer what to do, at what time, and with what data. Without software, the hardware is useless.

The main function of the operating system is to manage the information you enter into, store in, and retrieve from your computer. The scope of this management chore is shown in *Figure 2-1*.

**Figure 2-1.
Managing Files: DOS's
Main Job**

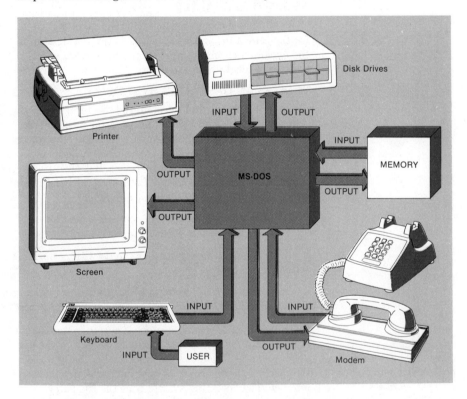

In the course of its work, the operating system is an interface between you, who understand what you would like to happen to the data you type in, and the mechanics of the computer, which demand that instructions be in a form that can be understood. Let's see how MS-DOS responds to this challenge.

Information Management

MS-DOS's major responsibility is to act as the master program for keeping all incoming and outgoing information in order. This task is accomplished by storing information in files.

The major responsibility of the operating system is to keep all the incoming and outgoing information in order. MS-DOS accomplishes this task by storing information in files. Computer files are no different from paper files; both hold a collection of related data. You give each file a name, and the operating system does the rest, storing the file where it can find it quickly, updating the file when you enter new information, and eliminating the file when you don't want it anymore. Computers may not be terribly interesting to converse with, but they are very good file clerks.

Let's compare this idea of a master program to something equally complex in everyday life. Suppose that instead of speaking of a DOS (DOS is an acronym for disk operating system), we were speaking of an ATC (air traffic controller). This ATC is in charge of all operations at a major international airport.

The controller is responsible for coordinating the overall traffic flow and is constantly aware of which planes are coming in, on which runways they'll land, their speed, and their arrival gates. An ATC must be sure those runways and gates have been cleared for landing, must know the relative position of each plane waiting to take off and which flight paths they will follow as they ascend, and must often make quick decisions so that all planes arrive and depart on schedule.

Listening to the conversation in a control tower can be confusing. You know that the instructions being passed back and forth are in English, but it's hard to believe these people are conversing sensibly. It might sound something like this:

> *"United 9er9er 7 heavy, clear for take-off on 2-1-left. You're number 3 behind the company."*

You can't really understand it, but obviously it's working.

The operating system is like an air traffic controller in the way it controls the system: it organizes, schedules, and updates information.

The operating system is like that controller. It monitors all the incoming and outgoing activity of your computer system. Just as the controller is in constant contact with the position of every plane in the air or on the ground, the operating system knows the location and size of all the files currently in its memory or stored on its current disk. And like the controller, the operating system constantly updates all of its information according to changing conditions.

The controller's job is to make sure that each plane scheduled to come into the airport does indeed arrive and that each plane scheduled to take off does. Again, the operating system does much the same thing for your computer programs and data files. It loads them, makes sure they start executing, and when one is finished, the DOS makes room for the next.

This kind of organizational control is a handy helper to have, whether you are navigating the skies over Chicago or attempting to get your accounting software to run. But just as the Wright Brothers had to struggle along on their own, so too did early computer operators. Operating systems are a fairly recent innovation in computer operation. Let's see how operating systems came to be.

HOW DID OPERATING SYSTEMS EVOLVE?

The earliest commercially available computers were huge yet simple-minded machines. You put your instructions on punch cards (all the cards in one group usually made up a program) and handed them to the computer operator. When it was time for your program to run, the first instruction "woke up" the computer. After the operator fiddled with some switches and controls, the computer started, read your instruction, executed your program, and then stopped. The operator would then clear the machine and prepare for the next program. Early computers could run only one program at a time. To them only the program in the computer at that time existed. The computer spent a great deal of time sitting idle, waiting for the operator to load another set of cards.

Many people in the small but quickly growing computer industry sensed the waste of all this "down time." They began to see the advantage of some type of standardized start-up procedure for the computer. If the instructions to run each program were the same, then several programs could be run in quick succession. What they needed was to take out the human's job and make the computer run itself. This was the birth of the idea of an operating system.

Monitor Programs

One of the earliest reported operating systems was devised in 1953 by IBM engineers and called a monitor program.

According to popular reports, the first mention of a computer operating system took place at the 1953 Eastern Joint Computer Conference. Sitting around in a hotel room, some IBM programmers came up with the concept of a monitor program. It was the first development of a program designed simply to "run the machine." The monitor program kept track of a number of jobs, or programs. When a job was completed, control returned to the monitor program, which then started up the next job.

Operating systems (expanded monitor programs) for mainframe computers became a reality, but this standardization was limited to its particular machine. This was fine for a while because there weren't very many computers, and the programs written were designed to run one specific type of computer. Shrinking in size, while gaining in power and ease of use, computers quickly became a vital part of business and government. With this growth came the need for increased standardization. No longer could a program be designed for one machine, not when the market was there to sell many copies to other users.

Common Operating Systems

One of the first home computers, called the AL-TAIR, appeared in 1975.

In 1975, the first home computer, named the ALTAIR, appeared on the cover of *Popular Electronics*. Manufactured by a company called MITS, this computer kit, designed for hobbyists, retailed for $397.00 and could be built (with sufficient technical knowledge) in your garage. Computer had come to the masses. Visionaries began to see a time when computers would be in every classroom and in every home. These computers would need to be easy to use. They would need to run many kinds of programs. They would need a standardized way to handle the information stored in their files. They would need, in short, a common operating system.

HISTORY OF MS-DOS

MS-DOS was originally called 86-DOS and was designed by Seattle Computer Products. In 1981, Microsoft Corporation purchased the rights to 86-DOS and renamed it MS-DOS.

One of those who was impressed by the possibilities of the ALTAIR computer was William Gates. In 1975, Gates was studying at Harvard. Gates and his friend Paul Allen had been working with computers since they were in seventh grade. But the introduction of the new, small ALTAIR really stirred their imaginations. They knew that hobbyist computers would need a simple, reliable programming language, so they adapted the widely used BASIC language to this new type of smaller machine. After convincing MITS that their adapted BASIC was up and running, Gates and Allen spent four frantic weeks writing a simulated program on an available mainframe computer. Incredibly, the language they devised worked on its first try. Today that BASIC is the standard programming language on millions of personal computers.

Microsoft

The success of their BASIC sent Gates and Allen into the computer business in earnest. Always aware of the escalating importance of standardization, they developed and sold several adaptations of programming languages. The company they formed was called Microsoft.

The first version of MS-DOS was released in 1982 for the IBM Personal Computer. Several versions of MS-DOS have been released since then.

In July 1981, Microsoft purchased the rights to 86-DOS, an operating system developed by Seattle Computer Products. In secret they began working with IBM, developing this system to be used as the PC-DOS operating system for IBM's personal computer (the IBM PC).

Microsoft released its version of the operating system (MS-DOS) to the general public in March 1982. In February 1983, an enhanced version of MS-DOS, Version 2.0, appeared. This is probably the version of MS-DOS that you have on your computer.

WHAT MS-DOS MEANS TO YOU

Every computer needs an operating system. But the fact that your computer uses the MS-DOS operating system brings you some extra advantages.

MS-DOS provides some clear advantages to microcomputer users today: a wide variety of commands, its availability for many different computers, and the availability of a great amount of compatible application software.

Because the operating system is the interface between you and your computer's operation, you want it to be easy to use. MS-DOS more than fills this bill. It is relatively clearly written and simple to learn. Most of the operations you want to accomplish can be performed with a few, easy-to-understand commands. Yet MS-DOS also incorporates some sophisticated and complex functions in its structure. As your computer knowledge grows, so will your appreciation of MS-DOS's capabilities.

One of the biggest advantages of MS-DOS is its popularity. Because MS-DOS is the chosen operating system of so many personal computer manufacturers, software programmers have responded with a deluge of application programs. This means you can usually find the programs you want, and they will work with no modifications on your machine.

SUMMARY

This chapter discussed the concept of an operating system. It told you that MS-DOS manages files to keep track of the information put into the computer. It also discussed the development of operating systems from their first use on mainframe computers to their use on the personal computers of today. Finally, it traced the growth of MS-DOS from a vision of Gates and Allen to its current popularity in the operating-systems market.

WHAT HAVE WE LEARNED?

1. The MS-DOS operating system manages the way in which you enter, retrieve, and store information as files within the computer system.
2. DOS is an acronym for Disk Operating System.
3. The first operating systems were standardized start-up programs for mainframe computers.

Quiz for Chapter 2

1. An operating system can be compared to the function of:
   a. an air-traffic controller.
   b. a circuit controller.
   c. a program controller.
   d. a file controller.
   e. any of the above.

2. Software is:
   a. a collection of instructions that tell a computer how to perform certain computing operations.
   b. soft and pliable if manipulated by a computer.
   c. an indispensable part of a computer.
   d. all of the above.

3. The main function of an operating system is to:
   a. manage all information that is input, stored, and output.
   b. take absolute control over the system on its own.
   c. show you how to operate the system.
   d. determine what information should be input and output.

4. MS-DOS maintains the order of incoming and outgoing information by using:
   a. special scale software.
   b. files.
   c. manual control.
   d. folders.

5. In the world of computers, DOS is used as an acronym for:
   a. disk optimizing software.
   b. density optically sensed.
   c. disk operating system.
   d. none of the above.

6. Because early computers didn't have operating systems, they had their information input and processed:
   a. one job at a time, manually.
   b. many jobs at a time, manually.
   c. one job at a time, automatically.
   d. many jobs at a time, automatically.

7. One of the first operating systems to be used was devised by IBM in 1953 and was called a program monitor. It gave computers the ability to input and process information:
   a. one job at a time, manually.
   b. many jobs at a time, manually.
   c. one job at a time, automatically.
   d. many jobs at a time, automatically.

8. In 1975, one of the first recognized home computers was introduced by a company called MITS and was called the:
   a. ALTAIR.
   b. IBM Personal Computer.
   c. Mark 1.
   d. PDP-8.

9. MS-DOS was originally called 86-DOS and was developed by:
   a. Seattle Computer Products.
   b. Microsoft Corporation.
   c. IBM Corporation.
   d. MITS.

10. After the rights to it were acquired in 1981 by Microsoft Corporation, the first version of MS-DOS was released for operation with the:
   a. IBM Personal Computer.
   b. ALTAIR.
   c. Apple II.
   d. IMSAI I-8080.

11. Some of the advantages of using MS-DOS include:
   a. a user interface with easy-to-use commands.
   b. its adoption for use by many computer manufacturers.
   c. the availability of a great amount of compatible application software.
   d. all of the above.

Getting Started with MS-DOS

ABOUT THIS CHAPTER

Using MS-DOS is very simple. In this chapter you will learn how to "boot" your system, how to activate the built-in calendar and clock, and how to get the computer to respond to MS-DOS commands. Two commands are introduced in this chapter, the DIR (directory) command and the CLS (clear the screen) command. (The CLS command isn't available on MS-DOS Versions 1.0 and 1.1).

BEFORE YOU BEGIN

Now that you are familiar with the basic facts about computer systems and you know that MS-DOS helps operate your system, it's time to begin computing. You probably agree that this sounds like a good plan, but you may have no idea about how to begin. Well, just as a pilot approaches take-off in a logical step-by-step fashion, you too are going to follow a simple "pre-flight" routine.

First, make sure that your machine is properly set up and ready to go (your user's manual will give you all the necessary instructions). Second, sit down at the controls, and try not to be intimidated by the intricacies of being in command of your computer.

BOOTING THE SYSTEM

The first step in getting MS-DOS off the ground is booting, or loading, the system. After the computer is powered up, or reset, it receives instructions from the "bootstrap loader" program stored in ROM on how to boot MS-DOS and reads the diskette in drive A for further instructions.

To begin using your computer, you must boot the system. This does not mean you deliver a sharp kick to the backside of the machine! The term is derived from "pulling oneself up by the bootstraps." In computereze, "booting" means getting the machine ready to accept your instructions.

This sounds very simple, but logically it creates a Catch-22 situation. How can the machine start, if the instructions it needs to begin are located inside the machine (which you can't get to until the machine starts)?

This problem is solved by a handy little program called, you guessed it, the "bootstrap loader." This small program located in ROM (that's the part of memory that is permanent) is the first thing the computer reads when the power is turned on. The bootstrap contains one simple directive—"start reading the instructions on the diskette in drive A." That's all MS-DOS needs to be up and running.

Right now you are looking at a blank screen. Let's put a little life into it.

Be sure you have handy the user's guide supplied by your manufacturer. Because not everyone has the same system, there may be slight differences in the wording or order of the messages which appear on the screen and the wording used in this book. If things seem inconsistent to you, just consult your user's guide.

The Operating-System Diskette

To begin the booting up process, locate your operating-system diskette. This will be labeled MS-DOS or some other variant of a DOS name. Because this diskette contains your operating system, it is the key to your computer's operation.

Next insert the diskette into disk drive A. If you have a question about how to insert the diskette or which drive is A, consult your user's guide. Every computer sage can recount a favorite story of trying for hours to get something to work, using all kinds of procedures, only to discover that the diskette was in wrong or was hiding in the wrong drive. Be sure to close the drive door after inserting the diskette; you can't get any information from a diskette unless the door is closed.

The Power Switch

Now you're ready to fire up. But where's the on switch? This is another question for your user's guide, but the switch is probably on the side or back of your machine. Turn on the power and wait patiently.

To help you through the booting up process, a checklist is provided in *Figure 3-1.*

**Figure 3-1.
Booting Checklist**

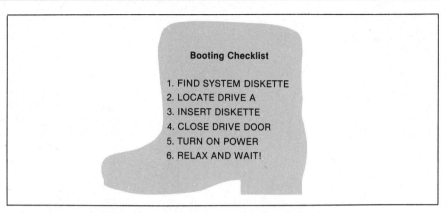

It takes a few seconds for the machine to wake up. Then, several things happen at once. You'll hear some whirring sounds as the cooling fan comes on, and you may be startled by a short electronic beep. Then a small line will start flashing on the screen. Good, this is the first sign of life. This line is the cursor, a small marker that indicates your place on the screen. Your cursor may or may not flash, and it may not be a line. More about the cursor in a moment.

You will also notice the drive's indicator light (usually red) flashing on and off. You can hear the drive moving when the light is on. All of this is quite normal. Your machine is just doing some self-checking and getting ready to receive instructions. (If none of the above occurs after a minute or two, check to be sure the machine is plugged in.)

When the activity stops, there will be a message on your screen.

Current date is Tues 1-01-1980 (The date may be different.)
Enter new date: _____

Notice that the cursor is now after the word "date." The cursor indicates the spot where the next incoming piece of information will appear on the screen. In this case, it means that when you type in a new date, it will be placed directly after the colon.

ENTERING DATA INTO THE MACHINE

The computer is waiting for some information. You will use the keyboard to enter data into the computer. Sometimes your entry is in response to a request such as the "enter new date" statement. Sometimes *you* initiate the interaction with a request of your own.

Understanding Instructions

At first, figuring out what information to enter and how and when to enter the information may seem mysterious. But there is no secret to deciphering the instructions in this book because *Table 3-1* is your official code breaker.

Table 3-1.
The Symbols Used in
This Book

Symbol	Meaning
A>Format another? [Y/N]	Information within the screen in black is supplied by the computer.
A>format b:	Information within the screen in color is supplied by you. When you type your entries be sure to include all punctuation and leave blank spaces where indicated.
< >	These brackets indicate a key on the keyboard (other than the letter or number keys).
<ENTER>	The <ENTER> key is your signal that you have finished typing in an entry. You must press the <ENTER> key before the computer can respond to your commands or instructions. The <ENTER> key may appear on your keyboard as <RETURN> or <⏎>.

Some Common Misconceptions

To the computer, each key means a different character. You must not type the 1 (number one) if you really mean the l (lowercase ell). The same is true of the 0 (number zero) and the O (uppercase oh).

The spacebar on your computer does not simply move the cursor across the screen. It also sends a message to the computer: "make this a blank space." If you want to move along a line, but not insert blank characters or erase existing characters, use the right arrow key < → >.

Correcting Mistakes

Because you are just beginning your exploration of the computer, it's natural that you will make mistakes (especially if you're also new at typing). So double-check your entries before you press the <ENTER> key. If you find a mistake just use the <BACKSPACE> key (it may look like this < ← >) to erase characters until you back up to the error. Then retype the entry.

If you can't get the keyboard to accept your data, or if you've lost track of what is going on, just press the <Esc> (Escape) key. If all else fails, turn off the machine and start over.

Take a moment to find these keys on your keyboard by looking at *Figure 3-2.*

**Figure 3-2.
Position of <Esc>,
<BACKSPACE>, and
<ENTER> Keys on
Keyboard**

SETTING THE CALENDAR AND CLOCK

Once you get the message to "enter new date" you have completed the boot.

```
Current date is Tues 1-01-1980
Enter new date: _____
```

The date you see on the screen will not be today's date. Let's say that today is August 1, 1984. This is the new date you want to enter. You can enter the date in a variety of ways:

    8-1-84   08-1-84   8/1/84   08/01/84

Almost all prompts displayed by MS-DOS requiring that you type in something on the keyboard, require that you press the <ENTER> key after you've finished typing your input.

Whichever method you use to enter the date, separate the parts of the date with hyphens or slashes. Notice that you don't enter the day of the week, just the numeric equivalents of the month, day, and year. Enter the date now.

```
Current date is Tues 1-01-1980
Enter new date: 8-1-84 <ENTER>
```

Immediately after you enter the date, MS-DOS returns the current time and asks you if you want to enter a new time.

```
Current time is 0:00:46.08
Enter new time: _____
```

At this point, the computer has no hours and no minutes, so enter the current time now. Our current hypothetical time is 9:30 in the morning. Here are the various ways you could enter the time:

    9:30:00.0   9:30:0   09:30:0   9:30

Your computer follows the international standard of the 24-hour clock. This means that the hours after midnight to noon are indicated by 0 to 12. After noon the hours go from 13 to 24 (midnight). You can enter the time according to the precise hours, minutes, seconds, and tenths of seconds, but for most applications the hour and minutes suffice. When entering the time, separate the hour, minutes, and seconds with a colon (:). If you do add the tenths of seconds, they are preceded by a period. Now enter the time.

> Current time is 0:00:46.08
> Enter new time: 9:30 <ENTER>

Your clock and calendar are now right on the mark; you did very well with your first computer encounter. After a while, setting the date and time will become second nature to you.

If your computer isn't equipped with a battery-powered clock circuit, the system will forget the current date and time once power is turned off. You'll have to reenter the current date and time when the system boots up again.

The computer does not remember the date and time after you shut off the power, so you need to set the date and time each time you boot the machine. While this is sometimes inconvenient, it's a good idea to set the calendar and clock each time you start working, because the computer uses the date and time to keep track of the data you enter, add, or update. However, if you want to skip the date and time settings, just press the <ENTER> key in response to the new date and time requests.

Some computers have a clock/calendar that is set once and then reports the time and date automatically. If your system has this feature, you will not have to set the time and date at the beginning of each computer session.

What we have been describing is the ideal sequence of events when setting the time and date. But what happens if you follow the instructions (you think perfectly), and this message appears on the screen.

INVALID DATE or INVALID TIME

or

ok

There is nothing to worry about, just try the entry again. You may have put a period where you need a slash. If you get the "ok" signal, you will need to boot the system again.

BOOT TEMPERATURE (COLD VERSUS WARM)

Using the power-off/power-on method of booting the system is called cold booting. The system can also be warm booted while power remains on by pressing the <Ctrl> key, and while <Ctrl>is held down, pressing the <Alt> and <Del> keys.

When you insert the operating-system diskette and then turn on the power, you are performing a cold boot, or starting the machine from a power-off position. There is another kind of boot that occurs when you are already working on the machine (the power is on), but you want to start over again from the beginning. This is called a warm boot. You might perform a warm boot if you had entered the wrong date or had gotten the "ok" message described above. To warm boot the system, press down the <Ctrl> (control) key, and while holding down <Ctrl>, press the <Alt> and <Del> keys. This brings you back to the "enter the date" message.

Control Key

You will find that the <Ctrl> key is always used in conjunction with other keys. When used with another key, it changes the message that key sends to the computer. Whenever you use <Ctrl> you must press and hold down this key while pressing another key or keys. All keys are released together.

ENTERING MS-DOS

After the system has been booted and the date and time have been entered (or have been loaded automatically), the main MS-DOS prompt will be displayed. In response to this prompt, you can enter MS-DOS commands.

Once the date and time are set, you are truly in the operating system. How do you know when MS-DOS is up and running and ready to receive commands from you?

After you enter the time your screen will look like this:

A>_____

Prompts

The capital letter A followed by the greater than symbol (>) is the MS-DOS prompt (some systems use a prompt that has the letter A followed by a colon, A:). A prompt tells you that the machine is waiting for you to enter some information. Notice that the cursor follows the prompt, indicating the location of the next entry.

Prompts vary with the program in use. "A" is the DOS prompt, "ok" is the prompt for the BASIC programming language, and "*" is the prompt for the EDLIN program, a special part of the MS-DOS operating system. (You will learn to use EDLIN in Chapter 5.)

In response to the A> prompt, you are going to give MS-DOS your first command. Commands are nothing more than instructions to the operating system. They consist of short words or abbreviations that tell MS-DOS to perform specific actions. Right now, you want to find out what's on a diskette.

COMMANDS

The DIR Command

The DIR command (short for DIRectory) displays a general diskette directory or lists the specific attributes of a single file on a specific diskette. Files, or collections of related data, are the way MS-DOS keeps track of which information is stored where. All the files on your system diskette come ready-made from MS-DOS. You will learn how to create your own files in Chapter 6. You use the DIR command to see the names of all the files that are on a diskette or to find out if a single file is located on a particular diskette.

Listing All the Files

The first command you should enter after having booted MS-DOS for the first time is the DIR command, which causes a list of files to be displayed on the screen.

Because our system diskette is already in drive A, let's use the DIR command to see what files are on this diskette. When you enter a command, you can use either upper- or lowercase letters (don't forget to include all punctuation and blank spaces). Enter this command now.

A> dir <ENTER>

MS-DOS responds with a listing of the files. Did the entire screen fill up and then move on quickly to another screen? No one can read anything that fast! What do you do now?

Scrolling

There is a simple explanation for this phenomenon. MS-DOS presents information to you one screen at a time. This is fine if the diskette contains only a few files; after they are listed the display stops. But when a diskette contains many files, they cannot fit on the screen at one time, and the display will scroll. Scrolling means that as the screen is filled with information, new data are added to the bottom of the display as old data roll off the top. There is a simple way to freeze the screen and stop this scrolling action.

Because lists of files generated by the DIR command can be lengthy, the list may scroll off the screen before you can read it. To stop the display at any time, press and hold down the <Ctrl>key, then press the S key. Press any key on the keyboard to resume scrolling.

To stop scrolling, you press and hold down the <Ctrl> key and then press the S key. Release both keys together. In some systems you stop scrolling by holding down <Ctrl> and pressing the <Num Lock> key.

Try using the DIR command to list the diskette contents again. If your display is more than one screen long, freeze the scrolling action by using the <Ctrl> S combination.

A>dir <ENTER>
<Ctrl> S

Press any key (<ENTER> is a good one to use) to begin the scrolling again until the display is finished.

SORT	EXE	1280	3-08-83	12:00p
FIND	EXE	5888	3-08-83	12:00p
MORE	COM	384	3-08-83	12:00p
BASIC	COM	16256	3-08-83	12:00p
BASICA	COM	25984	3-08-83	12:00p

23 File(s)   31232 bytes free A>

The Directory Listing

The exact names and numbers do not matter and may vary according to the diskette included in your system. The information on the screen describes the files that are on the operating-system diskette. *Figure 3-3* shows the pattern in which the files are listed.

Figure 3-3.
Directory Output
Sample

Volume in drive A has no label
Directory of A: \

filename	ext	size	date	time
COMMAND	COM	17664	3-08-83	12:00p
ANSI	SYS	1664	3-08-83	12:00p
FORMAT	COM	6016	3-08-83	12:00p
CHKDSK	COM	6400	3-08-83	12:00p
SYS	COM	1408	3-08-83	12:00p
DISKCOPY	COM	2444	3-08-83	12:00p
DISKCOMP	COM	2074	3-08-83	12:00p
COMP	COM	2523	3-08-83	12:00p
EDLIN	COM	4608	3-08-83	12:00p
MODE	COM	3139	3-08-83	12:00p
FDISK	COM	6177	3-08-83	12:00p
BACKUP	COM	3687	3-08-83	12:00p
RESTORE	COM	4003	3-08-83	12:00p
PRINT	COM	4608	3-08-83	12:00p
RECOVER	COM	2304	3-08-83	12:00p
ASSIGN	COM	896	3-08-83	12:00p
TREE	COM	1513	3-08-83	12:00p
GRAPHICS	COM	789	3-08-83	12:00p
SORT	EXE	1280	3-08-83	12:00p
FIND	EXE	5888	3-08-83	12:00p
MORE	COM	384	3-08-83	12:00p
BASIC	COM	16256	3-08-83	12:00p
BASICA	COM	25984	3-08-83	12:00p

23 File(s)   31232 bytes free

A >

If you are looking at the first page of the directory listing, you may see a short statement about the *volume label*. Ignore this for now. It will be discussed in Chapter 7.

The body of the listing is divided into five separate columns. Column 1 gives us the name of the file, for example, SORT, FIND, MORE, BASIC. This name identifies the contents of the file. Column 2 is an extension of the file's name. EXE and COM tell us what type of files these are. Pay no attention to these particulars right now. Filenaming is detailed in Chapter 6.

Column 3 tells us how big the file is. File size is measured in bytes; so the SORT file takes up 1280 bytes on the diskette. Columns 4 and 5 tell us the date and time that the file was last updated (this is the type of information that is supplied when you set the time and date at the beginning of a computer session).

Finally, MS-DOS performs a little housekeeping chore. It reports the total number of files on the diskette and the space available on the diskette for new files. This information will be very useful to you later, when you are deciding if a file will fit on a certain diskette.

That's a lot of information from one small three-letter command.

Notice that when MS-DOS is finished performing the DIR command, it returns you to the operating system. You know this has happened when you see the DOS prompt A>.

Listing a Specific File

When the DIR command is entered without qualifications, it causes the entire list of files on the disk to be displayed. You can also use DIR to see if a specific file exists on the disk by typing in the file's name.

In addition to listing all the files on a diskette, DIR can also tell you if a specific file is on a particular diskette. To get this information, enter the command followed by a filename. Although you already know the contents of your system diskette, let's assume that you are trying to find a file named COMMAND.COM. Enter the DIR command, leave a blank space, and enter the name of the file.

A>dir command.com <ENTER>

MS-DOS will reply to this command.

```
Volume in drive A has no label
Directory of A: \

COMMAND       COM      17664      3-08-83       12:00p
              1 File[s]                     31232 bytes free
```

And there it is—all of the same information listed in columns one through five, as they describe this particular file.

If the file you request is not on the diskette, MS-DOS returns this message:

File not found

Sorry, try again. Either you never put the file on this diskette or you are looking at a different diskette than you thought.

Now you are reaping the fruits of your labors (either a DIR of the entire diskette or a DIR of the COMMAND.COM file). But how do you remove this information from the screen? Our next command provides the answer.

CLEARING THE SCREEN

The CLS Command

To clear the screen, you can enter the CLS command at any time in response to the MS-DOS prompt. Using CLS does not alter any information stored in memory or on disk.

As you use your computer, you will realize that you don't need to save all the information after you have seen it. With mistakes and changes of mind, you can fill up a screen pretty quickly. For instance, in one use of the DIR command, you displayed all the files on your system diskette. You don't really need this information once you have looked at it. The CLS (CLear Screen) command is a handy way of getting rid of all the stuff on the screen. (The CLS command isn't available on MS-DOS Versions 1.0 or 1.1.) Try using CLS now to empty the screen.

A>cls <ENTER>

Like magic the screen is cleared. After you execute the CLS command, the cursor waits in the upper left-hand corner of the screen for the next entry. This is sometimes called the cursor's home position.

CLS affects only the information currently on the screen. It does nothing to data in memory or to information stored on diskettes. The corollary is that it also saves nothing. Use CLS only when you don't need the information on the screen.

SUMMARY

In this chapter you've learned how to insert your system diskette into the disk drive and how to perform a cold and a warm boot. You've learned some simple rules for entering data into the machine and gotten your "hands wet" by setting the calendar and clock in your system and entering your first MS-DOS commands. The DIR command allowed you to display the listing for a diskette, and <Ctrl>S showed you how to freeze that display. The CLS command cleaned up your screen when you were finished looking at the displayed information.

In the next chapter we are going to take a closer look at one piece of computer technology that helped spawn the personal computer revolution, the floppy disk.

WHAT HAVE WE LEARNED?

1. To boot your floppy disk system, you first place a copy of your MS-DOS disk into disk drive A.

2. To enter a new date, you must type absolutely correctly; use the backspace key to erase errors. You can enter the current date and time in several ways, but remember that the computer follows the international twenty-four–hour clock.

3. Cold boot refers to starting the machine from a power-off condition.

4. Warm boot refers to restarting the machine without having turned off power; to warm boot your machine, press the <Ctrl>key, the <Alt> key, and the <Del> key, all at the same time.

5. The A prompt indicates that MS-DOS is loaded and that the computer system is ready for your command.

6. The DIR command presents information on one or all of the files on a diskette in a given disk drive.

7. The CLS command removes all information displayed on the screen and places the cursor in the upper left-hand corner of the screen.

Quiz for Chapter 3

1. Booting the system is the process of:
  a. physically kicking the system.
  b. loading the MS-DOS operating system.
  c. applying polish to the system.
  d. dismissing the system.

2. The first program that is executed when the system is powered up is the:
  a. shoehorn loader.
  b. bootstrap loader.
  c. MS-DOS operating system.
  d. a predefined application program.

3. Having your computer manufacturer's reference documentation within easy reach while learning the system is important because:
  a. it can make interesting reading.
  b. it is the ultimate source of information on MS-DOS and its commands.
  c. because experimenting with a command without knowing how to use it can sometimes cause problems.
  d. it can help make you an expert MS-DOS user.
  e. all of the above.
  f. none of the above.

4. Your booting checklist should include:
  a. finding the system diskette.
  b. locating drive A.
  c. inserting the diskette.
  d. closing the drive door.
  e. turning on the power.
  f. relaxing and waiting for the boot process to complete.
  g. all of the above in the order shown.

  h. none of the above.

5. If your system doesn't have a battery-powered clock circuit, the first thing MS-DOS displays after it has been booted is the:
  a. blank screen.
  b. prompt requesting that you enter the current date.
  c. prompt requesting that you enter the current time.
  d. list of files stored on the disk.

6. Some keys can be easily confused with each other. They are:
  a. 0 and O keys.
  b. 1 (one) and l (lower case ell) keys.
  c. both of the above.
  d. none of the above.

7. You can correct typing errors at an MS-DOS prompt by using the <BACKSPACE> key and retyping the text:
  a. after pressing the <ENTER> key.
  b. after pressing the <Esc> key.
  c. before pressing the <ENTER> key.
  d. before pressing the <ScrollLock> key.

8. You can enter the date July 4, 1985, as:
  a. 7-4-85.
  b. 07-4-85.
  c. 7/4/85.
  d. 07/04/85.
  e. any of the above.

9. A cold boot means the system is booted:
  a. immediately after power has been turned on.
  b. without having to turn the power off.
  c. only in cold temperatures.
  d. using a cold floppy diskette.

10. A warm boot means the system is rebooted while power remains turned on and is accomplished by pressing the:
   a. <Del> key.
   b. <Ctrl> key.
   c. <Ctrl> key, and while holding it down, pressing the <Alt> and <Del> keys.
   d. <Ctrl> key, and while holding it down, pressing the <Alt> and <SPACEBAR> keys.

11. In response to the standard MS-DOS prompt A> that is displayed after the system has been booted you can:
   a. enter any text you want.
   b. enter only the DIR command.
   c. enter only MS-DOS commands.
   d. enter any operating-system command.

12. The DIR command is used to:
   a. look at the contents of files.
   b. display a list of files stored on the disk.
   c. erase files.
   d. copy files.

13. Pausing the scrolling of text on the screen is accomplished by:
   a. pressing and holding down the <Ctrl> key and then pressing the S key.
   b. pressing and holding down the <Ctrl> key and then pressing the <NumLock> key (on some computers).
   c. either of the above.
   d. none of the above.

14. The CLS command is used to:
   a. clear out memory.
   b. clear the screen.
   c. clear out the contents of a diskette.
   d. clear the CPU.

15. After pausing the scrolling of text on the screen, you can resume scrolling by:
   a. pressing any key.
   b. pressing and holding down the <Ctrl> key and then pressing the S key.
   c. pressing the <Esc> key.
   d. pressing the <SPACEBAR> key.
   e. any of the above.
   f. none of the above.

4

System Insurance

ABOUT THIS CHAPTER

There is a precaution that most of us take as a matter of course whenever we acquire something we want to protect: we take out insurance. Then, if the unexpected happens, we are protected.

The importance of protecting yourself by making a backup copy of your MS-DOS operating system disk cannot be overstated. It should be one of the first things you do when first using your system. Losing data that has not been backed up can be disastrous.

Your newly acquired operating-system diskette falls into the category of "valuable things you would be lost without." If there is no operating-system diskette, there is no computer operation. In this chapter you will learn how to insure your floppy diskette. In other words, you will make a *backup* copy of your operating-system diskette. By using this backup in your everyday computing, you always have the original to fall back on if your diskette is damaged or if you misplace it.

DISKETTES AND DISK DRIVES

It is staggering to think of how much information is stored on one magnetically coated piece of plastic. Detailed instructions about how the computer is to receive input, manage files, deliver output, and operate its equipment is all there on your operating-system diskette. In addition, the diskette still has room to store programming languages and maybe a utility program or two.

Before you actually insure this precious commodity, let's take a closer look at what makes up a diskette.

Just as the size, speed, and capabilities of computer hardware have undergone a remarkable technological evolution in the last three decades, so have the methods for storing the programs and data the computer needs to operate.

The use of floppy diskettes in today's microcomputers has made the task of backing up your data considerably easier than with older computers.

As mentioned in Chapter 2, earnest computer users of the 1950s and 1960s stored information on punch cards. These cards, 80 columns wide, were stored in long, oversized boxes. Transporting programs involved struggles with many unwieldy boxes, which were subject to agonizing rearrangement when dropped, or worse—"bent, folded, or mutilated." Information was also stored on punched paper tape.

Gradually, paper tape and cards were replaced by plastic-coated disks. By embedding information in the coating material on these disks, users could store large quantities of data in a safe way. Once the information was on a diskette, it could only be lost through mishandling or intentional erasing.

Floppies

Although floppy diskettes got their name because they are flexible, their flexibility should not be tested. Floppy diskettes should always be handled with care.

The first type of diskettes were 8 inches in diameter. Because they were flexible, they were termed "floppy diskettes." Constructed of thin plastic and surfaced with a magnetic coating, they could store information on only one side of the diskette. Typically, an 8-inch diskette held 50–100K bytes of information.

<u>Minifloppies</u>

"Floppies" rapidly got smaller and capable of holding more and more information. Modification to the reading heads of disk drives allowed both sides of a diskette to hold data. Today, "minifloppies" (5¼ inches in diameter) are used for most systems that operate using MS-DOS.

There are a variety of floppy diskette types. They differ in physical size, number of recordable sides, storage density, and data format.

The capacity of 5¼-inch diskettes varies according to their design. Some diskettes record on one side (single-sided), some use both sides to store data (double-sided). In addition, the amount of information on the diskette depends on the density of the storage. Some diskettes are single density. Others achieve twice as much storage by packing data in double density. The average double-sided, double-density diskette can contain about 360K of information. (Fixed disks with many, many times more storage are quite different and are discussed in Chapter 11.)

Microfloppies

The most common diskette size used with MS-DOS computers is 5¼ inches, and according to the data format used, storage capacity can range between 160K for single-sided diskettes to 360K for double-sided.

A more recent innovation is the microfloppy. These diskettes are approximately 3½ inches in diameter. They are held in a rigid, rather than flexible, sleeve. Microdisks are still in the process of standardization. Earlier 3½-inch disks use only one side for data storage. Double-sided microdisks with increased densities are now available.

The relative proportions of the three kinds of diskettes are shown in *Figure 4-1*.

**Figure 4-1.
Diskette Evolution**

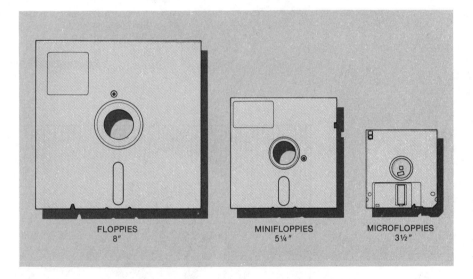

FLOPPIES
8″

MINIFLOPPIES
5¼″

MICROFLOPPIES
3½″

How data get put on diskettes is covered later in this chapter. For now, the only thing you need to know about your diskettes is what type your computer uses. Check your owner's manual for the specific types of diskettes you should buy.

PROTECTING YOUR DISKETTES

Whatever their size, sidedness, or density, all diskettes have several features in common. This discussion will describe the most common features found on 5¼-inch floppy diskettes. These features are illustrated in *Figure 4-2*.

Storage

While a diskette is not in use, it should always be placed in its protective jacket. Never touch the exposed surfaces of the diskette.

Diskettes are usually sold in convenient boxes (save these for storing your diskettes). Inside the box, each diskette is nestled a paper envelope. This is the diskette's storage jacket. It's a good idea to put this paper jacket on the diskette whenever you're not using it.

The diskette is completely enclosed in a square plastic protective jacket. The actual shape of the diskette is round. This protective jacket is permanent and should never be removed. In fact, you won't be able to remove it unless you are using a sharp instrument. If the diskette is not square, something dreadful has happened to the protective jacket (and undoubtedly to any information which was on the diskette).

Figure 4-2.
Features of Diskettes

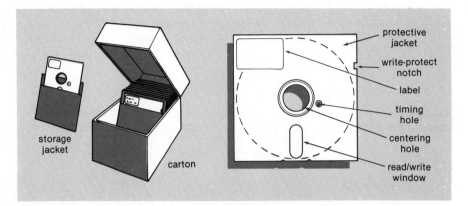

Handling

Figure 4-3 indicates the three areas where the recording surface is exposed on the diskette. Take care not to put your fingers (or anything else) on these sections. One exposed area is around the centering hole of the diskette. The disk drive uses this area to be sure the diskette is in the right place before it begins operation. The timing, or indexing, hole is just off to the side of the centering hole. This too is used to align the diskette correctly.

Figure 4-3.
Exposed Surfaces

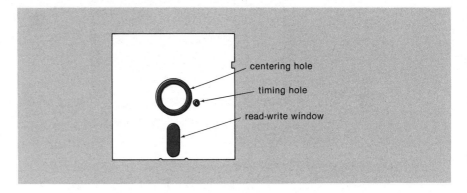

The third area is an oblong opening along one edge of the diskette. This area is a window used by the drive to read and write data on the surface of the diskette. As the diskette revolves, the special heads within the disk drive (just like the heads on a tape recorder) code the magnetic surface with information that contains the pattern of your data. It is especially important to keep this window free of dirt or dust. Imperfections in this window can be transferred to the drive heads and can damage your drives as well as your diskettes.

Write-Protection

When the write-protect notch on a 5¼-inch diskette is open, the computer may store data on the diskette as well as retrieve data from it. When the write-protect notch is covered with special write-protect tabs, data may only be retrieved from the diskette.

Along one edge of the diskette, you will see a distinct square cutout indentation. This is the write-protect notch. A clever design feature, this small space may prevent you from erasing vital information by inadvertently writing over it.

New information can overwrite, or erase, previous information. But before the computer writes to a diskette, it checks this notch. If the notch is covered, the diskette is write-protected; that is, it cannot receive new data. If the notch is open, the diskette is fair game for both reading and writing. *Figure 4-4* shows covered and open notches.

When you want to make sure that the contents of a diskette will not be altered, cover the notch with one of the write-protect tabs included in your box of purchased diskettes (there will be several oblong tabs stuck on one sheet; they are usually silver or black). These pieces of adhesive foil or paper seal off the notch and prevent any new information from being written to the diskette.

You may notice that some diskettes, especially those containing application programs, have no write-protect notch. If you can't write to the diskette, you don't run the risk of altering or destroying the program.

Figure 4-4.
Write-Protect Notch

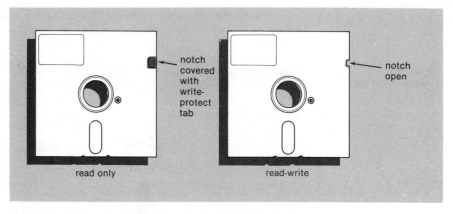

Labeling

Using adhesive labels written with clear information can help you organize your diskette library.

Also in your carton of purchased diskettes, you will find a packet of adhesive labels (they come in many colors and usually have lines on them). These are content labels, a means of identifying each diskette. Without labeling, most diskettes look alike. How much information you put on these labels is up to you, but your labeling should be clear enough so that you'll know what's on your diskette when you pick it up next month, or next year. Your label should be positioned as illustrated in *Figure 4-5*.

Figure 4-5.
Labeling

All these do's and don'ts may have you wondering if you will ever have the courage to pick up a diskette, let alone use it in your computer. But by following the rules listed in *Figure 4-6*, you should have little trouble with your diskettes.

Figure 4-6.
Rules for Disk Handling
and Usage

1. Do not rest heavy objects on diskette surfaces. Such objects include reference books, instruction manuals, and the omnipresent elbow.
2. Do not eat, drink, smoke, or comb your hair near your diskettes. These seemingly simple activities can cause deposits on the surface of a diskette.
3. Do not bend, staple, paper clip, or mutilate your diskettes by rough handling or improper storage.
4. Protect diskettes from the common forces of creation. This encompasses the peril of destruction by sunlight or exposure to acts of high temperature or humidity.
5. Do not allow your diskettes to be near X-ray machines (including those at the airport inquisition), telephones, or any other source of magnetic energy (beware the magnetic paper-clip dispenser). These "fields of force" can wreck havoc on your diskettes.
6. Handle your diskettes gently—by the edges only.
7. Label your diskettes properly. When transcribing labels, use only a felt-tip pen, for pencils and ballpoints damage diskettes. Unlabeled diskettes carrying precious information have been known to succumb to the destructive prowess of the FORMAT command.
8. Store your diskettes carefully. Specifically, refrain from resting them on their sides or crowding them too closely in their box.
9. When not in use, your diskettes should be kept in their storage jackets.
10. Remember that the quality of the performance of your diskettes is directly related to the quality of the care you give them.

STORING DATA ON THE DISKETTE

New diskettes are made compatible with MS-DOS by formatting them with the FORMAT command. The diskette formatting process establishes the data storage characteristics of the diskette, such as the number of tracks, the number of sectors per track, and the number of bytes per sector.

MS-DOS is a careful and efficient manager, so when it stores information on a diskette it does so in an orderly, logical way. Before any information can be put on a diskette, the diskette must be prepared using the FORMAT command (discussed later in this chapter). Your blank diskette, fresh from the box, is like a newly paved running track, one large, unmarked surface. The first thing that FORMAT does is divide this area into specific tracks. As shown in *Figure 4-7*, the tracks run in concentric circles around the diskette, much like the painted lanes that mark boundaries for runners on a running track.

The tracks are divided into small sections called sectors (also shown in *Figure 4-7*). This makes storage and retrieval of your data faster and more efficient because MS-DOS knows just what track and sector

Figure 4-7.
Tracks and Sectors

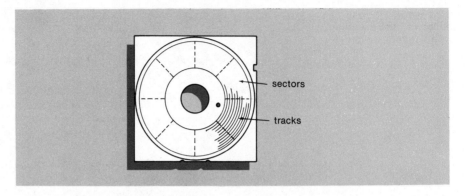

Figure 4-7.
Tracks and Sectors

holds each file. The amount of data stored in a sector is dependent upon your computer system. Most diskettes used with MS-DOS divide the diskette into 8 or 9 sectors per track. Each sector can hold either 512 or 1024 bytes.

The first section of the first track on every diskette is reserved for storage of the operating system. Thereafter, as data are written to the diskette, they are stored on a first-come, first-served basis. You do not need to remember the order in which you store data on the diskette, MS-DOS keeps track of that for you.

GETTING THE DISKETTE READY TO BE USED

It's easy to prepare your diskettes for use. Don't let this new challenge make you nervous. After all, you already know how to handle diskettes and how they go into your disk drive (remember how well you executed the DIR command). But a little planning can make things easier for you as you perform this procedure.

1. Have the computer up and running.
2. Have your computer instruction manual nearby.
3. Have ready the system diskette and several new, blank diskettes.

The instructions for the following MS-DOS commands are given in terms of the typical MS-DOS system. The typical system has two disk drives.

Disk Drives

Although your computer may be equipped with only one floppy diskette drive, most MS-DOS commands assume that two drives (A and B) are installed.

When asking questions and giving responses to commands, MS-DOS assumes that you have two disk drives, A and B. Operating with at least two drives is the most efficient method for MS-DOS because it simplifies transferring information from one diskette to the other and makes giving instructions easier. With two drives, MS-DOS can easily differentiate where the information is coming from and where the information is going.

The operating system is quite set in its ways on this point. So much so that even if you have a single drive, MS-DOS responds as though you have two. It always issues instructions in terms of drive A and drive B. How can single-drive owners use this system? *Figure 4-8* shows you how.

Figure 4-8.
Two Drives Versus One
Drive

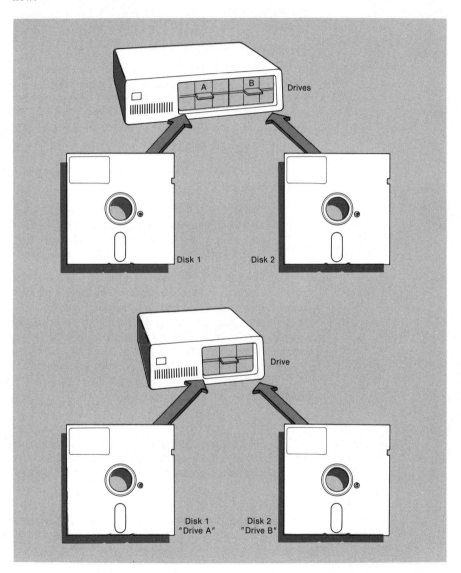

One easy way to do this is to think of your diskettes as drives. That is, one diskette represents drive A, and the second represents drive B. Then when the display tells you to do something with the diskette in drive A, you use the first diskette. When you need to do something with the diskette in drive B, you remove the first diskette and insert the second diskette before performing the action. Both the operating system and you are happy and no one is any the wiser.

With these preliminaries out of the way, you're ready to prepare some new diskettes. To accomplish this, you will call upon the FORMAT command.

The FORMAT Command

The FORMAT command readies a diskette to receive data by dividing up the diskette specifically for your type of computer system. This division of space is not standardized (i.e., not all MS-DOS systems use the same format). This is why it can be difficult to swap diskettes even between machines that are supposed to be compatible. When you buy already formatted diskettes, such as those containing application software, be sure they are formatted to your machine's specifications.

The FORMAT command is used in several situations. Here are the most common:

- the very first time you use a diskette
- when you wish to erase an entire diskette (be careful here)
- when you want to change the already existing format of the
- diskette (for instance, to use it on another machine)

You fit into the first category right now; so let's begin breaking in this command. Step one is to insert your operating-system diskette into drive A (single-drive owners see the discussion at the beginning of this section). Put your new blank diskette in drive B. (Refer to *Figure 4-9* for a graphic representation of the formatting sequence.) Now turn on the machine and let it cycle though the boot (you can use <Ctrl> <Alt> <Del> to reboot if your machine is already running). Enter the time and date. The computer will signal its readiness to accept commands by displaying the MS-DOS prompt.

A>

Now you are going to tell the operating system to FORMAT the diskette in drive B. You must include the letter B in your command or else you might destroy your system diskette. Enter the command.

A>format b: <ENTER>

Be sure to include the space between the command and the drive specifier, and the colon after the letter B. Now watch the screen. It will answer your command.

Insert new diskette for drive B:
and strike any key when ready

Because you have already put a new, blank diskette in drive B, you can press any key.

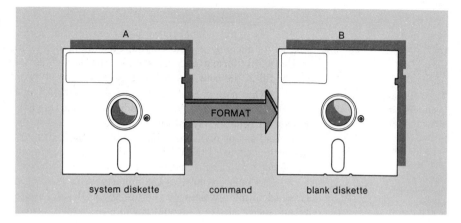

Figure 4-9.
The FORMAT Command

A

B

FORMAT

system diskette   command   blank diskette

The drive will click and whirr, and the indicator light will go on
and off. Do not interrupt this process, just let the machine do its work. The
operating system lets you know what is going on by displaying a message.

Formatting...

Once the formatting is completed, it tells you this also.

Formatting...Format complete

362496 bytes total disk space
362496 bytes available on disk

format another [Y/N]?

Let's take a moment to look at the messages MS-DOS is giving
you. First you are told that the formatting of the disk has been completed.
Then the total number of bytes on the disk is given. Because formatting
has not put any information on the diskette, but has only divided up the
space, the amount of total disk space and the amount available on the disk
are the same.

You must now make a decision. Do you want to format any
additional diskettes? If you answer Y, you will be instructed to insert
another diskette in drive B. It's a good idea to format several diskettes at
a time. Then, when you are working on a project and need a diskette, you
won't have to stop, insert your system diskette, and then prepare the
diskette. Go ahead and format several diskettes now.

Good for you. Everything is moving along smoothly, and you now
have several diskettes awaiting use. When you're finished formatting, just
answer N to the "Format another" question, and you will be returned to
the MS-DOS prompt.

Labeling Formatted Diskettes

Be sure to label those diskettes. This label can be short or long, just so its meaning is clear to you. One simple label consists of the letter F, or the word "formatted," followed by the date. This leaves lots of room for you to fill in the contents of the diskette as you store information on it.

The FORMAT command is an effective yet destructive command. If you format a diskette that contains data, the data will be destroyed after the formatting process has completed. Always make sure you are formatting a diskette that is blank or one that contains data you no longer need!

One note of caution in using the FORMAT command. When you tell MS-DOS to format, you are indicating that this is a new, blank diskette. FORMAT ignores any information already on a diskette and lays down new track and sector divisions. This can be useful if you want to erase an entire diskette. Just use FORMAT. But, this operation can also backfire. Once you format a diskette that contains something you really want, the data are gone. This only emphasizes the importance of labeling all diskettes. Keep this fact in mind whenever you use the FORMAT command: FORMAT treats each diskette as blank; it will erase any information on the diskette.

Occasionally, when you format a diskette, you will receive an unexpected message.

Bad sector on track xxx

or

xxxxx bytes in bad sector

If this message appears, do not continue to use the diskette. There is probably some manufacturing fault in the diskette (and possibly with the entire carton of diskettes). Return these diskettes to your dealer and request a refund or replacement.

INSURING THE SYSTEM DISKETTE

The DISKCOPY command provides a quick and effective method of making an exact copy of an entire diskette. As with the FORMAT command, DISKCOPY will destroy any data previously stored on the target diskette.

Before you do anything else, you are going to make that insurance copy of your system diskette. This copy will be an exact duplicate of the original diskette. You do not want to add or delete any information. Whenever you want to copy an entire diskette, use the DISKCOPY command.

The DISKCOPY Command

This command makes a duplicate of an entire diskette. Normally, before transferring any information to a diskette, you must prepare it using FORMAT. But in the case of the DISKCOPY command, the exception proves the rule. DISKCOPY automatically formats the diskette as it makes the duplicate copy. Because this is true, the same precautions exist when using this command: DISKCOPY erases any previous information on the diskette.

If you wish to copy only certain files to another disk, the COPY command should be used instead of DISKCOPY.

It's important to distinguish between DISKCOPY and COPY (an MS-DOS command introduced in Chapter 6). DISKCOPY automatically formats the diskette; it copies the entire diskette. COPY needs a formatted diskette; it copies only designated files. When you want to copy only part of the files on a diskette, use the COPY command.

Now let's make DISKCOPY jump through its hoops. If it's not already there, put your system diskette in drive A. Insert an unformatted, blank diskette in drive B.

Before you enter this command, take a close look at the exact wording of the example.

diskcopy a: b:

This DISKCOPY command tells MS-DOS to copy the entire contents from the diskette in drive A to the diskette in drive B. Be sure you enter the command in this exact order; otherwise you may erase your entire system diskette.

How can this happen? Well, as the DISKCOPY transfers the information, it wipes out anything previously on the diskette. So when you are using this command you must be sure to clearly indicate where the information is coming from and where it is going.

Source and Target Diskettes

The DISKCOPY command can be used with only one drive or with several drives to copy diskettes.

The diskette that holds the original information is your source diskette. It contains the information you want to copy. In this case the source diskette is your system diskette, currently in drive A. The diskette that receives the copy is your target diskette. It is the destination of the information you are copying. Your target diskette (as yet empty) is currently in drive B.

It's wise to become familiar with these terms because they are used in the instructions MS-DOS uses to perform copying commands. You'll see an example of this now as you execute DISKCOPY.

A > diskcopy a: b: < ENTER >

Include the blank spaces and colons. MS-DOS will remind you of what to do next.

Insert source diskette in drive A
Insert target diskette in drive B
Strike any key when ready

You already have the source and target diskettes in place, so press any key.

The operating system now performs the same sequence of events that accompanied the FORMAT command, and copies the contents of the diskette at the same time. Again the drives will whirr, and the indicator lights will flash on and off. When the light under drive A is lit, information is being read from the system diskette. When the light under drive B comes on, information is being written to this diskette. Do not attempt to open the drive doors or remove any diskettes while this command is in operation.

During this process, a message will be on the screen.

Copying 9 sectors per track, 2 side[s]

Depending on the type of diskette your system uses, your message may read a bit differently (it may have 8 sectors or copy on only one side). But in any case, MS-DOS tells you when the DISKCOPY command has finished copying the diskette.

```
Copy complete
Copy another [Y/N]?
```

At this point you are offered a choice. In the same way that you can use FORMAT repeatedly without retyping the command, you can use DISKCOPY to make more than one duplicate of the source diskette. If you answer Y to MS-DOS's query, you are instructed to insert a new target diskette in drive B and to start the copying process with a keystroke. If you answer N you are returned to the system prompt. If you want to be doubly protected, make an extra copy of your "insurance" diskette.

Now you are all set. You have taken out an insurance policy on your system diskette (properly labeled, of course). You can take your original system diskette and store it in a dry, safe place. Keep your backup system diskette and your newly formatted diskettes handy; you will need them in the very next chapter.

Drive Indicators

DISKCOPY is the first MS-DOS command you have encountered that requires the use of two diskettes, one in each drive. Many MS-DOS commands rely on this kind of transfer of information from one diskette to another. It is important that you understand exactly how MS-DOS identifies which drive is the source and which drive is the target. You inform MS-DOS as to which is the source and which is the target through the use of drive indicators.

After you complete a command, MS-DOS returns you to the system prompt:

```
A>
```

You are now back under the control of the MS-DOS operating system, that is, MS-DOS is ready for your next command. Besides being the system prompt, the A symbol gives you another important piece of information. It informs you that the system is working off the A drive. It expects that any information you request or store will be on this drive. So this A is also a drive indicator. *Figure 4-10* shows the position of the A and B drives in two different drive configurations.

Figure 4-10.
Drive Designations in
Different System Unit
Configurations

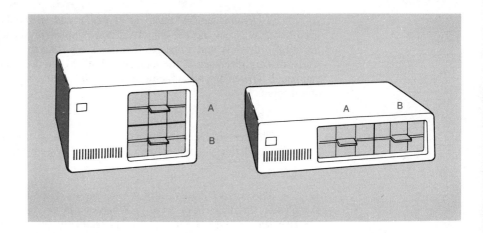

MS-DOS keeps track of
the current, or default,
drive by displaying the
drive's indicator (name) in
the MS-DOS prompt, such
as A> for drive A and
B> for drive B. The cur-
rent drive is always ac-
cessed by MS-DOS when
a command is entered
without indicating which
drive is to be accessed.

To keep track of itself, MS-DOS uses the concept of current drive.
The current drive is the one represented by the drive indicator. This is also
called the default drive because, unless you tell it otherwise, MS-DOS will
always look for information or store information on the current drive.

Take, for example, the DIR command. You want a listing of the
diskette in drive A. You ask for this information by entering the command,
followed by a drive indicator. Drive indicators in commands are separated
from the command by a space and must be followed by a colon.

A> dir a: <ENTER>

This command produces a listing of all the files on the diskette in
drive A. But you may be mumbling to yourself, "That's not the way I got a
listing of the system diskette." You are absolutely right. This is how you
entered the DIR command in Chapter 3:

A> dir <ENTER>

You did not include any drive indicator. These two versions of the
DIR command produce the same listings because of the default feature of
MS-DOS. The A system prompt tells you that A is the current drive,
therefore when you enter a command without any drive indicator, it lists
the files on the diskette in the current, or A, drive.

This default feature is very handy when you are working
extensively with one diskette. But it does have its drawbacks. You can
cause some pretty weird and unwanted file changes if you neglect to
include a drive indicator in a command. Because it does no harm to include
a drive indicator, when in doubt write it into the command. Even if the
operation involves only the current drive, it doesn't do any harm to include
the default indicator in your command. Specifying drive indicators is always
a good idea when you are transferring information from one diskette to
another, just as an extra measure of protection.

You can issue commands to be performed on the diskette in other drives without changing the current drive. Suppose you had your system diskette in drive A and a diskette holding some data files in drive B. If you want to see a directory of the data files, include the drive indicator in the command. The command is followed by a blank space, the drive indicator, and a colon.

A>dir b: <ENTER>

The screen displays the listing of the files on the diskette in drive B. After the listing you will be returned to the system prompt.

A>

The current drive is still A because you have only taken a peek at the files on the diskette in drive B. When you issue your next command, MS-DOS will look for the information or write the information to the diskette in drive A, as the A> prompt indicates that A is still the current drive.

The current, or default, drive can be changed at any time by entering the drive indicator followed by a colon. For example, to change the default drive from A to B, enter B: in response to the A> prompt, whereupon the prompt will change to B>.

When you are working extensively with the diskette in drive B, it can become inconvenient to keep including the drive indicator in every command; however, there is a simple solution—change the current drive. To make drive B the current drive, just type in the drive indicator in response to the system prompt.

A>b: <ENTER>

The new current drive will then appear as the system prompt.

B>

Don't get confused, this is still the MS-DOS system prompt, it does not mean that MS-DOS is not operating. It's just that your definition of system prompt has expanded. The MS-DOS system prompt is now the indicator of the current drive followed by >. So both A> and B> are MS-DOS system prompts.

Now that you have changed the current drive, what would be the result of the following command?

B>dir <ENTER>

This command produces a listing of the files on the diskette in drive B. Because B is now the current drive, and you did not include a drive indicator in the command, MS-DOS automatically performs the command on the diskette in drive B.

If you are still confused about when to include a drive indicator, think of it this way: the computer can do only what you tell it to. Including drive indicators is like making a will: you can only be sure the goodies go to the right recipients if you make your wishes known (preferably by writing them down). If you tell MS-DOS that drive A is the current drive, it will return to that drive after every command until you tell it differently. It will also perform the entered command on the data in the current drive unless you tell it to go to another diskette.

To return to A as the current drive, enter the drive indicator in response to the B prompt.

B>a: <ENTER>

The current drive is again A.

A>

As you become familiar with other MS-DOS commands, the significance and use of drive indicators will become clearer. This will be especially true as you move into more advanced MS-DOS commands in Chapter 6.

SUMMARY

This chapter has been about protecting yourself. This includes using and handling your diskettes wisely and making sure you back up your original system diskette. In addition, you have actually done something with a diskette. You've used FORMAT to prepare your diskettes and DISKCOPY to make your insurance copy. Finally, you have begun to see more of the inner operations of MS-DOS by learning the basics of source and target diskettes and the current drive indicator.

WHAT HAVE WE LEARNED?

1. Floppy diskettes reside inside of a permanent square plastics protective jacket. Parts of the floppy diskette are exposed through holes in the protective jacket; never touch those areas of the diskette.
2. You can prevent the disk drive from writing information on the floppy diskette by covering the write-protect notch that is cut out on one edge of the disk.
3. A disk must be formatted to define its tracks and sectors before it can store information.
4. If you format a diskette that already has files on it, you will erase all the information on the disk so be very careful not to reformat a disk that you still need to use.
5. To use the FORMAT command, specify the drive name: FORMAT B:
6. The DISKCOPY command will copy all information on one disk (the source diskette) to a second disk (the target diskette), and automatically format that second disk as part of the process.
7. To specify which disk drive you want to control with an MS-DOS command, include the name of the drive on the same line following the MS-DOS command.

Quiz for Chapter 4

1. Making regular backups of your diskette data is:
   a. always important.
   b. only occasionally necessary.
   c. to be done only if you have extra floppy diskettes.

2. Although floppy diskettes are flexible, testing their flexibility by bending them:
   a. never causes damage.
   b. may cause damage and is therefore not recommended.
   c. will always cause damage.

3. Touching the exposed surfaces of a floppy diskette:
   a. will most likely damage the disk and therefore must never be attempted.
   b. will probably not cause damage but shouldn't be attempted anyway.
   c. cannot hurt the diskette.

4. A covered write-protect notch on a floppy diskette will:
   a. not allow new data to be stored.
   b. not allow data to be erased.
   c. allow data to be retrieved.
   d. all of the above.

5. Clear labeling of your diskettes will:
   a. help keep track of what is stored on each diskette.
   b. be of marginal use.
   c. keep them nicely decorated.

6. The FORMAT command is used to establish:
   a. the data storage characteristics of a diskette.
   b. the number of tracks.
   c. the number of sectors per track.
   d. the number of bytes per sector.
   e. all of the above.

7. Although most MS-DOS commands assume that you have two diskette drives installed, the minimum number of drives an MS-DOS computer can have is:
   a. none.
   b. one.
   c. two.
   d. three.

8. Formatting a diskette with the FORMAT command will:
   a. copy any data stored on it.
   b. destroy any data stored on it.
   c. restore any data stored on it.
   d. leave any data stored on it intact.

9. The DISKCOPY command will:
   a. make an exact copy of a diskette.
   b. destroy any data originally stored on the target diskette.
   c. copy all files stored on a diskette.
   d. automatically format the target diskette if it wasn't previously formatted.
   e. all of the above.

10. Changing the current, or default, drive is accomplished by:
    a. typing the drive indicator.
    b. typing the drive indicator, followed by a colon (:).
    c. typing the drive indicator, followed by a colon (:), and then pressing the <ENTER> key.
    d. typing the drive indicator, followed by the greater than character (>), and then pressing the <ENTER> key.

EDLIN

ABOUT THIS CHAPTER

Computers, although powerful, are no more than tools that process and organize information. Likewise, software programs are tools that instruct the computer how to arrange, classify, and use your data.

Computers are simply machines that organize information. This is also the purpose of software packages and programming languages; they are tools to help you arrange, classify, and use your data. But before you can use your computer for this task, you have to get the data in there.

Most of the information you enter into the computer is in the form of text or combinations of numbers, letters, and punctuation marks. MS-DOS keeps track of data by placing it into files or groups of related data. (You were introduced to files when you used the DIR command in Chapter 3.) MS-DOS is a very efficient file organizer. You will learn how to name files and give MS-DOS commands to manage your files in Chapter 6.

But first you must learn how to create files. Included in the MS-DOS operating system is a special program called EDLIN. EDLIN is a text editor, and its sole purpose is to help you create and edit files.

WHAT IS A TEXT EDITOR?

Two common software tools used in a computer to enter and arrange information are text editors and word processors. MS-DOS includes a text editor called EDLIN, which provides you with the basic means of entering, editing, and storing textual information.

EDLIN belongs to that category of computer software tools called text editors. Editors are used to create new files and to add, delete, or modify text in existing files. In addition, editors can move text around inside a file or transfer information from one file to another. There are two different types of editors: full-screen editors and line editors.

Full-Screen Editor

A full-screen editor displays files so that the entire screen is filled with text (usually 23 lines at a time, the capacity of most personal computer monitors). Full-screen editors are also called word-processing programs. Each full screen is like a window displaying a specific section of your entire file. Getting around in a full-screen editor is quite simple. You have complete freedom of movement with your cursor, and you move from window to window with one or two keystrokes. To make changes in the text, you type directly into the window.

Line Editor

EDLIN, however, is a line editor (EDit LINes). Line editors are more limited than full screen editors and a bit more difficult to use. Each line of text is handled separately and is identified by a line number. You use these line numbers to create your own window.

One time-consuming part of using a line editor is that before you can perform any command, you must define the exact location where the operation is to occur. Then you enter instructions to move to this section and display the specified part of the text document. Only then can the editing changes be made.

Actually, using a line editor is not as complicated as it sounds, but these extra steps can slow you down and be frustrating until you are familiar with the EDLIN commands. If most of your work on the computer will be with large files, you should consider purchasing a word-processing program. For smaller jobs, EDLIN does just fine. *Table 5-1* compares the features of the two types of editors.

Table 5-1.
Two Types of Editors

Full Screen Editor	Line Editor
Displays entire screen	Displays designated block of lines
Edits anywhere on screen	Edits within one line
Sophisticated editing features	Limited set of commands
Adds special characters	Uses ASCII code
Long loading time	Built-in and compact
May use lots of memory	Doesn't take up much space
Can be expensive	Free with MS-DOS
Good for large files	Good for small editing jobs

BACKUP FILES

One important feature of the EDLIN editor also found in many other MS-DOS–compatible programs is its built-in safety mechanism of automatically creating a backup file whenever a text file is modified. A file with a name ending in .BAK is always a backup file.

One feature of the EDLIN editor is a built-in safety device. This feature is the automatic creation of a backup file whenever you modify an EDLIN file. This backup has the same name and contents as your text file but is identifiable by a three-letter addition to the filename. Not surprisingly, this extension is .BAK. When you list your files using the DIR command, you will see these "insurance" files listed with the .BAK extension.

```
Volume in drive A has no label
Directory of A: \
```

BILLS	TXT	46976	3-08-83	12:00p
SCORES	TXT	4608	3-08-83	12:00p
LETTERS	TXT	33920	3-08-83	12:00p
BILLS	BAK	45568	3-08-83	12:00p
SCORES	BAK	1408	3-08-83	12:00p
LETTERS	BAK	33792	3-08-83	12:00p

     6 Files(s)   193024 bytes free

Backup files can often prove to be a blessing. Should the computer lose power or malfunction while a file is being edited, only the work during the current edit session is lost; the .BAK backup file will remain intact and can later be copied or renamed to the original name of the file that was being edited.

An EDLIN.BAK file contains a duplicate version of the latest text in a file, not including changes made in the current editing session. Use a .BAK file whenever you lose the contents of an EDLIN file.

Imagine that you have worked long and hard to create a file and are just about ready to call it quits when there is a power blackout. Of course, your computer goes off, and with it go all the changes and modifications you have been patiently entering for the last hour (they were in transient RAM). EDLIN can't miraculously recover those changes, but it can help you "cut your losses." Because your original file still exits in the .BAK version, you will lose only the modifications entered during this current editing session.

EDLIN also has another built-in safety feature. It won't let you edit a file with a .BAK extension. If you could get into the backup files and randomly make changes to this last version, you wouldn't have that unedited copy when you needed it. To use a backup file, you must first give the file a new name, removing the .BAK designation. (You'll learn how to do this using the RENAME command in Chapter 6.) Once the file is no longer the backup, you can begin the editing process all over again.

An EDLIN .BAK file contains a duplicate version of the latest text in a file, not including changes made in the current editing session. Use a .BAK file whenever you lose the contents of an EDLIN file.

Although a .BAK backup copy of a file is always created by EDLIN, it is nevertheless good practice to always make a backup copy of your diskette so that your file can be retrieved even if the original diskette is damaged.

Of course, if anything happens to your diskette, your insurance is canceled because both the original and backup files are stored on the same diskette. It's a good practice to have reserve copies of your files on separate diskettes (the COPY command in Chapter 6 explains how to do this).

Although EDLIN is not as efficient or comprehensive as some full-screen editors, there are some advantages to using it.

One is that EDLIN is free—it is built in as part of MS-DOS. Another advantage is that some word-processing programs make subtle changes to the text files. These are not changes you can see; they are internal changes usually involving modification of the way the file is stored. This can be a problem if you try to use a word-processed file with another program, want to share a file with someone who has a different editor, or attempt to display the file using the MS-DOS TYPE command. These word-processed changes can cause the display of the file's contents to resemble some as yet undiscovered language.

ASCII FILES

EDLIN, like almost all MS-DOS programs that manipulate text data, uses ASCII text that is stored in what are called ASCII files. The ASCII code for representing text is the most commonly used method of manipulating text in today's computers. Using ASCII provides you with the greatest flexibility of transferring text files to many different types of computers.

To eliminate some of these problems, most text files are stored in a format known as an ASCII file. ASCII (American Standard Code for Information Interchange) is a specific code scheme that the computer uses to recognize letters, numbers, and the punctuation marks that make up a text file. ASCII files contain their text information in exactly the same format as it is entered. When displayed, ASCII files make perfect sense.

ASCII is the most widely used format for computer files and is used by most personal computers. One big advantage of entering your data in ASCII code is that these files can be used by many types of programs. This increases the flexibility of your data files. EDLIN enters and stores files in ASCII code.

In addition to the letters, numbers, and punctuation marks that you enter into an ASCII file, there are a few characters that ASCII itself adds to help format the text in a way it can easily understand.

ASCII indicates the end of each line by inserting two characters, the carriage return and the line feed. These characters carry the message "stop this line and move down to the next line."

At the conclusion of each file, ASCII inserts a marker to indicate the end of the file. This character is Ctrl Z, often written with a caret (^) to indicate the control key (^Z = Ctrl Z). These ASCII punctuation characters are hidden; you do not see them when you display or print out ASCII text files.

ASCII text files are used in three main areas of data entry: text files, written source code for programs (source code means the way the programs look as you type them in), and batch-processing files (batch processing is covered in Chapter 8). When you create your files with EDLIN, you are using ASCII to make your files as useful as possible. But now, onto the nitty gritty of actually using EDLIN.

LINE NUMBERS

As with all line-oriented text editors, EDLIN identifies with line numbers each line of text in a text file, numbering them sequentially from the beginning of the file to the end. When text is changed in a text file, EDLIN automatically renumbers the lines as necessary.

Because EDLIN is a line editor, it identifies all information in terms of line numbers. You do not enter these line numbers as you enter text; they are automatically supplied by EDLIN. Line numbers are only reference points within the file; they are not part of the data contained in the file.

1: This is the first line of text.
2: You do not enter the line number as part of the file.
3: The numbers are supplied automatically by EDLIN.

Lines within the file are numbered in sequence. When lines are inserted or deleted, EDLIN remembers the lines automatically. But it doesn't show you the renumbering until you ask to see the file again. This is a bit confusing at first.

Suppose you want to add a new line at the beginning of an existing file (you'll learn how to do this in just a minute). This is a file about computer history, and right now, the first line reads:

In the beginning there was ENIAC...

When you create or display this file using EDLIN, the first line begins with a number.

1: In the beginning there was ENIAC...

If you decide to change your opening and now want the first line to read: "And on the eighth day She created computers," the line number would change.

1: And on the eighth day She created computers.
2: In the beginning there was ENIAC...

Thereafter, if you wanted to modify "In the beginning there was ENIAC . . .," you would need to refer to it as line 2.

GIVING COMMANDS

EDLIN accomplishes its editing tasks by receiving your instructions in the form of commands. Some commands are entered by themselves; others must be accompanied by a line number or range of line numbers.

EDLIN receives its instructions from you in the form of commands. Commands are indicated by one-letter abbreviations as shown in *Table 5-2*. Many commands also require that you indicate which line or line numbers are to be affected by the command. The format of EDLIN commands is simple. First you enter the beginning line number, then the ending line number (when line numbers are present, they are separated by commas), and finally the single letter abbreviation indicating the command. Here are simple examples of EDLIN commands:

**Table 5-2.
Format of EDLIN Commands**

Command	Meaning
1D	Delete line 1.
1,9L	List the file starting with line 1 and ending with line 9.
4I	Insert a new line before line 4.
E	End the editing session

Each EDLIN command is discussed in detail in this chapter.

Current Lines

The line of text currently being worked on inside EDLIN is called the current line and is identified by an asterisk following the line number. When commands are entered that affect the current line, the current line number need not be entered.

Inside EDLIN, the current line (the line you are working on or the last line you modified) is indicated by an asterisk (*) after the line number and preceding the text on that line. If line 2 is your current line, it appears like this:

2:*In the beginning there was ENIAC...

Using the current line as a marker can help you move through your file quickly. For instance, to make modifications to your current line you do not need to enter the current line number. Instead you enter a period.

.D tells EDLIN to delete the current line.

A shortcut to referencing other line numbers from the current line is to use the plus symbol to refer to a number of lines after the current line, or the minus symbol for a number of lines before the current line.

You can use the current line in place of a starting line number as a shortcut to get to a new location. To do this, you indicate the new location relative to the current line using a plus or minus sign and a number.

+35 refers to the line that is 35 lines after the current line.

−54 refers to the line that is 54 lines before the current line.

Until you have become more familiar with EDLIN, you can use actual line numbers to get to the line you want. Later you might find using the current line useful for faster moving in a large file.

Command Prompt

The EDLIN command prompt is identified by a single asterisk appearing on a line of its own on the far left of the screen. It is in response to this prompt that EDLIN commands are entered.

In addition to being a marker of the current line, the asterisk is used as a command prompt. When EDLIN is waiting for a command or for you to enter some information, the asterisk appears on the far left of the screen and is not associated with a line number. When the asterisk is located after a line number, it is indicating the current line.

With this brief introduction to line numbers, commands, and current lines you are all warmed up to begin using EDLIN.

GETTING ORGANIZED

Although using EDLIN and its commands may seem strange at first, the best way to learn any program is to practice on useful but non-important text files.

In earlier chapters you have learned the advantages of hands-on learning. Each use of MS-DOS commands becomes easier when you participate. Up until now you have been learning the fundamentals, and this book has encouraged you to take part. Because this book is based strongly on the "immersion" theory of learning, you are now going to take this participation one step further. Not only will you be learning through practice, you will be doing it in the guise of a series of "personae," each designed to demonstrate an important aspect of MS-DOS.

In your first role you are an overworked, underpaid, harried worker who is definitely in need of some timesaving organization. Sound familiar?

Every Friday you leave the office with fresh determination to accomplish all those chores that you have been putting off. Every Monday morning you wonder "where did the weekend go?" All of this is about to change. As the owner of a new personal computer, you are about to get organized. In fact, that was one of the reasons you bought your computer in the first place. On this early Friday evening you begin by making a list.

CHORES

Jody's soccer game, 9:00
Chad's Little League Game, 12:00
go to grocery store
mow lawn
put up hammock
dog to vet
get dog flea collar!
tennis with Annie, 2:00

SETTING UP

To begin, you must get your computer set up and ready to run. Take your system diskette (your write-protected backup version of your system diskette) and insert it in drive A. Using the DIR command, make sure this diskette contains the EDLIN.COM program.

A> dir edlin.com <ENTER>

Volume in drive A has no label
Directory of A: \

EDLIN	COM	4608	3-08-83	12:00p
	1 File[s]		31232 bytes free	

Next take a formatted diskette with plenty of space available and put it in drive B.

As you contemplate creating your first file, you may find yourself in a quandary. What should you call this new creation? Let's call it "chores." With that decided, you're ready to begin. To create a file, EDLIN needs two facts, the name of the program and the name of the file.

Opening the File

Is the A prompt on the screen? The A drive should be your current drive. You are going to create this file on the diskette in drive B, so you must include the drive indicator (b:) in the command.

A> edlin b:chores <ENTER>

EDLIN responds promptly with one of the messages listed in *Table 5-3*.

New file
*

So far so good: this is a new file, and the asterisk is the EDLIN prompt, which tells you the program is waiting for further instructions.

EDLIN informs you of the status of your text file by displaying messages, such as "New file" if you've just created a new file, and "End of input file" if you've reached the end of the file currently being edited.

EDLIN returns this new-file message after it searches the diskette on the indicated drive and does not find an existing file with the entered filename. In other words, because there is no "chores" file on the diskette in drive B, EDLIN assumes this is a new file.

If you enter the name of an existing file, EDLIN reads this file into memory, then returns a different message.

End of input file

**Table 5-3.
EDLIN's Opening
Messages**

IF EDLIN displays:	It means:
New file	There is no file by this name on the designated diskette.
End of input file	The file has been loaded into memory.
*	The file is too large to fit into memory; memory is filled up to 75% capacity. The remainder of the file is still on the diskette.

If a file that takes more that 75% of available memory is loaded by ED-LIN, a single asterisk will be displayed (the original file remains intact, however).

There is only one instance in which you do not receive a message from EDLIN in response to entering a filename. This is when your file is so large that not all of it can fit into the computer's memory at one time. When this is the case, and it is rare that a beginner would have files this large, EDLIN reads in as much of the file as can fit, reserving 25% of the memory. EDLIN operates with this 25% safety reserve at all times. If this instance should occur, EDLIN will simply display the asterisk prompt with no additional message. Later we will describe some commands for creating space within memory and moving data around when your file is very large.

EDLIN has given you the prompt and is awaiting your command.

ENTERING INFORMATION

The I command is used to place EDLIN into insert mode. Once EDLIN is in insert mode, any text typed on the keyboard will be inserted into the text file.

Now you are ready to type your list of chores into the file. You inform EDLIN that you want to begin entering text by typing in the letter I. As in MS-DOS commands, you can use upper- or lowercase letters to enter commands.

I stands for insert. While you are not strictly inserting information (since no information currently exists in the file), this is the command that EDLIN uses to begin new files. As you might suspect, you also use the I command to insert information into existing files.

```
*i <ENTER>
```

EDLIN accepts your instructions and presents you with the first line number.

```
New file
*i
    1:*_____
```

Begin to type in your list. The first line of your file is your title "chores." You must indicate the end of every line with <ENTER>. Each time you press the <ENTER> key, EDLIN will automatically supply a new line number for the next entry.

```
1:*Chores <ENTER>
2:*
```

If you make typing mistakes, just use the <BACKSPACE> key to erase characters (before pressing <ENTER>) and type the entry again.

When you have entered all the items, you will have nine lines of text. EDLIN will be waiting for line 10.

```
1:*Chores
2:*Jody's soccer game, 9:00
3:*Chad's Little League game, 12:00
4:*go to grocery store
5:*mow lawn
6:*put up hammock
7:*dog to vet
8:*get dog flea collar!
9:*tennis with Annie, 2:00
```

The <Ctrl> C function (or <Ctrl> <Break> on IBM computers) is used while in insert mode to return to EDLIN's command mode.

After you have entered the last chore, you are ready to exit from the insert mode. To return to command mode (EDLIN is ready to receive commands), you use the ^C (<Ctrl> C) function. (IBM users use the <Ctrl> <Break> key combination.) Remember that you must hold down the <Ctrl> key while you press the letter key. Both keys are released together. Enter this <Ctrl> C combination now in response to the prompt for line 10.

```
10:* ^C
   *
```

The asterisk, which has been keeping track of the current line, returns to the prompt position at the far left. You are now back in the command mode.

EXITING EDLIN

There is one more step to take before leaving the EDLIN program completely. You must tell EDLIN that this is the end of the file. You do that by using the E (END) command.

The E (END) Command

To save all edited text to the file stored on disk, the E command must be entered. Once entered, the E command causes EDLIN to update the text file and then display the MS-DOS prompt. The DIR command can then be used to verify the existence of the newly created or updated text file.

This command indicates the conclusion of an editing session. When you finish entering text in an EDLIN file, you must first exit the insert mode (using ^C) and then give the end-of-the-file signal to EDLIN by entering the E command. End the "chores" file now.

    *e <ENTER>

As soon as you enter this command, EDLIN returns control to the operating system (indicated by the A> prompt).

    A>

Table 5-4 lists the steps to take to go into EDLIN, and to return again to MS-DOS at the completion of the EDLIN program.

Table 5-4.
In and Out with EDLIN

A>	Start out in operating system.
edlin *filename*	Call the EDLIN program.
i	Enter the "insert" mode.
lines of text	Enter the content of the file.
^C	Exit the "insert" mode.
e	Exit the EDLIN program.
A>	Returned to operating system.

Now, use DIR to check for the present of a file named "chores." Remember you indicated that this file was to be on drive B when you entered the original filename. Don't forget to include the drive letter now that you are looking for the file.

    A>dir b:chores <ENTER>

Use MS-DOS's TYPE command to display the contents of a text file created or modified by EDLIN. You can also display the contents of your file while in EDLIN by entering EDLIN's L command.

There is your "chores" list on the directory.

Volume in drive B has no label
Directory of B: \

CHORES   175   12-17-84   8:50a
        1 File[s]   361472 bytes free

Checking File Contents

There are two ways to check the contents of an EDLIN file. The first requires the use of the MS-DOS TYPE command discussed in full in Chapter 6. Here is a sneak preview of TYPE. Enter the TYPE command and watch what happens.

A>type b:chores <ENTER>

Chores
Jody's soccer game, 9:00
Chad's Little League game, 12:00
go to grocery store
mow lawn
put up hammock
dog to vet
get dog flea collar!
tennis with Annie, 2:00

There is your file, exactly as you entered it. But notice one thing. There are no line numbers. That's because line numbers are not part of the data in EDLIN files, they are simply reference points to use when editing or creating EDLIN files.

The second way to see the contents of your file is to use the EDLIN L (List) command. More about this command a little later in this chapter. Right now you are going to learn about another way to end an editing session.

The Q (Quit) Command

In addition to the E command, there is another way to end an editing session using EDLIN: you can use the Q (Quit) command. Choose the Q command when you want to stop editing, but don't care about saving the new file or any changes you have made to an existing file. The Q command does not write your file back to the diskette, it simply cancels the current editing session.

You might want to stop a session because you find that you don't really want to make any changes or because things have gotten very mixed up, and you just want to throw this session away. This is the time for the Q command.

Don't confuse the E (End) and the Q (Quit) command.

E is for END.
Save for the next day.
Q is for QUIT.
Toss this #%&* thing away.

EDLIN provides a safeguard to prevent the loss of changes that
you really intend to keep. When you enter the Q command, EDLIN asks a
question.

Abort edit [Y/N]?

This is your last chance. A Y response destroys the information
entered in this editing session. An N response lets you continue with the
edit.

MAKING CHANGES

Now that you have created a file and stored it, it's time to learn
how to make changes in an EDLIN file. Be sure your system diskette
(containing the EDLIN.COM file) is in drive A and the diskette containing
your "chores" file is in drive B. Now ask for the file.

A>edlin b:chores <ENTER>

Because the file named "chores" already exists, EDLIN responds
with the appropriate message.

End of input file
*

The asterisk prompt indicates that EDLIN is waiting in the
command mode. It's ready to make any required modification. There is one
problem though: where is the text of the file?

You must remember that EDLIN moves one step at a time. All
you requested was access to the file. Now EDLIN is waiting to find out
which part of the file you want to see. You have to issue a command to
look at your file.

LOOKING AT THE FIRST DRAFT

The L (List) Command

The L command lists the contents of an EDLIN file and allows
you to look at a file, or a section of a file, while the EDLIN program is in
operation (TYPE lets you look at the contents from MS-DOS). As with
many EDLIN commands, LIST requires the use of line numbers so that
EDLIN can find the correct location in the file. As discussed earlier,
EDLIN commands follow this pattern: starting line number, comma, ending
line number, letter of the command (some commands require additional
information).

EDLIN's L command can be used to list the entire contents of the text file, a range of lines, or a specified number of lines after the current line.

Following this pattern, enter the L command to display the "chores" file.

```
*1,9L <ENTER>

1:*Chores
2: Jody's soccer game, 9:00
3: Chad's Little League game, 12:00
4: go to grocery store
5: mow lawn
6: put up hammock
7: dog to vet
8: get dog flea collar!
9: tennis with Annie, 2:00
*
```

The command told EDLIN to list lines 1 through 9 of the file. If you enter the L command without any line numbers, EDLIN lists the 23 lines centered on the current line number. (The asterisk indicates that line 1 is the current line, which makes sense since you have just opened the file.) Displaying the section immediately surrounding the current line makes working with large files easier when you want to see an overview of the section you are editing. Because "chores" is so short, you could have entered L without a line number, and the entire file would have been displayed. Longer files require that you limit your range of line numbers to 23, the maximum number of lines that can be displayed at one time.

There are other ways to use the L command. The L command with one line number lists the 23 lines starting with that line number, no matter what the current line number is. For example, *43L would list from line 43 through line 65.

Getting the Right Line

Okay, as the weekend moves closer, it's time to get those chores in order. Glancing over your list, you detect a few minor conflicts. You decide that while you can most definitely go to the soccer game at 9:00 and, barring excessive overtimes, make the Little League at 12:00, there is no way you can play tennis at 2:00 and get anything else done. So you make a quick call, "Sorry Annie, how about a bit of twilight tennis?" Because it is forecast to be in the high 90s tomorrow afternoon, Annie quickly agrees, "Tennis at seven."

To edit a specific line within EDLIN, enter the number of the line in response to EDLIN's command prompt. To edit line 10, for instance, simply type 10 and press <ENTER>, and the contents of line 10 will be displayed, followed by a blank line in response to which new text can be entered.

Now it's time to update your file. To edit a specific line within an EDLIN file, enter the line number in response to the asterisk prompt. This command has no letter of the alphabet, simply enter the single line number. Your tennis match is on line 9.

```
*9 <ENTER>
```

EDLIN immediately displays a copy of that line, in its current version. You are then offered a seemingly blank line, preceded by the same line number.

```
9:*tennis with Annie, 2:00
9:*
```

This new line will contain the edited version of the current line. To update your list, you want to change the time of this appointment to 7:00. For now, type in the line again, changing the time. (There are some nice shortcuts you can use in editing lines in EDLIN files. You will learn about these tricks in the section on special keys in Chapter 7.)

```
9:*tennis with Annie, 7:00 <ENTER>
*
```

A newly edited line is not immediately displayed by EDLIN. The L command preceded by the line number of the newly edited line (or a range of lines) must be entered to displayed the new text.

This is all that EDLIN shows you, it doesn't show you the correction right now. To see how changes affect the contents of an EDLIN file, you must use L to list the file again.

```
*1,9L <ENTER>
  1: Chores
  2: Jody's soccer game, 9:00
  3: Chad's Little League game, 12:00
  4: go to grocery store
  5: mow lawn
  6: put up hammock
  7: dog to vet
  8: get dog flea collar!
  9:*tennis with Annie, 7:00
  *
```

If you don't want to make any changes in a line once you have called for it, press <Ctrl> C. The line remains unchanged, and you are returned to the prompt (*).

INSERTING MATERIAL

The I (Insert) Command

What if you remember another thing that you really want to do this weekend—to go to the computer store to get that how new game your son was telling you about. Well, let's add it to the list. To add new lines in an EDLIN file, use the I command, the same one you use to create a new file.

You have to give some additional information to EDLIN when you use the I command to insert new information into an existing file. You must tell EDLIN where to insert the new line. You indicate the line number before the line where you want to make the insertion.

Because your list shows you going out to the grocery store anyway, why not put the computer store right above the grocery store. As with other EDLIN commands, enter the line number first and then the command. You want to insert this new line before line 4.

Line numbers can also be specified with the I (Insert) command to instruct EDLIN to begin the insertion of text at specific line numbers regardless of the current number of the line.

```
*4i <ENTER>
```

The screen displays the line number and waits for the new line.

```
4:*
```

Now type in your addition.

```
4:* go to computer store <ENTER>
```

EDLIN will continue to supply you with new line numbers for insertions until you exit the insert mode using the ^C keys.

```
5:* ^C
*
```

Use the L command to display the changes.

```
*L <ENTER>
  1: Chores
  2: Jody's soccer game, 9:00
  3: Chad's Little League game, 12:00
  4: go to computer store
  5: *go to grocery store
  6: mow lawn
  7: put up hammock
  8: dog to vet
  9: get dog flea collar!
  10: tennis with Annie, 7:00
  *
```

The new line is line 4, and all the remaining items on the list have been moved down one line number. There are now a total of ten items on the list.

The # character can be used with many of ED-LIN's commands instead of a specific line number or range of numbers to indicate the end of the file. To begin inserting text at the end of the file, for example, enter #I in response to EDLIN's command prompt.

Sometimes you may want to add new information at the end of a file; however, no line number currently exits that you can insert before. EDLIN solves this problem by providing the # symbol. The # in conjunction with an editing command means "do this operation at the end of the current file in memory." If you had wanted to add the store trip to the end of the file, you would have entered this command.

    *#i <ENTER>

In response to this command, EDLIN presents a line number that is one higher then the current total number of lines in the file.

    11:*

You would then type in the new line or lines. EDLIN keeps supplying line numbers after every <ENTER>. But you don't want this item on your list twice. So just press ^C to tell EDLIN you are finished with entering new information. Line 11 will remain blank and will not be included in the file. If you are skeptical, check your file using the L command. If the line somehow is included in there, the next command tells you how to get rid of it.

ELIMINATING MATERIAL

The D (Delete) Command

The D command is used to delete the current line, a specified line or number of lines, or a range of lines.

Look over your list. Does it seem like things are beginning to pile up? After all, this is the weekend; you deserve some time off. Maybe you can get the kid next door to mow the lawn and put up the hammock. You're in luck, your neighbor agrees to do those chores. That's two things you can eliminate from your list.

To delete lines in EDLIN, use the D command. This command deletes lines from an EDLIN file. Enter a starting line number an ending line number. In effect, these two line numbers form a block of the information you want to eliminate. This block concept is useful for performing several commands in EDLIN. A block can also be only one line, in which case the starting and ending line numbers are the same and need be entered only once.

First double-check the line numbers of the items you want to delete by displaying the file with the L command.

    *L <ENTER>
    1: Chores
    2: Jody's soccer game, 9:00
    3: Chad's Little League game, 12:00
    4: go to computer store
    5: go to grocery store
    6: mow lawn
    7: put up hammock
    8: dog to vet
    9: get dog flea collar!

10: tennis with Annie, 7:00
*

In the current version of the file (since you added the computer store), "mow lawn" and "put up hammock" are line numbers 6 and 7. Enter a command to delete these lines.

*6,7d <ENTER>
*

To check to see that they are really gone, use the L command.

*L <ENTER>

You will see your revised listing.

1: Chores
2: Jody's soccer game, 9:00
3: Chad's Little League game, 12:00
4: go to computer store
5: go to grocery store
6:*dog to vet
7: get dog flea collar!
8: tennis with Annie, 7:00
*

Notice that in this new listing your original items 6 and 7 are deleted and the remaining items have been renumbered.

Table 5-5 is a comparison of the I and D commands.

**Table 5-5.
Comparison of Insert
and Delete**

	Insert		Delete
i	begin a new file	d	delete the current line
6i	insert a new line 6	6d	delete line 6
	line 6 becomes line 7		line 7 becomes line 6
#i	add new lines at end	1,6d	delete lines 1 through 6
			line 7 becomes line 1

SEARCHING FOR STRINGS

Strings

The S command is used to instruct EDLIN to search for a specified string of characters or words. The text that is to be searched for is entered after the S command, followed by <ENTER>.

Often when you are using EDLIN, you want to find a specific place in a file by searching for a particular word or pattern of characters within the file. In computereze, a group of characters (whether or not they make up an English "word") is called a string. You might, for instance, want to edit a section of a file dealing with the string "Christmas," or you may want to check that you changed "Strong and Sons" to "Strong and Associates" in a letter. To do this you use the S command.

In addition to the string, which tells EDLIN what it should search for, EDLIN also needs to know where to search. You provide this information by indicating the starting and ending line numbers of the block to be searched.

Because you have made several modifications to your "chores" file, you want to make sure that the trip to the vet is still on the agenda. You want to search the entire file (lines 1 through 8) for the string "dog."

The S (Search) Command

By preceding the S command with a line number, a range of line numbers, or the # character, EDLIN is instructed to search a specific line, a range of lines, or the entire file. If the string of text is found, the first line on which the string occurs becomes the current line. If the string is not found, EDLIN informs you of that fact. To continue searching through the text file for the same text string, simply enter the S command without any limits.

The S command, which searches for a string in an EDLIN file, follows this pattern: line number to begin the search, a comma, line number to end the search, the S command, and then the string to be searched for. Enter the S command to find "dog."

　　*1,8sdog <ENTER>

EDLIN begins searching at line 1 and reports the first match.

　　6:*dog to vet
　　*

If you want to continue the search for other occurrences of "dog," enter the S command again.

　　*s <ENTER>

EDLIN displays the next match.

　　7: get dog flea collar!
　　*

When you enter S without any new string, EDLIN uses the last string it was told to search for.

There is one catch with the S command. It finds only *exact* string matches. If "dog" appeared in our file as "Dog" or "DOG" or as part of another word, these instances would not be reported by EDLIN.

Each time you enter the S command, EDLIN continues searching for string matches until it reaches the last line number entered. If it does not find the string, it sends a message that tells you so.

　　Not found

Global Search

There is a variation to the S command that allows you to continue searching after each occurrence of the string without reentering the S command. To do this "global search," insert a question mark (?) in the initial S command. Try looking everywhere for "dog."

        *1,8?sdog <ENTER>

The S command can be used to search for all occurrences of a particular text string by preceding the S command with a question mark—after any line numbers specified. At each occurrence of the specified text string, EDLIN displays a prompt asking you if the line number displayed is the one you want.

Notice that the question mark is entered before the S command. Because you included a ? in the S command, EDLIN asks you if this is what you were looking for or if you want to continue searching.

        6: dog to vet
        O.K.?

If you answer N, EDLIN continues to make matches. A Y answer indicates this is where you want to be, and the search ends.

The R (Replace) Command

The R command is related to the S command in that it too goes through the file searching for the specified pattern. R, however, allows you to replace every instance of your string and another string.

As you are reading over your list you realize that the cat needs a shot too, and she certainly needs a flea collar. To put this information on your list you want to search through "chores" for "dog" and replace it with "dog and cat."

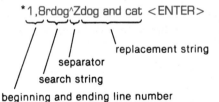

        *1,8rdog^Zdog and cat <ENTER>

        replacement string
        separator
        search string
        beginning and ending line number

The R command performs the same function as the S command with the added capability of replacing the searched-for string of text with new text. The command is entered the same way as the S command except that the <Ctrl> Z function is pressed after the searched-for string, followed by the replacement text string.

The beginning line number is followed by the ending line number. Then comes the R command preceding the string to be searched for. The R command requires one additional piece of information, the replacement string. A ^Z character separates the two strings. The R command automatically replaces every occurrence of the old string with the new string.

        6: dog and cat to vet
        7: get dog and cat flea collar!
        *

As with the S command, you can use ? with the R command. This is useful if you are not certain you want to replace every occurrence of the string. When you include ? in the command, EDLIN asks if you want to make the replacement.

        *1,8?rdog^Zdog and cat <ENTER>

6:*dog and cat to vet
O.K.?

Use the question mark
with the R command if
you're not certain you
want to replace all occurrences of a text string
throughout the entire file
or within a range of lines.

Use Y to approve the replacement and instruct EDLIN to continue with the search. It then displays the next occurrence of the string.

7: get dog and cat flea collar!
O.K.?

If you answer N to this query, no replacement occurs in this line, but the search continues until the ending line number is reached.

These commands, I(nsert), D(elete), S(earch), and R(eplace), are useful editing tools when you are dealing with small changes in just a few lines. But there are times when you will need to make changes involving large sections of a file. These require additional EDLIN commands.

MAJOR REVISIONS

The M (Move) Command

You use the M command when you want to relocate a block of information within an EDLIN file. Because you want to accomplish all your car-related chores at one time, you decide to move the animal items right up there with the store items. It's much more efficient to have your list in neat chronological order.

Entire lines or blocks of
text can be moved within
a file by using the M command. The command is
entered by preceding the
M command by the line or
range of lines to be
moved, a comma, and the
line number before which
the moved text is to be
inserted.

The M command requires beginning and ending line numbers to define the block to be moved. You must also indicate the place you want the block to be moved to. Just as in the I command, you indicate the line number before which you want the items to appear. Because the vet is farther away than the computer store, you move lines 6 and 7 to before line 4.

```
*6,7,4m <ENTER>
*
```

Notice that in addition to the comma separating the beginning and ending line numbers, you must also put a comma between the ending line number and the line number indicating the new location.

Now you have modified your list a lot. Time to see what the newest version looks like.

```
*L <ENTER>
```

```
1: Chores
2: Jody's soccer game, 9:00
3: Chad's Little League game, 12:00
4: *dog and cat to vet
5: get dog and cat flea collar!
6: go to computer store
7: go to grocery store
8: tennis with Annie, 7:00
*
```

The C (Copy) Command

Using the same rules for the M command, the C command can be used to copy, not move, a line or a range of lines to any part of the file.

Another useful way to move lines around inside an EDLIN file is with the C command, which duplicates lines within an EDLIN file. Just like the M command, the C command requires three line numbers, the starting and ending line numbers of the block, and the line number before which the copied lines should appear.

In our "chores" file, there is really no need to put duplicate lines elsewhere in the file, but for practice let's copy lines 2 through 4 and put them before line 7.

```
*2,4,7c <ENTER>
*
```

The resulting list will have eleven items.

```
*L <ENTER>
   1: Chores
   2: Jody's soccer game, 9:00
   3: Chad's Little League game, 12:00
   4: dog and cat to vet
   5: get dog and cat flea collar!
   6: go to computer store
   7:*Jody's soccer game, 9:00
   8: Chad's Little League game, 12:00
   9: dog and cat to vet
  10: go to grocery store
  11: tennis with Annie, 7:00
   *
```

Using the rules for specifying a number of lines or a range of lines with the D command, an entire block of text can be deleted.

The three copied lines appear twice in the list, in their original location as lines 2, 3, and 4 and as new lines 7, 8 and 9. But this makes no sense, so delete lines 7, 8, and 9.

```
*7,9d <ENTER>
*
```

OTHER EDITING COMMANDS

The remaining EDLIN commands require two files or one very large file, so you won't actually perform these commands. Be sure to read through the description of these three commands so that you will be familiar with their capabilities when you need to use them.

The T (Transfer) Command

A line or several lines can be transferred to another file by using the T command.

T is yet another line-moving EDLIN command, but in this case it moves lines from one EDLIN file to another, not to different locations within a file.

Here is a hypothetical situation where you would use this command. You have another file on the diskette in drive B entitled "schedule." This contains a list of appointments that you want included in your "chores" file. You want to merge these two files.

You are going to add the contents of "schedule" to the "chores" file right before your tennis engagement, which is line 8. The T command requires you to give EDLIN these pieces of information: the line before which you want the transfer made, the drive containing the diskette that holds the file, and the filename (with extension if necessary) of the file to be transferred. To merge these two files, you would use the following command:

*8tb:schedule

The contents of "schedule" would now appear in the "chores" file, located immediately before line 8.

The W (Write) Command

As mentioned earlier, you may at some point be working with EDLIN files that are so large that they exceed the 75% memory capacity that EDLIN allocates for file size. In this case you will need to work with your file in parts.

You know that an entire file is not in memory, because EDLIN does not return the "end of input file" message after you load a file. Instead only the asterisk appears.

To access the part of your file that is still on the diskette, you must first clear out some space in memory by writing lines back to a diskette. This is the function of the W command. To use W, enter the number of lines that are to be written back to the diskette followed by the command W.

*2222w

In response, EDLIN writes the first 2222 lines back to the diskette. If you enter W without any line numbers, EDLIN writes back lines until memory is 25% full.

The A (Append) Command

After you have made room using the W command, you want to transfer the next section of your file into memory. The A command adds new text from a diskette to the EDLIN file currently in memory. This command also uses the specified line numbers as a total count of lines to be moved. To add 2222 lines to the file, enter the number of lines to be transferred followed by the command A.

*2222a

If you don't specify any line numbers here, EDLIN automatically fills memory up to its 75% working capacity.

It is unlikely that you will be using the W and A commands in the near future, as they are required only when editing very large files.

SUMMARY

In this chapter you have learned what an editor is and how to use the MS-DOS EDLIN editor. In addition to knowing how to create a new file, you now know how to use all the EDLIN commands, E, Q, L, I, D, S , R, M, C, T, W, and A. If you can make a word out of that, go to the head of the class!

In the next chapter you are going to learn facts about files and how to use MS-DOS commands to manage the files you create and edit with EDLIN.

WHAT HAVE WE LEARNED?

1. The EDLIN line editor is included with MS-DOS utilities; it allows you to create and change text files.
2. The EDLIN backup feature automatically creates a protected duplicate of a file and names the file similarly but with the .BAK extension.
3. EDLIN stores text characters as standard ASCII codes, which associate keyboard characters with specific numbers. EDLIN stores text as lines, which it numbers. In using EDLIN, you must refer to a line or to a range of lines by number.
4. To open a file using EDLIN, type EDLIN <filename>. You will be in the command mode.
5. In the command mode, EDLIN presents an asterisk prompt and an End of Input File message if the file is not too large for memory and accepts single-letter (upper- or lowercase) commands such as I (insert), L (list), and D (delete).
6. To add text to a file, specify a line number followed by the insert command: *4i
7. To delete lines of text from a file, type the range numbers and the delete command: *5,9d
8. You can search for strings of text within a file with the S command and replace strings of text with other text by using the R command. You can move blocks of text within a file by using the M command and copy blocks of text within a file by using the C command.
9. The transfer (T) command moves lines from one file to another; the write (W) command writes lines from memory to a file on the disk; the append (A) command writes lines from a file on the disk into memory.

Quiz for Chapter 5

1. The MS-DOS program EDLIN is a:
   a. full-screen text editor.
   b. line-oriented text editor.
   c. word processor.
   d. text formatter.

2. EDLIN automatically creates a backup file of an existing file being edited so that:
   a. one file can be used for input and the other for output.
   b. the disk can be filled to capacity faster.
   c. the original text can be retrieved should the system lose power or malfunction during an edit session.
   d. MS-DOS is made happy with two copies of everything.

3. EDLIN, and most other MS-DOS–compatible programs, store text in:
   a. ASCII.
   b. ANSI.
   c. EBCDIC.
   d. Hollerith code.

4. EDLIN receives its instructions through:
   a. MS-DOS commands.
   b. EDLIN commands.
   c. COPY commands.
   d. FORMAT commands.

5. Line numbers can be referenced in EDLIN before or after the current line by specifying:
   a. * and the number of lines after the current line, or ¦ and the number of lines before the current line.
   b. + and the number of lines after the current line, or − and the number of lines before the current line.

   c. / and the number of lines after the current line, or \ and the number of lines before the current line.
   d. $ and the number of lines after the current line, or % and the number of lines before the current line.

6. When EDLIN displays an asterisk (*), it means that:
   a. the line of text displayed is the current line if the * follows the line number.
   b. EDLIN is in command mode and is waiting for you to enter a command if the * is the only character on the line.
   c. both of the above.
   d. none of the above.

7. The EDLIN command I is used to:
   a. place EDLIN into insert mode so that you may begin entering text that is to be inserted into the file.
   b. cancel insert mode.
   c. place EDLIN in interrupt mode.
   d. none of the above.

8. The <Ctrl> C function (or <Ctrl> <Break> on IBM systems) is used to:
   a. cancel EDLIN.
   b. cancel insert mode and return to command mode.
   c. stop the system.
   d. write data to the disk.

9. To instruct EDLIN to save all text to the file on disk and return to MS-DOS, the:
   a. W command is entered.
   b. S command is entered.
   c. I command is entered.
   d. E command is entered.

10. The Q command is used only if:
- **a.** you don't want to save any text to the file before terminating EDLIN.
- **b.** you want to store text to the file at any time.
- **c.** you want to save text to the file without terminating EDLIN.

11. To display the contents of a text file, use the:
- **a.** L command while in EDLIN.
- **b.** TYPE command while at the MS-DOS prompt.
- **c.** either of the above.
- **d.** none of the above.

12. With many of EDLIN's commands, a series of lines is specified by entering the:
- **a.** total number of lines to be affected before or after the current line.
- **b.** first line number, followed by a comma, and then the last line number, so that all numbers in between are included.
- **c.** a specific line number.
- **d.** any of the above.
- **e.** none of the above.

13. The D command is used to:
- **a.** delete all lines of text.
- **b.** delete a line of text.
- **c.** delete a range of specific lines of text.
- **d.** delete a specified number of lines before or after the current line.
- **e.** any of the above.
- **f.** none of the above.

14. The S command can be used to:
- **a.** search for any string of text.
- **b.** search for only certain commands.
- **c.** automatically replace text.
- **d.** none of the above.

15. The R command searches for strings of text much like the S command does but with the added capability of:
- **a.** ignoring the text string once found.
- **b.** replacing the text string once found.
- **c.** simply deleting the text string once found.
- **d.** duplicating the text string once found.

16. The character that optionally precedes the S or R command to cause repetitive searches or searches and replacements is:
- **a.** ?
- **b.** #
- **c.** *
- **d.** +

17. In EDLIN, the C command differs from the M command in that:
- **a.** C copies a file, whereas M moves a file.
- **b.** C copies a block of text to another location, whereas M moves a block of text by copying the text and then deleting it.
- **c.** either of the above.
- **d.** none of the above.

18. The T command is used to transfer text within EDLIN to:
- **a.** another file.
- **b.** another location inside the file being edited.
- **c.** the screen.
- **d.** the printer.

19. The W command is used to clear memory and save current text to the file, and the A command is used to retrieve new text from the same file only when:

a. there is plenty of memory in the system.

b. the text loaded from a file exceeds 75% of memory.

c. the system has failed.

d. the file is deleted.

Getting the Files in Shape

ABOUT THIS CHAPTER

The term "file" is not unknown to you. You've been working with files for a while now. You listed files with DIR, copied files with DISKCOPY, and created files with EDLIN. In this chapter you will learn about the intricacies of naming files and how to use MS-DOS to manage your files. First a quick summary.

WHAT IS A FILE?

A file stored on a magnetic disk is much like a paper file folder placed in a file cabinet, in that it stores a group of related data and is stored in one location. When the DIR command is used to display a list of files stored on disk, the effect is similar to opening a file drawer and visually scanning its contents.

A file is a group of related data stored together in one location. Files are not restricted to the high tech world of computers; as illustrated in *Figure 6-1,* you use files every day in a variety of ways. When you stack all your phone bills in one pile, you're creating a file. When you add a memo to a project report at work, you're expanding a file. When you delete from your address book the names of people who moved away ten years ago, you're updating a file.

Computer data files perform this same organization and storage function, but they happen to reside on diskettes. When DIR displays the contents of a diskette, it details the information about each file: its filename, its size in bytes (remember each byte represents one character in a file), and the time and date the file was created or last modified. To MS-DOS all data are part of one file or another.

Figure 6-1.
Types of Files

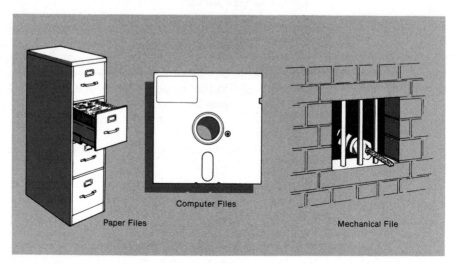

Paper Files

Computer Files

Mechanical File

FILENAMES

To keep MS-DOS from getting confused, each file stored on a particular disk must have a unique name.

To create, store, and retrieve files, they must be named. Otherwise how would MS-DOS differentiate among the thousands of files it has to keep track of? And how would you know what was in each of those files? To alleviate confusion, there is a very simple rule:

Each file on a diskette must have a unique name.

If two or more files share the same name, MS-DOS is totally confused. You have to be very specific.

Imagine a group of participants all milling around at the beginning of a track meet. If the announcer calls over the loud-speaker, "Racers to their marks, please," confusion reigns. Which racers for which race to which marks? This problem is solved by adding specific information that clarifies the instructions: "Attention participants in the 400-yard dash. Racer 2 report to lane 1, racer 4 report to lane 2, racer 6 report to lane 3, and racer 8 to lane 4." Adding specific identifications clears up ambiguities and assures that everyone is in the correct location. This same confusion might happen within DOS.

One of the commands you will learn about in this chapter is COPY.

Many of MS-DOS's commands must be followed by a filename or a group of filenames. Otherwise, MS-DOS doesn't understand what you are trying to accomplish.

A > copy

If you type in this command like this, MS-DOS cannot respond. Copy what, from where, to where? You'll see how to enter this command with all the necessary information in just a second.

Rules and Regulations

When you assign each file a unique filename, both you and MS-DOS know exactly which file is to be created, modified, operated upon, or stored away. A filename must follow a specific pattern.

filename.extension

The filename can be from one to eight characters. An optional extension, not exceeding three characters, may be added to the name. When you give a filename an extension, use a period to separate the extension from the filename itself.

Filenames must be made up of valid characters. *Figure 6-2* is a list of these characters. The exact list of special characters may vary, depending on your computer type and the version of MS-DOS on your machine.

In general, the symbols listed in *Figure 6-3* may not be used in filenames. These symbols have special meanings in MS-DOS and are misinterpreted if included within a filename.

There are also some special groups of characters, listed in *Figure 6-4* that MS-DOS reserves for its own use. One group is the names of the MS-DOS commands and program files. You can't use such already existing filenames. Another group consists of device names. These are abbreviations that MS-DOS uses to refer to specific pieces of computer equipment. By the time you finish reading this book, you'll know 50% of these terms.

All file naming follows a set pattern: filename.extension. The filename must consist of at least one character but may not exceed eight characters. The extension is optional; it may be omitted, or it may contain one, two, or three characters. When a file contains an extension, a period must be used to separate it from the filename. Not all characters may be used in a filename or extension. Some symbol characters have special meaning for certain MS-DOS command functions.

**Figure 6-2.
Valid Characters for Filenames**

All letters of the alphabet, numbers 1 through 9 and 0, and the following special characters:

@ (at sign)	' (single quote)
# (number sign)	P (grave accent)
$ (dollar sign)	~ (tilde)
% (percent sign)	((opening parenthesis)
^ (caret)	) (closing parenthesis)
& (ampersand)	{ (opening brace)
- (hyphen)	} (closing brace)
_____ (underscore)	

Figure 6-3.
Invalid Characters for
Filenames

. (period, except to   / (slash)
delineate an extension)   \ (backslash)
, (comma)   ¦ (vertical bar)
: (colon)   " (double quote)
; (semicolon)   + (plus sign)
* (asterisk)   = (equal sign)
? (question mark)   [(opening bracket)
< (less than)   ] (closing bracket)
> (greater than)

Figure 6-4.
Reserved Filenames
and Device Names

Files:

ASSIGN	DATE	GRAPHICS	RD
BASIC	DEBUG	LINK	RMDIR
BASICA	DEL	MKDIR	SET
BREAK	DIR	MODE	SORT
CD	DISKCOMP	MORE	TIME
CHDIR	DISKCOPY	PATH	TREE
CHKDSK	EDLIN	PRINT	TYPE
CLS	ERASE	PROMPT	VER
COMMAND	EXE2BIN	RECOVER	VERIFY
COMP	FDISK	RENAME	VOL
COPY	FIND	REN	
CTTY	FORMAT	RESTORE	

Devices:

AUX	CON:	LPT3:
COM1:	LPT1:	NUL:
COM2:	LPT2:	PRN:

Some filenames are reserved by MS-DOS as command names or device names. Attempting to name new files the same as the reserved names will either cause immediate errors or future errors.

If you use these combinations of characters in filenames, MS-DOS gets confused. Again, this list may vary from system to system. To be sure about filename limitations, check your computer's user's guide.

Except for these special cases, you can name your files almost anything; for example, "bills," "scores,", "games," "letters."

For convenience and to make typing them in easier, this book always shows filenames in lowercase letters. When you are using filenames in commands, you can enter them in either upper- or lowercase. When filenames are included in the text, they are enclosed in quotation marks (" ").

A FILE BY ANY OTHER NAME

DAN DISK AND HIS DISKETTES

Extensions

A file's extension is normally used to identify the type of file. Some file extensions always mean certain things to MS-DOS; others can be determined by you according to your preferences.

A three-character extension in any filename is optional. Extensions are useful for clarifying or categorizing the contents of a file. For example, you have a file named "letters." Now, if you put all your letters into this one file, not only would it be very large, it would also be extremely difficult to use. Each time you wanted to look at a specific letter, you would have to search through the entire file. By subdividing this file into three smaller files with identifying extensions, you can save yourself a lot of time and trouble.

letters.bus   These are your business letters.
letters.sue   These letters are of a more personal nature.
letters.tax   Legal correspondence concerning tax shelters.

At first glance it would seem that these three files violate the uniqueness rule for filenames. All the files are named "letters." But the extension, as a part of the filename, can be the differentiating factor.

Sometimes it is even desirable to use similar filenames to group related files together. However, be prudent in doing so, because too many similar filenames can cause confusion.

Although you can use any valid character in an extension, there is a loose sort of convention that has grown up among software designers to give certain types of files certain extensions. A few extensions are mandatory because they tell MS-DOS what to do with a file. For example, .BAS refers to a file that is written in BASIC source code. All BASIC files must have this extension. MS-DOS recognizes files with a .BAT extension as "batch files" (batch files are discussed in Chapter 8). Some of the most frequently used filename extensions are shown in *Table 6-1*.

Table 6-1.
Most Frequently Used
Filename Extensions

Extension	Meaning
.BAK	A backup copy of a text file
.BAS	A BASIC source code file
.BAT	A batch processing file
.COM	An executable program in memory-image format
.DAT	A general data file
.EXE	An executable program in relocation format
.TXT	A text file from a word processor

Don't worry if you don't understand these explanations. The only reason these extensions are mentioned at all is so you won't be alarmed if some strange extension shows up on one of your directory listings.

Probably the most important rule of naming files is to assign a name that makes sense to you. Although you can use many special symbols in filenames, what good is a file when you can't remember what's inside it?

Figure 6-5.
What's Wrong With
These Filenames?

ZZZ#9HUH.YUK	This is a legal filename, but what's in it?
MYOWN/.TEXT	Two things are wrong here: / is an illegal character, and there are too many characters in the extension.
FASTNOTES	A filename can have only eight characters.
COPY.BAT	Although COPY can be used in a filename, the file must not be an executable file (also like COPY.COM or COPY.EXE), because COPY is a reserved command name.
DING.BAT	This is a perfectly valid filename, and you're sure to remember what you put in it.

File Specification

Filenames are often specified to MS-DOS com-
mands with preceding
disk-drive identifiers.

The name of a file is made up of the filename (up to eight characters) and the optional extension (up to three characters). But when you use a filename in a command, MS-DOS must have one more piece of information: which drive contains the diskette that holds the file? You direct MS-DOS to the correct drive by including the letter of the drive (the drive indicator a: or b:) in the filename. You were introduced to this concept in Chapter 4 when you learned about the current drive and source and target diskettes. A quick review of drive indicators is presented in *Table 6-2.*

Table 6-2.
Drive Indicators

Drive Indicator	Meaning
A > a:games	The drive indicator is optional because A is the current drive (as shown by the A prompt).
A > games	Produces the same results as the above command.
A > b:games	The drive indicator is mandatory because the file is not on the diskette in the current drive.
B > a:games	The same situation in reverse.
A > format b:	Drive indicator is mandatory for MS-DOS to perform the operation on the correct diskette.
A > diskcopy a: b:	Whenever you are transferring data from one diskette to another, it is a good idea to include both drive indicators.

Because you are going to use the COPY command later in this chapter, learning to use drive indicators takes on added significance. These three elements of a filename—the filename itself, the optional extension, and the drive indicator—make up a file specification. And that's all you really need to know about naming files. This is one area where you can let your imagination run free; just remember a few special rules:

1. Give each file a unique name.
2. Make filename easy to remember.
3. Include a drive indicator if necessary.
4. No more than eight letters in a filename.
5. No more than three characters in an extension.
6. Don't use invalid characters or reserved names.
7. Separate the filename from the extension with a period.

Now that you've conquered filenaming, it's time to expand your routine and learn more about commands.

INTERNAL AND EXTERNAL COMMANDS

Not all of the MS-DOS's commands are stored on the disk in the same manner. Some, called internal commands, are built into MS-DOS itself, whereas others, called external commands, are stored in their own individual files.

Just as "file" was familiar to you from earlier chapters, so is the term "commands." You've been issuing commands since your first DIR experience. But now you are going to expand on that knowledge.

"Command" is another word that is not restricted to computer use. Any of you who have been in the Army or have suffered through dog-obedience courses with lovable Rover know about commands. Commands are simply clear and comprehensible instructions.

Commands in MS-DOS are instructions to the computer. As mentioned earlier, MS-DOS, while true and loyal, is rather stupid. It can understand instructions only when they follow a preordained pattern. The commands that you give MS-DOS must be very specific. Fortunately for users, MS-DOS commands make sense in English too. It's pretty simple now that you have used them a few times to remember that DIR stands for DIRectory, and CLS stands for CLear the Screen. FORMAT and DISKCOPY are self-explanatory. You'll find the commands in this chapter just as clear and concise.

Internal Commands

The advantage of internal commands is that they can be accessed at any time, regardless of the disk inserted in a drive, because they are accessed directly from memory.

There are some commands that are resident in your computer's RAM (transient memory) whenever you are operating under MS-DOS control, that is, whenever you are responding to the MS-DOS prompt (A> or B>). These commands are called "internal" because they are inside the machine's memory, ready for use whenever you are operating in MS-DOS. *Table 6-3* shows the "typical" MS-DOS internal commands.

**Table 6-3.
Internal Commands**

Command	Action
COPY	Makes copies of files
DATE	Sets or displays the date
DIR	Displays a list of files
ERASE (DEL)	Eliminates a disk file
RENAME	Changes a file's name
TIME	Sets or displays the time
TYPE	Displays the contents of a file

The internal commands in your version of MS-DOS may include other commands. Check your user's guide for the internal commands associated with your system.

As indicated in *Figure 6-6*, the important thing to remember about internal commands is that you can use them any time after you have booted your system, without reinserting your system diskette. For instance, you might be running a program off the diskette in drive A, let's say a word-processing program. You have finished with the file, which is on the diskette in drive A, and you want to copy it to drive B. After exiting the word-processing program, you return to the MS-DOS system prompt. Your word-processing program is on diskette 1, now in drive A. The file you want to copy is also on diskette 1. Diskette 2 is in drive B. It contains text files and is the target diskette for your newly completed file.

**Figure 6-6.
Using an Internal
Command**

*Boot system
with MS-DOS
diskette.
Internal
commands
are always
available.*

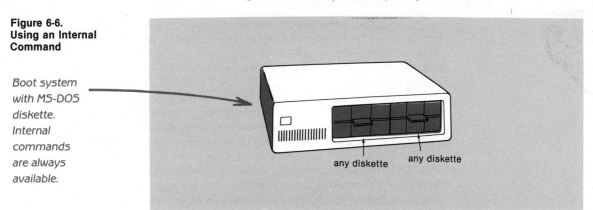

Because COPY is an internal command, you can use it without removing your word-processing diskette from drive A. The command is in memory, available for use no matter which diskettes are in the drives. Use caution, however; there is more to copying files than this. See the section on the COPY command before you copy anything.

External Commands

Most MS-DOS commands do not make their home inside RAM memory. This means they are not available when you are in MS-DOS. These external commands must be loaded from the operating system diskette when you need them. As shown in *Figure 6-7*, to use these commands, you must have a system diskette in drive A.

**Figure 6-7.
Using an External
Command**

*Boot system
with MS-DOS
diskette.
Must have
system
diskette in
drive A for
external
commands.*

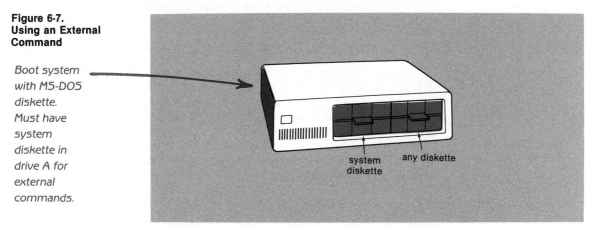

When you enter a command, MS-DOS first checks its list of internal commands. If the command is not found, MS-DOS searches the default disk for a matching external command. If MS-DOS is not able to find the command specified, it displays an error message.

When you enter a command, MS-DOS first checks to see if the command is internal. If the command is not found, MS-DOS goes out to the system diskette to find and load the command. If it is not on the diskette, or you don't have a system diskette in the drive, MS-DOS sends you an appropriate error message.

Bad command or file name

FORMAT is an example of an external command. In the hypothetical example above (word-processing diskette in drive A, and data diskette in drive B), you may want to transfer the file on diskette 1 to a new diskette, diskette 3, but first you need to FORMAT a diskette to receive the data.

Because FORMAT is an external command, you must have a system diskette in a drive to make use of this command. (That is why you should have several formatted diskettes handy at all times.) To execute the FORMAT command, you must first remove your word-processing diskette and insert the system diskette. Only now are you ready to use the FORMAT command. (Of course, you should also remove the data diskette from drive B and insert a new blank diskette before entering the FORMAT command, or else you will lose the data currently on the diskette in drive B.)

If you enter a command that you know is an external command, you can instruct MS-DOS to retrieve the command from a disk drive other than the default by preceding the command with a disk-drive identifier.

Before you begin studying specific commands in detail, here are some helpful hints for entering all MS-DOS commands:

- Wait until you see the MS-DOS prompt (A> or B>) before entering a command. The prompt means DOS is up and waiting.
- When a command requires a filename to operate, be sure you include all the necessary parts of the file specification (drive indicator, filename, and extension).
- Use a blank space to separate the different parts of a command: Leave a space between command and drive indicator. Leave spaces between command, filename, and drive indicator.
- You can enter commands in either upper- or lowercase.
- When commands don't work, check your typing. Is the command correct, did you leave the appropriate spaces, did you spell the filename correctly? Are you trying to use an external command without inserting the system diskette?
- End each command with the <ENTER> key.

This chapter covers four MS-DOS commands: COPY, TYPE, ERASE, and RENAME. They are all internal commands. But before you start copying, typing, erasing (especially erasing), and renaming files, you need a file to use with these commands. So let's put your EDLIN skills to work and create a new file.

Put your backup system diskette in drive A. Be sure it contains a copy of the EDLIN.COM program. The file you are creating will also be located on this system diskette.

CREATING A NEW FILE

Assume that you are a writer just embarking on a literary career. You are using your new personal computer to write your first work. Your book text will be contained in a file called "novel." Using EDLIN, enter the text of this file. The first line of text is the title of this work, "EVEN MONEY."

```
A>edlin novel <ENTER>
New file
*i <ENTER>
        1:*EVEN MONEY <ENTER>
```

As EDLIN returns new line numbers, enter the remainder of the text. You're going to get through only the opening paragraph in this session.

```
2:*There was a 50/50 chance the world would end today. <ENTER>
3:*It was down to just the three of us now. <ENTER>
4:*The "Stranger" kept watching the darkening sky. <ENTER>
5:*Finally he saw the signal. <ENTER>
6:*Tossing the quarter in the air, he laughed "Call it"...<ENTER>
7:*
```

Use ^C to exit the "insert" mode.

```
7:^C
```

Now give EDLIN the end of file command.

```
*e <ENTER>
```

The system prompt tells you that MS-DOS is now back in control.

```
A>
```

If you want to, you can use DIR to verify that the file is on the diskette.

```
A>dir novel <ENTER>

Volume in drive A has no label
Directory of A: \

NOVEL        242      12-17-84  10:11a
     1 File[s]                30720 bytes free
```

If you are eager to see your work in print, you can use a new MS-DOS command to see the contents of this file. You had a preview of this command in Chapter 5.

REVIEWING WHAT YOU WROTE

The TYPE Command

With the commands such as EDLIN and TYPE, computers equipped with MS-DOS can be excellent tools for the creation of text files for many applications such as letters, recipes, reports, documents, and books.

TYPE is a very straightforward command. Used in conjunction with a filename, it displays the contents of the file. The text of the file must be in ASCII format, or you'll have a tough time deciphering it. If you missed it earlier, ASCII file format is discussed in detail at the beginning of Chapter 5. Because EDLIN creates files in ASCII code, you will have no trouble reading your "novel."

A>type novel <ENTER>

The file contents appear (without line numbers).

EVEN MONEY
There was a 50/50 chance the world would end today.
It was down to just the three of us now.
The "Stranger" kept watching the darkening sky.
Finally he saw the signal.
Tossing the quarter in the air, he laughed "Call it". . .

Figure 6-8.
The TYPE Command

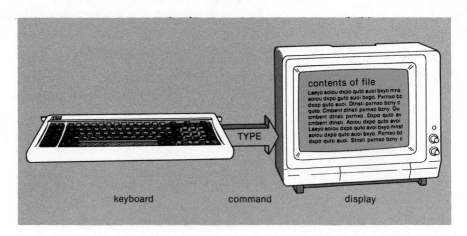

By including a drive indicator in the TYPE command, you can view files on other diskettes. If you had created "novel" on the diskette in drive B, you would ask to see the file by adding b: after the command.

A>type b:novel <ENTER>

Because you don't currently have the file on the diskette in B, this command will not work. But how do you go about making a backup of this copy to put on another diskette?

MAKING COPIES

The making of regular backup copies of all your disks each time they're updated cannot be over-stressed. If you are able to retrieve backed-up files if the disk containing the original files is damaged, you will save time and money and reduce consid-erably the amount of irri-tation computer mishaps can cause.

In today's world of information proliferation, rarely do you make just an original of anything. From term papers to tax forms, it's always smart to keep a copy. When the documents are on paper, you type multiple copies or, more likely, run down to the copy machine.

Copies are useful for many reasons. They are handy if two or more people are referring to the same document. They allow you to share with someone else information that might not otherwise be available to them. They provide a record of interaction between two companies or communication between two people. But by far the most persuasive argument for copies is that they provide insurance in case something should happen to the original. (This was discussed in some detail in Chapter 4.)

All of these reasons for making copies hold true for your computer files too. It is just as easy to copy a computer file as it is to copy a paper file, but you don't need any extra copying equipment. All you need is another diskette. How important are copies? Let's go back to your rule as a writer.

Much as you would like to, you can't earn a living as an unpublished author. So your writing times are squeezed between the demands of the office and the need for sleep. Naturally, this time is precious to you. Late one evening, you start to work on some changes that your agent has suggested. After hours of work, you have incorporated the revisions into the text. But the very next day your agent phones and says, "Scratch those changes, there may be a question of libel involved."

Unfortunately, while you were editing the work, you entered and exited the EDLIN program several times, so even the EDLIN backup file no longer contains your original version. You do have a printout of the first few chapters, but that means entering lots of text again. To avoid situations such as this, it is important that you make a backup of your original file (on a separate diskette) before you make any significant changes.

Now you finally have your book back in order. You have been talking to a friend in Chicago about the possibility of turning this book into a screenplay. Your friend is eager to see the latest revision, so you send your diskette to Chicago. Your friend spills a cup of coffee on your diskette, and it is ruined. This is why you should make a copy of all files before they leave your possession.

Are you beginning to get the picture? The thing that is helpful to remember about diskette files, as opposed to paper files, is that unless you make one, there is no copy of anything in the file. You can't hunt through the wastepaper basket for the piece of information you deleted. You should make copies for insurance, in case a diskette is accidentally damaged; in case you need a copy of an earlier version of the files; and to reorganize files. There are other reasons to make copies. You might copy files when you want to put them in new groups on a diskette or use parts of a file to reorganize its contents. Some of these reasons are shown in *Figure 6-9.*

Figure 6-9.
Making a Backup Copy
of a File

Copy entire
file to a
different
diskette

erase
unneeded
section of
file

give file a
new name

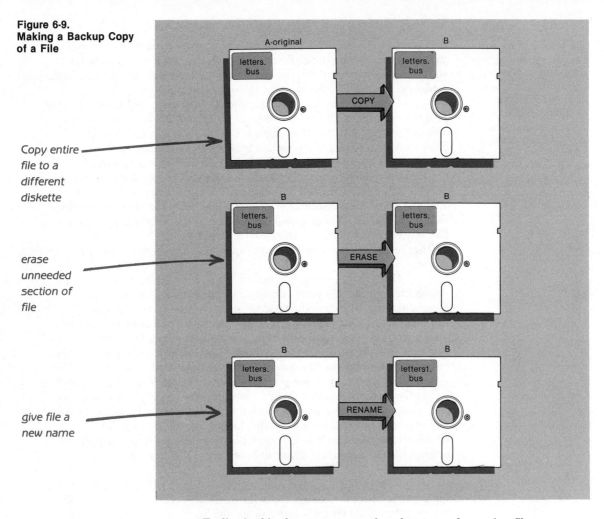

Earlier in this chapter you saw the advantage of grouping files using extensions.

letters.bus, letters.sue, letters.tax

Suppose the "letters.bus" file has become too large to be efficient. Here's how you would use a copy to solve that problem. Of course, you already have an updated backup of this file.

First, you make a copy of the entire "letters.bus" file. You want to make a new file that contains only the letters from the Live Now, Die Later company. By deleting all the other correspondence in your newly copied file you are left with only the relevant letters. You then give this file a new name using RENAME (a command discussed later in this chapter). Your results are one file, "letters1.bus," which holds only a part of your original file, "letter.bus."

In most cases, you will be copying from one diskette to another. This means you have to tell MS-DOS where to find the original and where to put the copy.

Source and Target Diskettes

The DISKCOPY command provides a method of backing up entire diskettes that is quicker than using the COPY command to copy files individually.

You were introduced to the concept of source and target diskettes when you used the DISKCOPY command. They are equally important in the use of the command you are about to execute, the COPY command, and deserve a brief review here.

The source diskette contains the original file. The target diskette is the destination of the copied file. Where there are two drives, the source is usually the diskette in drive A, and the target is the diskette in drive B. MS-DOS reminds you to keep track of your source and target.

Insert source diskette in Drive A
Insert target diskette in Drive B

The source and target diskettes are indicated by drive specifiers (a: and b:).

If you have a single-drive system, refer back to the discussion of DISKCOPY (in Chapter 4) to review how MS-DOS "pretends" you have two drives.

With this theoretical discussion of why and when to make copies behind you, revert to your novelist's role as you learn to use the COPY command.

The COPY Command

Use the COPY command to copy individual files or a group of files between disks.

The COPY command is versatile. It makes copies of a file or a group of files. One use of this command that you will make very frequently is to copy a file from one diskette to another, keeping the same name. (This is the backup.) Let's try this now. You will need your system diskette containing the created "novel" file and a formatted blank diskette to perform these copying exercises.

You want to make an insurance copy of your first edition of "EVEN MONEY." Take the diskette containing "novel" (in this case, your system diskette) and put it in drive A. This is your source diskette. It is just a coincidence that "novel" is on your system diskette. Because COPY is an internal command, it is not necessary to have the system diskette in a drive when you are executing this command. Put the diskette that will contain the copy in drive B. This is your target diskette.

The A> prompt shows you that drive A is your current drive. It is not necessary to include the drive indicator a: when referring to a file on this diskette in this drive. Just to keep things clear, however, it's easier to include the drive indicator in these copy commands. As you become more at ease with MS-DOS, you will probably not include the drive indicator when it is unnecessary.

Okay, now copy "novel" to the target diskette.

A> copy a:novel b: <ENTER>

With this command you tell MS-DOS to copy the file "novel" now on the diskette in drive A to the disk in drive B. The name of the copied file will also be "novel."

MS-DOS will respond to this command.

1 File[s] copied

Short and simple but to the point. This message says, "fine, your request has been honored." This message is a convenient part of MS-DOS, because it lets you know several things at once. It tells you that the specified file was found on the indicated diskette, that there is no problem with the target diskette, and that the copying procedure is completed. If anything had gone wrong, such as an incorrect diskette inserted in A or an unformatted diskette in B, you would have received an error message. The COPY command procedure is depicted in *Figure 6-10*.

**Figure 6-10.
Copy to a Different
Diskette**

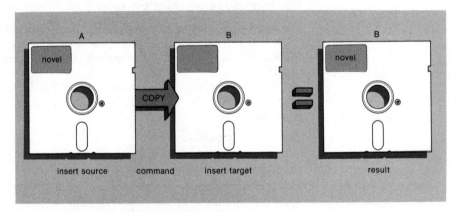

As a nervous writer, you may want to be sure the copy is on the diskette in B. Relieve your skepticism by requesting verification with the DIR command.

A > dir b: < ENTER >

MS-DOS will respond.

Volume in drive B has no label
Directory of B: \

NOVEL   242   12-17-84   10:11a
        1 File[s]   361472 bytes free

The COPY command can be used to copy and rename a file at the same time. Copying and renaming can be accomplished on the same disk or between two disks.

Changing the Filename

You don't have to use the same name when you copy a file. Suppose you want to copy the file and try changing sections of it. You want both a copy of the original and a copy to fool around with. You can copy the file and give it a new name. To do this include a new filename in the COPY command. Try copying your file, but change the name to "bestsell." The procedure is shown in *Figure 6-11*.

A>copy a:novel b:bestsell <ENTER>

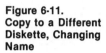

**Figure 6-11.
Copy to a Different
Diskette, Changing
Name**

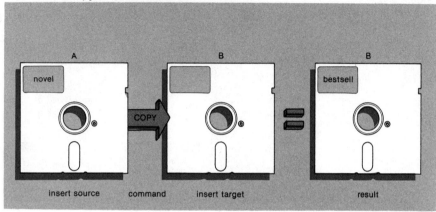

Again your instruction will be confirmed.

1 File[s] copied

If you have done both of the preceding exercises, you now have two files copied on the target diskette. One is called "novel" and the other is "bestsell." Both files contain exactly the same information. To make sure both copies are on the diskette, use the DIR command.

A>dir b: <ENTER>

Volume in drive B has no label
Directory of B: \

NOVEL   242   12-17-84 10:11a
BESTSELL   242   12-17-84 10:11a
         2 File[s]   360448 bytes free

You can also have two copies of a file on the same diskette. But to copy a file to the same diskette, you have to give the file a new name because no two files on the same diskette can have the same name. Let's make a duplicate copy of "novel" on the diskette in drive A. In this case, the diskette in drive A is both the source and target diskette. This time try leaving out the drive indicator.

A>copy novel bestsell <ENTER>
                1 File[s] copied

You now have two copies of the file on the same diskette. Only the names are different; the contents are the same. *Figure 6-12* shows how this is done.

**Figure 6-12.
Copy to Same Diskette,
Changing Name**

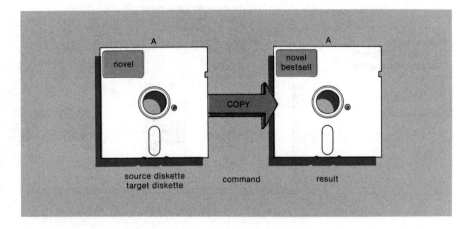

Use the RENAME command when you don't want to copy a file but want only to change its name. When renaming a file, the new filename must also be unique.

If you attempt to copy a file to a diskette and that diskette already contains a file with an identical filename, MS-DOS will respond with an error message.

```
File cannot be copied onto itself
      0 File(s) copied
```

If you want to be sure that all your files are, in fact, duplicate copies of the same diskette, you can check their contents using the TYPE command.

```
A> type novel <ENTER>
A> type bestsell <ENTER>
A> type b:novel <ENTER>
A> type b:bestsell <ENTER>
```

The results of all these commands are the same because you have not altered the contents, just the filenames. The next command also allows you to change the name of a file.

RENAMING FILES

There are several reasons you might want to rename a file. It could be that you have files with similar names and there is danger of confusing them. Perhaps you have given your file an esoteric name and now can't remember what's in it. Or you may want to group a set of files together under a new name, as when the Handydandy Company becomes At Your Service Company, and you need to change their name in all your files dealing with them.

The RENAME Command

This command, abbreviated REN, changes the name of a file. RENAME is also the command you use to remove the .BAK extension from files so that you can use backup files for editing purposes. See "Safety in Numbers" in Chapter 5.

As an aspiring writer, you realize that there is another novel you want to write. The filename "novel" is now too limiting. You want to know *which* novel. So you decide to give your file the specific name "opus1." Using the RENAME command, change the filename. You can enter this command with its entire name, "RENAME," or you can use the abbreviation "REN." You must include the old and new name. To rename the file on the current drive you don't need to include drive indicators.

A>ren novel opus1 <ENTER>

This is a silent job by MS-DOS. It simply returns you to the A>prompt after renaming the file. To verify the name change you must use DIR.

A>dir <ENTER>

This gives you a listing of the entire diskette. Notice that the listing no longer contains "novel" but does contain "opus1."

You can also make sure that the change has occurred by using DIR with the new filename.

A>dir opus1 <ENTER>

MS-DOS confirms that the filename has been changed.

Volume in drive A has no label
Directory of A: \

OPUS1   242   12-17-84   10:11a
        1 File[s]   30208 bytes free

If you want to be absolutely sure that "novel" no longer exists, you can ask for a directory of that file.

A>dir novel <ENTER>

If no file by that name is on the diskette, MS-DOS will tell you.

File not found

As you can with the other commands, you can rename a file on a drive other than the current drive by including a drive indicator. Now, rename the file "novel" that is on the diskette in the B drive by including the drive indicator in the command.

A>ren b:novel opus1 <ENTER>

"Novel" is no more. Again you will be returned to the system prompt. You still have two copies of the file on each diskette, but they are named "opus1" and "bestsell." A listing of the files on the diskette in B confirms this change.

A>dir b: <ENTER>

Volume in drive B has no label
Directory of B: \

OPUS1	242	12-17-84	10:11a
BESTSELL	242	12-17-84	10:11a
2 File[s]		360448 bytes free	

You may be confused as to how this command is different from using the COPY command with a new filename; both change the name of the file. *Table 6-4* outlines the distinction.

Table 6-4.
COPY Versus RENAME

Command	Action
A>copy novel bestsell	Creates a duplicate file with a new name
A>ren novel opus1	Changes the name of the existing file

ERASING FILES

Files seem to multiply at an alarming rate. Many of the files you use, such as program files, will serve you well for many years. Other files quickly become outdated or irrelevant. Even the worst pack rat cannot save every file forever. Sooner or later you will want to do some housekeeping and clean up your files. You eliminate unneeded files with the ERASE command.

The ERASE and DEL commands provide the identical function of erasing a file or group of files on a disk. However, only when erasing "all files" with either of these commands will a prompt ask you if this is what you want. These commands should therefore be used with caution.

The ERASE Command

The ERASE command, which is identical to the DEL (Delete) command, deletes files from a diskette. The DEL (Delete) command is identical to the ERASE command.

Before using this command, make sure that the file to be erased is a duplicate or useless file. Also, enter the filename with care; if your files have similar names, a simple typing error can cause you grief because you cannot get back files once they have been erased.

At this point, you have duplicated copies of your file on both diskettes. You want to do a little tidying up, so you are going to erase one of the files on each diskette. You decide to stick with the name "opus1" because it most clearly defines the file for you. Before you do any erasing, it's a good idea to make sure exactly which files are on a diskette. If you have a directory in front of you, you're less likely to enter a filename by error and find out too late that you made a mistake. A directory also confirms that the file you want to delete actually resides on the diskette.

With all of the copying and renaming that you have done on this file, you may be confused as to which names are still valid filenames. Get a directory of each diskette.

A>dir<ENTER>

```
Volume in drive A has no label
Directory of A:\
```

COMMAND	COM	17664	3-08-83	12:00p
ANSI	SYS	1664	3-08-83	12:00p
FORMAT	COM	6016	3-08-83	12:00p
CHKDSK	COM	6400	3-08-83	12:00p
SYS	COM	1408	3-08-83	12:00p
DISKCOPY	COM	2444	3-08-83	12:00p
DISKCOMP	COM	2074	3-08-83	12:00p
COMP	COM	2523	3-08-83	12:00p
EDLIN	COM	4608	3-08-83	12:00p
MODE	COM	3139	3-08-83	12:00p
FDISK	COM	6177	3-08-83	12:00p
BACKUP	COM	3687	3-08-83	12:00p
RESTORE	COM	4003	3-08-83	12:00p
PRINT	COM	4608	3-08-83	12:00p
RECOVER	COM	2304	3-08-83	12:00p
ASSIGN	COM	896	3-08-83	12:00p
TREE	COM	1513	3-08-83	12:00p
GRAPHICS	COM	789	3-08-83	12:00p
SORT	EXE	1280	3-08-83	12:00p
FIND	EXE	5888	3-08-83	12:00p
MORE	COM	384	3-08-83	12:00p
BASIC	COM	16256	3-08-83	12:00p
BASICA	COM	25984	3-08-83	12:00p
OPUS1		242	12-17-84	10:11a
BESTSELL		242	12-17-84	10:11a

```
        25 File(s)          30208 bytes free
```

Now take a look at the other diskette.

A>dir b: <ENTER>

```
Volume in drive B has no label
Directory of B:\
```

OPUS1	242	12-17-84	10:11a
BESTSELL	242	12-17-84	10:11a

```
        2 File(s)          360448 bytes free
```

First eliminate the "bestsell" file from the diskette in drive A.

A>erase bestsell <ENTER>

You don't get any response from MS-DOS when you use the ERASE command. To make sure the file is gone, use the DIR command.

A>dir bestsell <ENTER>

The ERASE procedure is shown in *Figure 6-13*.

**Figure 6-13.
The ERASE Command
Result**

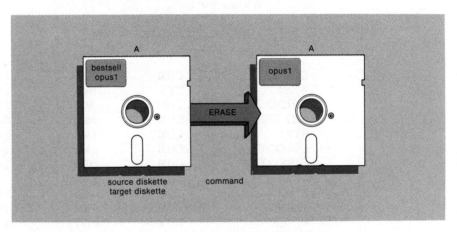

If the ERASE command has been executed properly, you get this message:

File not found

Are you worried that you have eliminated all traces of your book? Just ask for it by name.

A>dir opus1 <ENTER>

Volume in drive A has no label
Directory of A: \

OPUS1   242   12-17-84   10:11a
         1 File[s]   361472 bytes free

Perform the same procedure on the diskette in drive B.

A>erase b:bestsell <ENTER>

Use the DIR command either way you want to make sure the file is gone.

A>dir b: <ENTER>

Volume in drive B has no label
Directory of B: \

OPUS1   242   9-29-84   1:29p
         1 File[s]   361477 bytes free

When using the COPY, RENAME, or ERASE (or DEL) commands, always use the DIR command beforehand to verify what it is that you're trying to accomplish. Use the DIR command again afterward to make sure that the command you entered accomplished what you wanted.

Everything is as it should be. You're right back where you started, with two copies of the file, one on the diskette in drive A and the backup on the diskette in drive B.

If you are a bit confused, it is worth your time to create, copy, type, rename, and erase some more files. These commands are the "bread and butter" of your everyday work with MS-DOS. COPY, especially, is essential because you will be making frequent backups of your files. You may be surprised by how often you use TYPE to see the contents of a file. RENAME and ERASE are commands that become increasingly useful as you accumulate more and more files and want to clarify and clean your various directories.

SUMMARY

This chapter has set a new pace for your conquest of MS-DOS. First you discovered files and learned the ins and outs of filenaming. You were then introduced to MS-DOS commands in general and the difference in the use of internal and external commands. In the guise of a struggling writer, you used EDLIN to create a file. Using this file you put MS-DOS to work by using the TYPE, COPY, RENAME, and ERASE commands. At the conclusion of this chapter, you are well on your way to effective file management using MS-DOS.

WHAT HAVE WE LEARNED?

1. Every file must have a unique name, which can be up to eight characters followed by a period and an extension of up to three characters.
2. DOS does not allow a colon, asterisk, hyphen, or many other punctuation characters in a filename.
3. Certain names are reserved for DOS use and may not be used for any other purpose.
4. In using a command to manipulate a file, you need to specify the name of the disk drive in which the file is currently stored.
5. Internal commands reside with the disk operating system in memory, ready for use.
6. External commands are associated with the utility programs that accompany the DOS command program on the MS-DOS diskette.
7. The type command is an internal command that prints the contents of a file to the screen: A > type b:fancy.one.
8. The copy command is an internal command that lets you copy the contents of a file to another disk or to its own disk under a different name.
9. The rename and erase commands are internal commands that let you change the names of files and delete files, respectively.

Quiz for Chapter 6

1. Data stored in files by MS-DOS can be compared to:
   a. files stored in a file cabinet.
   b. files stored within folders.
   c. a stack of files in the in-basket.
   d. a stack of files in the out-basket.
   e. any of the above.
   f. none of the above.

2. A filename can have up to:
   a. no characters.
   b. eight characters.
   c. twenty characters.
   d. any number of characters.

3. A file's extension is an optional part of a file's name and is normally used to indicate the type of file. An extension can be composed of:
   a. no characters (if not used).
   b. one character.
   c. two characters.
   d. three characters.
   e. any of the above.
   f. none of the above.

4. Filenames and extensions can be made up of:
   a. any characters.
   b. only numerical characters.
   c. all alphabetic and numeric characters and some special symbol characters.
   d. only alphabetic characters.

5. MS-DOS internal commands are those that are:
   a. built into MS-DOS itself.
   b. stored in external files.
   c. always stored on ROM.
   d. stored in the CPU.

6. External commands are those that are:
   a. built into MS-DOS itself.

   b. stored in external files.
   c. always stored in ROM.
   d. always stored in RAM.

7. MS-DOS will execute an internal command:
   a. regardless of the disk inserted in any of the disk drives.
   b. only if a specific disk is in the default drive.
   c. only in two-drive systems.
   d. only in hard-disk systems.

8. Considering the importance of regularly backing up your data files, MS-DOS provides the following commands to help you in this task:
   a. DIR
   b. COPY
   c. DISKCOPY
   d. all of the above

9. The COPY command can be used to:
   a. copy a file between two disks.
   b. copy and rename a file at the same time between two disks or on the same disk.
   c. copy all files or a group of files between disks.
   d. all of the above.
   e. none of the above.

10. The REN, or RENAME, command provides the function of:
    a. copying a file.
    b. renaming a file.
    c. deleting a file.
    d. listing a file.

11. The ERASE command, which is used to erase a file, a group of files, or all files on a disk, can also be accessed by entering:
    a. DEL
    b. DELETE
    c. DESTROY

Special Keys and Key Combinations

ABOUT THIS CHAPTER

This chapter is going to refine your computing skills. In the preceding two chapters you have been working with files, creating them with EDLIN, and managing them with the basic MS-DOS commands. Through your experience with MS-DOS you have already become acquainted with some of the special keys on your computer keyboard. By this time you are probably becoming familiar with the location of the standard alphabet, number, and punctuation keys.

This chapter teaches you how to use your keyboard more effectively by presenting some special keys and key combinations that make file creation and editing easier. In addition, it expands your knowledge of commands by showing you how to use switches with the DIR and FORMAT commands. Finally, three new commands are discussed: SYS, CHKDSK, and MODE.

A QUICK REVIEW

The two most commonly used keys on an MS-DOS system are the <ENTER> and <BACKSPACE> keys.

The first two special keys are already in your repertoire. They are illustrated in *Figure 7-1* and included here as a brief review.

Figure 7-1.
The <ENTER> and <BACKSPACE> Keys

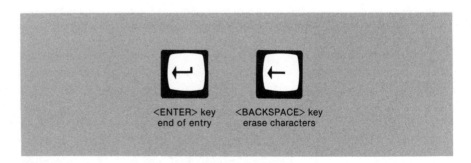

<ENTER> key
end of entry

<BACKSPACE> key
erase characters

The <ENTER> Key

You wouldn't be this far along unless you had already mastered the <ENTER> key. This important key indicates the end of an entry and must be pressed to give the go ahead signal to MS-DOS. This key may look like this < ↵ > on your keyboard.

The <BACKSPACE> Key

And unless you are perfect, you've probably had a lot of experience with the <BACKSPACE> key as well. This key is an easy way to erase characters to correct mistakes. It moves the cursor to the left along a line and erases characters as it moves. You will learn some additional mistake-correcting procedures later in this chapter. This key may be represented as a left arrow <←> on your keyboard.

SPECIAL KEYS

Now we are going to introduce some other keys that make using MS-DOS and EDLIN more convenient. One word of caution: your keyboard may not contain some or any of these keys. But by reading through the entire section on editing characters, you will find out how to use your keyboard to the best advantage.

Most of these keys are operational only when you are using MS-DOS or EDLIN, although there are exceptions. They are usually inoperative or perform different functions in other programs. After a little experience in a variety of computing applications, you will learn the quirks of each key and its uses.

The <Caps Lock> Key

The <SHIFT> and <Caps Lock> keys on a computer keyboard often operate a little differently from those on a typewriter.

When <Caps Lock> is in effect, pressing <SHIFT> causes all alphabet keys to be entered in lowercase. You have used the <SHIFT> key to enter uppercase letters, but you may not know that there is another key that also lets you type in uppercase. This is the <Caps Lock> key, which is located for you in *Figure 7-2*. When <Caps Lock> is not in use, all letter and number keys are normally entered in lowercase. When you turn on <Caps Lock> mode by depressing this key, all letters are entered in uppercase. <Caps Lock> affects only the letter keys on your keyboard; it does not affect number or punctuation keys. <SHIFT> is still required to enter the punctuation symbols found above the number keys and on the upper section of other keys. <Caps Lock> mode stays in effect until you depress the key again.

Figure 7-2.
<Caps lock> Key

<Caps Lock>

Here is one unique result of using the <Caps Lock> key that may surprise you: when you are in the <Caps Lock> mode, pressing the <SHIFT> key causes all letters to be entered in lowercase. Try using <Caps Lock> to enter some information just to get the general idea.

In Normal Mode (<Caps Lock> off), pressing <M> results in m; pressing <SHIFT> <M> results in M; and pressing <SHIFT> <2> results in @.

In Caps Lock Mode (<Caps Lock> on), pressing <M> results in M; pressing <SHIFT> <M> results in m; and pressing <SHIFT> <2> results in @.

The <Esc> Key

The <Esc> (Escape) key is used for many programs to "escape" from a particular operation. If you press <Esc> while typing a command at the MS-DOS prompt, a backslash (\ ) is displayed, indicating that the command is canceled.

Suppose you discover that you have made a mistake on an entry as you just finish typing in the entire line. Of course, the mistake is way back at the front of the line. You just don't feel like sitting there using <BACKSPACE> to erase the whole thing. There is a way to cancel an entire line.

To eliminate the current line you use the <Esc> (Escape) key. (<Esc> must be pressed before the <ENTER> key.) <Esc> puts a backslash (\ ) on your command line to indicate that the command is canceled. It then moves the cursor down one line so you can enter a new command. When you cancel a line with <Esc> it is not received by the computer. The <Esc> key is located for you in *Figure 7-3*. Try this now: imagine that you are looking for a file on the directory called fishing.123. As you enter the extension you realize that you have made a mistake.

A> dir wishing.123 <Esc>

The <Esc> key cancels this command and moves you down to the next line. The cursor appears waiting for a new command.

A> dir wishing.123 \

You could now enter the correct information and continue with your work. Additional editing commands will be explained later in this chapter.

Figure 7-3.
The <Esc> and <PrtSc> Keys

The <PrtSc> Key

The <PrtSc> key (only on IBM-compatible keyboards) is used in combination with other keys to cause text displayed on the screen to be output to a printer.
<SHIFT> <PrtSc> prints entire contents of the screen to the printer, whereas
<Ctrl> <PrtSc> causes each line on the screen to be printed as it is entered.

Often, when you are entering or editing commands or text, you may want to have a printed copy of what is being displayed on the screen. To do this, you use the <PrtSc> (Print Screen) key. This key is located for you in *Figure 7-3*. If you do not have this key, there is also a way for you to print out your display. See the <Ctrl> P description on page 114.

To print out everything that is currently displayed on your screen, be sure your printer is turned on and ready. When you print out the contents of a display it is known as "dumping the screen." To perform this dump, hold down one of the <SHIFT> keys and press <PrtSc>.

You can also make a printed copy of everything you enter on the screen, at the same time as you enter each line. This is called "echoing the screen" to the printer. To echo each line as it is entered, hold down the <Ctrl> key and press the <PrtSc> key. All typed-in entries are echoed to the printer until you press <Ctrl> <PrtSc> again.

The <Num Lock> Key

The <Num Lock> key is used on IBM-compatible keyboards to switch the modes of the keypad between numeric input and cursor control.

The keys on the numeric keypad on your machine have a dual purpose as shown in *Figure 7-4*. They may be used to enter numbers as input or to control the movement of the cursor. These keys will have a set of arrows and terms such as "Home," "End," "PgUp" (page up), and "PgDn" (page down). The <Num Lock> key controls which function these keys perform.

Figure 7-4.
The Numeric Keypad

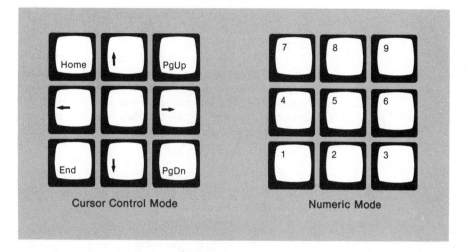

Cursor Control Mode · Numeric Mode

Normally <Num Lock> is in the cursor control mode. This means that pressing the keys moves the cursor up, down, left, right, or to a certain location on the screen or in a file. These cursor control keys are not normally used in MS-DOS operation but they are used in many application programs.

Pressing <Num Lock> while it is in this cursor control mode shifts the keyboard to the numeric mode. Now, when you press these keys, the numbers are entered as input. However, when using MS-DOS you will probably use the number keys across the top of the keyboard for numeric input.

When you look at a piece of information that is more than twenty-three lines long, the screen will scroll. As new information appears on the bottom of the screen the entries at the top disappear. Remember what happened the first time you used DIR to look at the contents of your system diskette? To stop the screen from scrolling, use the <Ctrl> <Num Lock> key combination. To "unfreeze" the screen, press the <SPACEBAR> key or <Ctrl> <Break>.

If you do not have <Num Lock> on your keyboard, you can stop the screen from scrolling too. See the <Ctrl> S description on page 114.

CORRECTING YOUR MISTAKES

Whether you are writing the great American novel, figuring how you can make the most of your new tax shelter, or creating your first BASIC program, most of your interactions with the computer take place via the keyboard. And unless you are a typing champion, you will frequently make mistakes while entering your information.

Most computer programs provide some help for you in correcting these mistakes. A word processor, for example, allows for certain keys that help you move forward and backward in a line or around in a file to change information, or even provide internal spelling checks. BASIC, the programming language your computer most likely uses, has a built-in editor to help make error correction easier. MS-DOS also provides some special keys to speed up the editing process when you are entering commands or using the EDLIN program.

Any line that you type into the computer is stored in a special place in the computer's memory. This location is called the input buffer. As soon as you press <ENTER>, the last line you typed is retained in the input buffer. The line currently stored in the input buffer is called a template. By recalling this template, you can use it as a pattern to make minor changes within a line using just a few keystrokes. This storage sequence is shown in *Figure 7-5*.

**Figure 7-5.
Template in the Input
Buffer**

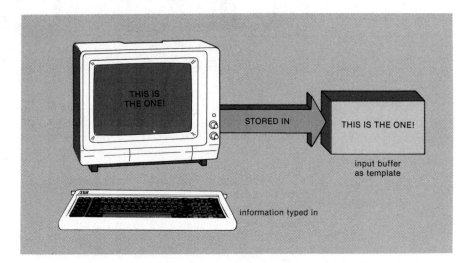

How can this template help you? Well, most of the commands and other information you enter into MS-DOS consist of very short lines. Commands, after all, are rarely more than four letters, and filenames will never exceed twelve characters. MS-DOS editing keys are designed to make correcting mistakes in these short lines easier and faster.

THE FUNCTION KEYS

Some of the editing keys are already familiar to you. You know about using <Esc> to cancel the line you are typing, and you have used <BACKSPACE> to erase characters on a line. The other editing operations require the use of function keys, those strange keys with F1, F2, and so forth enscribed on them, or a combination of two keys. The function keys on two different keyboards are located for you in *Figure 7-6*.

The function key pad (the <F1> through <F10> keys) are assigned special functions according to whether you're at the MS-DOS prompt or are running a program.

One problem with explaining the editing keys is that they are one of the least standardized parts of personal computer systems. That means, unfortunately, that this discussion can tell you how the editing keys work, but it can't identify exactly which keys perform these functions on your computer. Here is another situation where you must check your user's guide to find out the specifics for your machine.

Figure 7-6.
Location of Function
Keys

If you have numerous function keys on your keyboard, you are probably in luck. Most often these function keys provide the editing operations with one keystroke.

The reference chart on page 113 lists the most frequently used key for each function. If the keys your computer uses are different from those listed, write down the keys you use in the blank box before the description of each operation.

When positioned at the MS-DOS prompt, the system always retains the last command entered in the part of memory called the input buffer. By using the function keys <F1> through <F5>, you can retrieve all or part of the previously entered command and reissue it or edit it and turn it into a new command.

How do you actually use the editing keys? Let's look at a hypothetical situation. You have a file in which the last line reads like this:

This is the final line. <ENTER>

Now you want to make some editing changes in that line.

The <F3> (Copy All) Function

This function copies the entire template. Once you have pressed the <ENTER> key, the last line on the screen becomes the template in your input buffer. But then you decide you want to add more information at the end of the line. First you need to recall the line from the template. To retrieve the entire line you use the copy all function.

This is the final line.

You press <F3> (copy all).

MS-DOS returns the template. To add more information, first erase the period using the <BACKSPACE> key, then type in the new text.

> This is the final line.
> This is the final line
> This is the final line of this program. <ENTER>

Now "This is the final line of this program" is your template.

The <F1> (Copy One Character) Function

You can use the editing keys to copy part of a line. There are several ways to do this. The simplest is to copy one character at a time.

> This is the final line of this program.

Press <F1>.

> T

If you press <F1> four times.

> This

The <F2> (Copy Up To) Function

There is a quicker way to copy part of the template, however. You can use the copy up to function, <F2>. "Copy up to" means retrieve all of the template up to the first occurrence of the specified character. The specified character is not included in the new template.

> This is the final line of this program.

Press <F2> and then f.

> This is the

"Copy up to" copies up to the first occurrence of the indicated letter.

> This is often the final line of this program.

Press <F2> and then f.

> This is o

• The characters in the template are copied up to the first occurrence of f in the word "often." To copy up to the word "final" you would enter <F2> and f once more.

> This is o

You press <F2> and then f.

> This is often the

The <Del> (Skip Over One Character) Function

You can also use the editing keys to skip over part of the template. You use the <Del> key to skip over one character.

> This is the final line of this program

You press <Del> and then <F3> to copy the remaining characters.

his is the the final line of this program.

Press <Del> and <F3> again.

is is the final line of this program.

The <F4> (Skip Up To) Function

Just as you can copy up to, you can also "skip up to." To do this you use the <F4> key and indicate the character you want to skip up to. The specified character is not included in the template.

This is the final line of this program.

You press, <F4> and then n. Press <F3> to copy the remaining characters.

nal line of this program.

Just as "copy up to" copies up to the first occurrence of the character, "skip up to" skips all characters up to the first occurrence of the letter given.

This is the final line of this program.

You press <F4> and then 1. Press <F3> to copy the remaining characters.

1 line of this program.

You may have been intending to skip up to the word "line," but the 1 in "final" is encountered first. Pressing <F4> and 1 again brings you up to the desired location in the template.

The <Ins> (Insert a New Character) Function

By combining the use of function keys <F1> through <F5> to manipulate the input buffer with other keys such as <BACKSPACE>, <Del>, <Ins>, and <Esc>, you can significantly cut down on the amount of typing required to issue similar commands over and over again.

You can also insert new information into the middle of the existing template. To do this you use the <Ins> key. This may seem tricky. See if you can follow this example.

This is the final line of this program.

You press <F2> and then o.

This is the final line

Press <Ins>, type "and end" and then press <F3>.

This is the final line and end of this program.

Did you get all that? If not, just take another look. First you copied the template up to the first occurrence of the letter o (in the word "of"). Then you pressed the <Ins> key to indicate that you wanted to add new characters. The characters added are "and end." <F3> then copies all the remaining characters in the template, resulting in the new line. Once you get used to them, these function keys will cut your editing time.

The <F5> (Create a New Template) Function

The <F5> editing key makes the most recently entered line the new template. In the previous example, pressing <F5> after you had finished editing the line, but before you had pressed <ENTER>, would make "This is the final line and end of this program" the template. Note that although this line is now the template, it has not been sent to the computer. If the new line was a command, it would not be executed by the computer.

COPY a: b:

You do not press <ENTER> at the end of the line, but do press <F5>. Then you press <F3>.

COPY a: b:

This is the new template but the command has not been sent to the computer.

The <Esc> (Escape) Function

You already know how to use this function. This is just a reminder that <Esc> is a function as well as a key. When you <Esc> to cancel a line, the template is not changed (that is, it is not canceled and left blank). The last line entered is still the current template. The backslash on the line indicates that it has been canceled.

This is the final line

You press <Esc>.

This is the final line \

The line entered just before this one would still be the template.

Using editing keys takes a bit of getting used to, and you may be confused until you get the hang of it. But these keys can be useful when you are entering duplicate or repetitive commands or when you want to correct mistakes without typing in the entire line again. Experiment with these keys and see if they are helpful to you.

Table 7-1 is a reference chart of the editing functions and the probable keys used to perform each function.

<Ctrl> KEY COMBINATIONS

Throughout this book you have been gradually introduced to the <Ctrl> key in its various guises. You used <Ctrl> <Alt> <Del> to perform a warm boot, and you used <Ctrl> S to stop the screen from scrolling.

**Table 7-1.
Editing Functions and
Keys**

Your Key	Key	Function	Explanation
	<Esc>	Cancel	Cancel the last line.
	<BACKSPACE>	Back up	Erase the last character.
	<←>		
	<F3>	Copy all	Copy the entire template.
	<F1>	Copy one	Copy one character.
	<F2>	Copy up to	Copy up to a specified character (character is not included in the copied template.
	<Del>	Skip one	Skip one character in template.
	<F4>	Skip up to	Skip up to the specified character (specified character not included in the template).
	<Ins>	Enter new characters	Insert new information in the middle of the template.
	<F5>	New template	Make this line the new template (if a command, not executed until <ENTER> is pressed).

An alternative to using the <Ctrl><PrtSc> key function to cause lines of text to be printed as they are entered on non-IBM-compatible keyboards is the <Ctrl> P function.

Some computer keyboards use specific keys to perform specific actions such as <PrtSc> and <Num Lock> described previously. But if your machine does not have these special keys, you can use <Ctrl> in conjunction with another key to perform these actions. Even if you do have these special keys, you can use the <Ctrl> combinations too, because these keys are standard on all computers using MS-DOS. These control functions operate not only in MS-DOS but also in a wide variety of other programs. They are presented in *Table 7-2* for a quick reference.

Table 7-2.
Control Functions and
Keys

Keys	Explanation
\<Ctrl> \<Alt> \<Del>	Reboots the MS-DOS system.
\<Ctrl> C	Cancels the current line (like the \<Esc> key) or cancels the currently running program.
\<Ctrl> H	Moves the cursor to the left and erases the last character, just like the \<BACKSPACE> or \<←> key.
\<Ctrl> P	Echoes the display to the printer, line by line.
\<Ctrl> N	Turns off the echoing function.
\<Ctrl> S	Stops the scrolling on the screen; to resume scrolling, press any key.
\<Ctrl> Z	End-of-file marker.

WILDCARD SYMBOLS

MS-DOS provides a simple method of specifying a group of files within a filename when used with a command. Like the jokers in a deck of cards, the * and ? characters are used to represent wildcards (also called global characters). A wildcard means "any character." The * wildcard is used to represent a group of characters, whereas the ? wildcard represents a specific character position. Using wildcards can greatly enhance the capabilities of file-related commands.

Special keys, function keys, and control key combinations help you use MS-DOS and EDLIN with little wasted motion. Not surprisingly, filenames also have shortcuts that can increase your efficiency.

You probably haven't thought of your experience in computing as resembling a card game, although you have taken a few chances. But now you are going to learn to use wildcards.

Like their playing card antecedents, wildcards can stand for something else or a lot of something elses. When used in filenames, wildcards replace one or more specific characters in the filename or extension.

As you know, each file's name must be unique, but many of your filenames probably have a lot in common. Wildcards allow you to use one command to perform an action on a group of similarly named files. The wildcard replaces one or more characters in the filename. Wildcards are especially useful when you are using the DIR, COPY, ERASE, and RENAME commands, because in these situations you are frequently referring to groups of files.

The wildcard symbols (sometimes called "global characters") are the question mark (?) and the asterisk (*).

The question mark is used to match one character in one specific character position in a filename or extension. For example, assume you had all your monthly salary records on one diskette.

```
JA-MAR.SUM
JANSAL.
FEBSAL.
MARSAL.
MARTOT.
JA-JUN.SUM
```

You want a directory of all the files that concern monthly salaries. You could look at the whole directory or use DIR to check on the presence of each individual salary file. But you can get this information much quicker by entering a wildcard command.

A>dir ???sal <ENTER>

A directory would appear.

```
Volume in drive A has no label
Directory of A:\
JANSAL        128        8-1-84        12:24p
FEBSAL        128        8-1-84        12:24p
MARSAL        128        8-1-84        12:24p
              3 File[s]        294912 bytes free
```

This command tells MS-DOS to look through the directory of the diskette in drive A and list all files that end in "sal." Any characters may be used in the first three positions. The use of the question mark in the first three positions means that each of these files fulfills the qualifications of the command. This is the key to the question mark wildcard; any character can occupy the position indicated by the ?, but the rest of the name must be exactly the same. If you had entered

A>dir mar????? <ENTER>

then files beginning "mar" would have been listed.

```
Volume in drive A has no label
Directory of A\:
MARSAL        128        8-1-84        12:24p
MARTOT        128        8-1-84        12:24p
              2 File[s]        294912 bytes free
```

In response to this command, MS-DOS looks for files that have "mar" in the first three positions and any characters in the last five positions.

The * and ? wildcards can often be combined in a filename specification to provide specific instructions to a file-related command.

When you include the ? wildcard as the last character in a filename or extension, you must account for all eight characters in the filename proper or all three characters in the extension.

The asterisk wildcard is just like using a lot of question marks. When you include an * in a filename specification, any character can occupy that position or any of the remaining positions in the filename or extension. An asterisk pretends that there are as many question marks in the filename as there are positions.

Asterisks do not include the extension of a filename unless you specify this with another asterisk after the period. Then it will accept any extension.

A>dir ja*.* <ENTER>

If, for our above files, you entered this command, MS-DOS would list the following files beginning "ja."

```
Volume in drive A has no label
Directory of A:\
JA-MAR      SUM     128     8-1-84      12:24p
JANSAL            . 128     8-1-84      12:24p
JA/JUN      SUM     128     8-1-84      12:24p
            3 File[s]       294912 bytes free
```

Here MS-DOS is looking for any files that contain "ja" in the first two positions. Any characters can occupy the remaining positions int he filename. Since you also included an asterisk in the extension, the filename can contain any extension.

You can also use a completely wild filename.

        .

As you have probably guessed, this means all files.

Wildcards can be useful because of their power, but they can also be dangerous. When you want to copy all the files on a diskette (copy *.*) or to list an entire directory (dir *.*), they can make your task easier.

Beware of the use of wildcards with the ERASE command. As you probably have guessed, ERASE*.* would mean goodbye to all the files on your diskette; however, when you use *.* with the ERASE command, MS-DOS gives you a chance to back out.

        A>erase *.* <ENTER>

When you enter this command, MS-DOS asks a question.

        Are you sure [Y/N]?

Enter Y if you are really sure or N if you have any doubts about what you're doing.

The keys functions, and tools described in this chapter increase your knowledge of MS-DOS. Now you're going to learn some new uses of familiar commands.

Switches

Many of MS-DOS's commands can be entered with optional switches. A switch usually consists of a single character and is preceded by a slash (/). The DIR command, for example, has two optional switches: /w is used to display the directory in several columns across the screen, and /p is used to instruct DIR to pause at every screen full of text. Both switches can be used together if desired.

As you become better acquainted with MS-DOS, you not only are able to use it more easily, but you come to appreciate some of its finer points. Up until now, you have been using commands in their simplest form. These are valid uses of commands, but there are some command options that make them even more useful.

Commands can contain switches. As the name implies, switches can turn on and off certain operations within a command. When you add a switch to a command you indicate it with a slash (/) and a letter. Switches always follow the command and any drive indicators.

The DIR Command

You are familiar with the DIR command. You know this command lists the files on a directory, displaying their names, extensions, sizes, and the time and date they were last accessed. If the directory contains more files than will fit on one screen, the display scrolls until it reaches the end of the listing.

There are two optional switches you can include in the DIR command that alter how the directory is displayed, /w and /p. The /w switch lists the files in several columns across the screen. Only the filenames are displayed.

The /w Switch

Assume that the diskette listing you want to see is in drive A and this is your current drive. Enter the DIR/w command.

A>dir/w <ENTER>

If this diskette is a typical system diskette, the command will produce a multicolumn list of filenames.

```
Volume in drive A has no label
Directory of A: \
COMMAND  COM  ANSI      SYS  FORMAT    COM  CHKDSK  COM  SYS      COM
DISKCOPY COM  DISKCOMP  COM  COMP      COM  EDLIN   COM  MODE     COM
FDISK    COM  BACKUP    COM  RESTORE   COM  PRINT   COM  RECOVER  COM
ASSIGN   COM  TREE      COM  GRAPHICS  COM  SORT    EXE  FIND     EXE
MORE     COM  BASIC     COM  BASICA    COM
            23 File[s]     31232 bytes free
```

This horizontal layout of the directory is useful when the diskette holds a lot of files and you want to see only their names. Note that this directory does not give you any information about file size or the date or time the file was last accessed.

The /p Switch

The other switch used with the DIR command is /p. The /p switch operates like an automatic scroll control. It stops the display of a directory when the screen is filled. This switch is useful when you want to look at the listing of a large directory. You can study the display and then indicate when you are ready to proceed. Again, the switch follows the command. (*Figure 7-7* illustrates the effects of the /w and /p switches.)

Figure 7-7.
The DIR Command

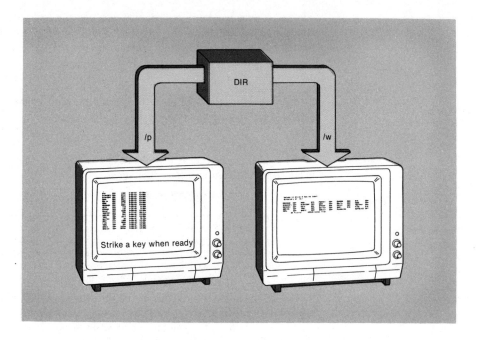

A>dir/p <ENTER>

This command results in a list of filenames and attributes.

Volume in drive A has no label
Directory of A: \

COMMAND	COM	17664	3-08-83	12:00p
ANSI	SYS	1664	3-08-83	12:00p
FORMAT	COM	6016	3-08-83	12:00p
CHKDSK	COM	6400	3-08-83	12:00p
SYS	COM	1408	3-08-83	12:00p
DISKCOPY	COM	2444	3-08-83	12:00p
DISKCOMP	COM	2074	3-08-83	12:00p
COMP	COM	2523	3-08-83	12:00p
EDLIN	COM	4608	3-08-83	12:00p
MODE	COM	3139	3-08-83	12:00p
FDISK	COM	6177	3-08-83	12:00p
BACKUP	COM	3687	3-08-83	12:00p
RESTORE	COM	4003	3-08-83	12:00p
PRINT	COM	4608	3-08-83	12:00p
RECOVER	COM	2304	3-08-83	12:00p
ASSIGN	COM	896	3-08-83	12:00p
TREE	COM	1513	3-08-83	12:00p
GRAPHICS	COM	789	3-08-83	12:00p
SORT	EXE	1280	3-08-83	12:00p
FIND	EXE	5888	3-08-83	12:00p

MORE	COM	384	3-08-83	12:00p
BASIC	COM	16256	3-08-83	12:00p
BASICA	COM	25984	3-08-83	12:00p

When the entire screen is filled, MS-DOS gives a message.

Strike a key when ready . . .

You press any key and the directory continues.

23 File[s] 31232 bytes free

While DIR/p takes up more space then DIR/w on your screen, it has the advantage of allowing information on all files to be displayed in a fashion that is convenient to read. It also provides complete information on each file.

By now, you're probably beginning to understand switches. Another command you are familiar with also has optional switches.

The FORMAT Command

The /v Switch

The FORMAT command is used to set up the data storage characteristics required by MS-DOS on a floppy diskette. Formatting a diskette is normally required only for new diskettes, although sometimes it is needed to reformat older diskettes.

As you know, FORMAT readies your diskette to receive information. Up to this point we have not discussed a very important capability of FORMAT—the ability to put a name on a diskette.

How many times have you looked at the results of a DIR command and wondered why the volume in drive A doesn't have a label. You keep getting this same message and think you can't do anything about it.

The volume name (which simply means the name of the diskette) can be helpful to you in identifying the contents of a diskette. To put a volume name, or volume label (as MS-DOS refers to it), on a disk, you use the /v switch.

Let's put a volume label on a diskette we're going to use for examples in Chapter 10. Put your system diskette in drive A and a new, unformatted diskette in drive B. Be sure it is empty because the FORMAT command will erase any existing information on a diskette.

The optional FORMAT switch /v is used to store a volume label on a newly formatted diskette. The nature of a diskette with a meaningful volume label can be easily identified using the DIR command.

Begin the procedure by entering the FORMAT command and including the /v switch.

A>format b:/v <ENTER>
Insert new diskette in drive B:
and strike any key when ready

You've already put in your new diskette.

Formatting...Format complete

So far everything seems exactly normal. But now MS-DOS inserts a new message.

Volume label [11 characters, ENTER for none]?

Here is your chance to individualize your diskette. You can name the diskette anything you want up to eleven characters. Name your diskette "wine cellar." If you had decided against including a volume label, you would just press <ENTER>. Type in the volume label now.

Volume label [11 characters, ENTER for none]?wine cellar <ENTER>

The formatting then continues as usual.

362496 bytes total disk space
362496 bytes available on disk
Format another [Y/N]?n

The diskette is now ready to receive data. How do you know the volume label of a diskette? Enter the DIR command and you'll find out.

A>dir b: <ENTER>
Volume in drive B is WINE CELLAR
Directory of B: \

The contents of the diskette would then be listed. Because you don't have any files on this diskette yet, MS-DOS responds with an appropriate message.

File not found

The /s Switch

The optional FORMAT switch /s is used to instruct FORMAT to automatically copy the MS-DOS operating system to the diskette after it has been formatted.

The /s switch on the FORMAT command allows you to put a copy of the operating system on a diskette during the formatting procedure. This can be a timesaver because it allows you to boot the system from any diskette that has been formatted this way. To put the system on a diskette, you *must* include the /s switch at the time you format the diskette.

For example, you may write a program that you know you will use quite often. This program requires you to input information from a data diskette. If you have the system on your program diskette, you can just insert it in drive A, insert the data diskette in drive B, turn on the machine, and proceed. No more inserting the system diskette in drive A, then removing this diskette to put in your program diskette, and then beginning to run the program.

When you include the /s switch in the FORMAT command to set up a system diskette, it transfers three files to the new diskette. Two of these files are hidden. It doesn't mean DOS can't find them. It means you won't see them listed among the files on a diskette when using the DIR command. The CHKDSK command will tell you if a diskette contains any hidden files. These files cannot be accessed by you; that way you can't change them or do anything to make the system fail to operate properly. The third file transferred by the /s switch is COMMAND.COM. This file does appear as part of a diskette's contents when you use DIR to look at the diskette. All three of these files make up the system.

Putting the system on the diskette does take up some space. Not every diskette needs to have the system on it. However, if you think you are likely to be booting from a diskette or you know you will need the internal commands handy when you are using the diskette, put the system on it. You can take the COMMAND.COM file off (using ERASE) if you find you need more space on the diskette.

To format the diskette in drive B and make this diskette a system diskette, enter the command and the switch.

A> format b:/s <ENTER>

MS-DOS follows the usual steps in the formatting sequence.

Insert new diskette for drive B:
and strike any key when ready

Formatting...Format complete

The new twist is an added message.

System transferred

The space occupied by the system is included in the message at the completion of the formatting operation.

362496 bytes total disk space
 40960 bytes used by system
321536 bytes available on disk

FORMAT another [Y/N?] n

And that's all there is to it. You now have a self-booting diskette ready for your data or programs.

You can put a volume label and the system on the same diskette. Simply enter both switches at the time you FORMAT the diskette.

A> format b:/v/s <ENTER>

On some computers the order of the switches does not matter. Others require the /s to come last. You can never go wrong by indicating the /v first and the /s second.

You will see the "system transferred" message and be asked for a "volume label" during the formatting procedure. The difference between the two FORMAT switches is illustrated in *Figure 7-8*.

Remember, the /s switch is only for transferring the system to a new, blank diskette. Because you will quickly find how convenient it is to have the system on a diskette. You may want to know how to put the system on diskettes that already contain information.

Figure 7-8.
The FORMAT Command

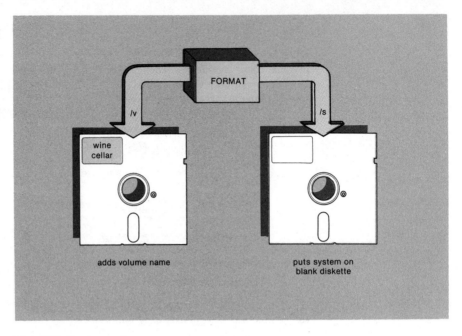

The SYS Command

An alternative to using
FORMAT with the /s
switch is the SYS com-
mand, which can be used
after a diskette has been
formatted to transfer the
MS-DOS operating sys-
tem. One drawback, how-
ever, is that, unlike
FORMAT, SYS does not
copy the file COM-
MAND.COM to the new
diskette, thus requiring
that it be copied sepa-
rately with the COPY
command.

The SYS Command

The SYS command performs the same function as the /s switch in the FORMAT command; that is, it transfers the operating system onto a designated diskette but does not transfer the command files of MS-DOS. Because the use of FORMAT erases all previous information on a diskette, you cannot use FORMAT /s to put the system on preprogrammed or application diskettes. Many of these diskettes cannot be copied to customized diskettes because they are "copy protected." But, by using SYS, you can have the system on most of these diskettes.

Just like the /s switch in FORMAT, SYS transfers two hidden files to the specified diskette. You can't see these files, but don't worry, MS-DOS knows if they are there. System files occupy a unique position on the diskette; they are always located in the first track, at the very beginning of the diskette. Even if the files are not on the diskette, MS-DOS allocates this space to them when you format the diskette. When you use the SYS command, you put the system in this already available location. Most preprogrammed or application diskettes are produced with this pre-defined location for the system files. If you save data to a formatted diskette, this reserved area will be written over, and you will not be able to transfer the system files successfully.

SYS transfers the hidden files, but unlike the /s switch, it does not transfer any of MS-DOS's command files. To have a diskette that is self-booting, you must also transfer the COMMAND.COM portion of the operating system. First use SYS to put the system on the diskette, and then use COPY to transfer the COMMAND.COM file. You may also use

COPY to transfer other files that you use a great deal, such as FORMAT.COM or DISKCOPY.COM. (The difference between FORMAT /s and SYS is outlined in *Table 7-3*.)

**Table 7-3.
Putting the System on a
Diskette**

Using FORMAT/s	Using SYS
On a blank diskette, FORMAT/s transfers the COMMAND.COM file and two hidden files.	On a blank diskette, SYS transfers two hidden files.
	Use the COPY command to transfer the COMMAND.COM file.

Because SYS is an external command, you must have your system diskette in drive A before issuing the command. Don't forget to put your target diskette in drive B.

A>sys b: <ENTER>

MS-DOS tells you when the transfer has been completed.

System transferred
A>

When you look at the directory of this diskette, you will see that COMMAND.COM is now one of its files. But how can you be sure that the hidden files were also transferred? The next command gives you that information.

The CHKDSK Command

The CHKDSK command is a very useful multifunction command. When CHKDSK is entered without any switches, it displays the characteristics of a disk and informs you of any errors it may encounter. Special switches can be used with CHKDSK to correct detected errors.

This command is used to check the condition of the File Allocation Table (FAT) and directories on a diskette. CHKDSK is useful for finding out exactly how much room is taken up on a diskette, how much room is still available, and what types of files are currently on the diskette. As a nice extra, CHKDSK also reports on how much memory is taken up and how much is still free, but this has nothing to do with the diskette itself.

As the name implies, you use CHKDSK to find out if everything is okay on a diskette. This is especially useful if you are having trouble using a diskette and want to try and locate the problem and save the information.

The first thing CHKDSK examines is the FAT. MS-DOS uses the FAT to keep track of the available space on a diskette. The FAT records where a file is on the diskette; it's like a table of contents. It also records unused space on the diskette. MS-DOS tries to make the most out of each diskette, so it does not like to have wasted space or noncontiguous files. CHKDSK checks on space allocation and reports any problems to you.

Because CHKDSK is an external command, you must have your system diskette in a drive to use it. To check on the status of a diskette, just enter the command and the drive indicator.

A> chkdsk a: <ENTER>

The report CHKDSK displays after it checks the characteristics of a disk include such things as total disk space in bytes, the number and amount of space occupied by hidden files, the number and amount of space occupied by normal files, and the amount of free space remaining on the disk. Included in the CHKDSK report is the amount of memory installed in the system and the amount of free memory currently not being used.

The resulting display reports on the diskette.

```
179712 bytes total disk space
 22016 bytes in 2 hidden files
126464 bytes in 23 user files
 31232 bytes available on disk

262144 bytes total memory
237568 bytes free
```

This diskette seems to be in good shape. CHKDSK gives us lots of information on the status of the diskette. We know how much total disk space is taken up, how many files are on the diskette, and how much space is still available. This is followed by the information on memory. Of course, all these numbers depend on the specifics of your computer system.

The second line of the display gives the information on hidden files. Because this diskette has two hidden files, it is reasonable to assume that the system is on this diskette. Remember that FORMAT/s and SYS transfer two hidden files when the system is placed on a diskette.

So far, our diskettes have been in good shape. If there is a problem, an appropriate message will be displayed.

A>chkdsk b: <ENTER>

The screen reports this condition:

```
Disk error reading FAT 1
362496 bytes total disk space
 38912 bytes in 6 user files
323584 bytes available on disk

262144 bytes total memory
237568 bytes free
```

CHKDSK encountered a problem as soon as it began reading the diskette. Here is another status report which you might receive:

```
362496 total disk space
     0 bytes in 1 hidden file
 10240 bytes in bad sectors
352256 bytes available on disk

262144 bytes total memory
237568 bytes free
```

In this example, the problem is not in the FAT, but in the disk sectors.

Occasionally, the data stored on a disk can become corrupted because of such things as excessive magnetism, a scratched disk, or a malfunctioning program. In many cases the data on a corrupted disk can be recovered by first using CHKDSK to detect the nature of the error, and then reissuing CHKDSK with the /f switch to correct the problem.

The f/ Switch

CHKDSK does have the ability to attempt to correct some errors. If you want MS-DOS to check for errors and attempt to repair the problem, you issue the CHKDSK command with the /f switch. The /f switch means fix if possible.

```
A>chkdsk b:/f <ENTER>
```

If an error is found, MS-DOS asks permission to fix it. There can be many types of errors and consequently many types of error messages. Here are two more error messages that might result from CHKDSK:

```
xxx lost clusters found in xxx chains
Convert lost chains to files[Y/N]?
```

or

```
Allocation error for file, size adjusted
```

When you use CHKDSK with the /f switch you will need to refer to your computer's operating system manual to understand the error message. Your manual will also advise you about what action is appropriate for each error condition.

The v/ Switch

You may also use another switch in conjunction with the CHKDSK command. /v gives you more information about the error it has found. When you use this switch, CHKDSK lists each directory and the files in that directory as part of the status report.

```
A>chkdsk b:/v <ENTER>
Disk error reading FAT 1
Directory B:
    B:\SAMPLE.BAK
    B:\LETTERS.BAK
    B:\SAMPLE
    B:\LETTERS

362496 bytes total disk space
 38912 bytes in 4 user files
323584 bytes available on disk

262144 bytes total memory
237584 bytes free
```

You can combine both CHKDSK switches in one command.

```
A>chkdsk/f/v <ENTER>
```

This command not only lists the contents of the diskette but also attempts to fix any problems noted.

It's a good idea to use CHKDSK often. It can prevent minor problems from growing into major ones. The various applications of CHKDSK are shown in *Figure 7-9*.

Figure 7-9.
The CHKDSK Command

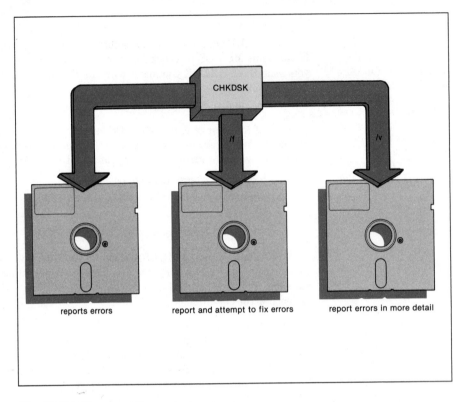

The MODE Command

The MODE command is a multipurpose command used to establish the modes of certain types of devices attached to the computer. In IBM-compatible computers, several MODE commands are available to change characteristics of the monitor. In all MS-DOS computers, MODE can be used to change the characteristics of input/output ports such a parallel printer port or a serial port to which another printer or a modem is attached.

The MODE command is unique in MS-DOS in that it has nothing to do with disks or diskettes. Instead, MODE is used to control the way your input/output devices operate. For instance, some computer systems allow you to use a printer in a variety of ways. You use the MODE command to tell your system how to operate the printer.

A>mode LPT1:80,6 <ENTER>

This may seem like gibberish to you, but MS-DOS understands it.

Broken down, this command tells MS-DOS to set the printer (LPT is the system's designation for printer) that is number 1 (some systems can have more than one printer attached at one time) so that it outputs 80-character lines at the vertical spacing of 6 lines per inch. Don't worry about using MODE like this right now. Your operations guide describes your system's use of MODE when dealing with printers and other input/output ports.

There is one instance of using MODE that is more usual, however. This is to adjust your display screen. You are probably saying that there's nothing wrong with your display. Chances are you are right. In most situations, your display is perfectly all right. If, however, you use a color/graphics monitor adapter you may need the MODE command.

On a television set or color monitor, you may occasionally notice that the first few characters of the display line are somewhere off the left edge of the screen. Even the prompt may be out of sight. You use the MODE command to correct this alignment problem. Assume that the prompt is there even if you can't see it.

A>mode ,r,t <ENTER>

Be especially careful when entering this command; you must leave a space after mode and put a comma in front of the letter r as well as a comma separating the two letters. This command is telling MS-DOS to move the display to the right. MS-DOS responds.

Resident portion of MODE loaded
0123567890123567890123567890123567890123567890123567890123567 89

Do you see the leftmost 0? [Y/N]

If you still need to move the display to the right, enter N. If you can see the zero at the far left, enter Y.

If you can't see the characters to the far right of your screen, use MODE to move them to the left. Issue the same command, but substitute an L for the R.

A> mode ,l,t <ENTER>
0123567890123567890123567890123567890123567890123567890123567 89

Do you see the rightmost 9? [Y/N]

Respond Y if you can see the 9, or N to move the display farther to the left. After you have adjusted the display and answered Y, MS-DOS returns you to the operating system.

In addition to setting up your printer and aligning your display, MODE can also be used for setting up additional advanced applications, such as communications. You can find this additional information in your user's manual or in the *MS-DOS Bible,* published by Sams.

SUMMARY

You have expanded your knowledge of MS-DOS significantly in this chapter. You now use the keyboard and special keys to edit, to list your files to your specification (DIR/w and DIR/p), to FORMAT with new options (/v and /s), and to put the system on preprogrammed diskettes (SYS). To verify that your diskettes are holding up, you can use CHKDSK, and if your display is askew, you can fix that too. In the next chapter we will present a new idea about how to use MS-DOS files—batch processing.

WHAT HAVE WE LEARNED?

1. The <Esc>, <Num Lock>, Home, End, PgUp, PgDn keys and the ten function keys are used to reduce time and effort at the keyboard.
2. Using the ? and * wildcards enhances the capabilities of file-related commands.

3. The special switches for DOS commands, such as dir/w, dir/p, format/v, and format/s, are timesavers.
4. The SYS command transfers the two hidden system files onto a disk.
5. The CHKDSK command (and its optional switches /f and /v) lets you inspect and repair the File Allocation Table (FAT) and directories of a diskette.
6. The MODE command lets you define the way MS-DOS controls input and output devices such as printers and modems.

Quiz for Chapter 7

1. In addition to the special keys <ENTER> and <BACKSPACE>, other special keys are commonly used, such as:
   a. <Caps Lock>.
   b. the left and right <SHIFT> keys.
   c. <Esc>.
   d. <PrtSc>.
   e. <Del>.
   f. all of the above.

2. The <PrtSc> key is used in the following ways:
   a. <SHIFT><PrtSc> prints everything currently displayed on the screen.
   b. <Ctrl><PrtSc> causes each line displayed on the screen to be printed as it is entered.
   c. When pressed by itself, it causes the * to be displayed.
   d. all of the above.

3. <Num Lock> is a toggle key that is used to:
   a. switch between numeric and cursor control modes.
   b. switch between special and normal characters.
   c. switch between insert and command modes.
   d. lock and unlock all numbers.

4. The area in memory where MS-DOS stores the last command entered is called the:
   a. transient buffer.
   b. input buffer.
   c. output buffer.
   d. input/output buffer.

5. The function keys used to manipulate the input buffer are:
   a. <F1> through <F5>.
   b. <F6> through <F10>.

   c. <F1> through <F10>.
   d. There aren't any.

6. While positioned at the MS-DOS prompt, the function keys <F1>through <F5> are used to manipulate the input buffer in what ways?
   a. <F1> is used to retrieve the previously entered command one character at a time.
   b. <F2> is used to retrieve all of the previously entered command up to the character subsequently specified.
   c. <F3> is used to retrieve the entire previously entered command.
   d. <F4> is used to skip over characters of the previously entered command up to the first occurrence of the character subsequently specified.
   e. <F5> puts a newly edited command back into the input buffer.
   f. all of the above.
   g. none of the above.

7. While at the MS-DOS prompt, the <Esc> key is used to:
   a. execute the typed command.
   b. cancel the typed command.
   c. ignore the typed command.
   d. either a or b.
   e. both b and c.
   f. either a, b, or c.
   g. none of the above.

8. For non-IBM-compatible computers, an alternative command to the <Ctrl><PrtSc> function is:
   a. <Ctrl> S.
   b. <Ctrl> C.
   c. <Ctrl> P.
   d. <Ctrl> Z.

9. The * and ? characters, used as special characters in file names specified with file-related commands, are called:
   a. wildcards.
   b. global characters.
   c. aces.
   d. jokers.

10. The * wildcard is used to specify:
    a. a single character position.
    b. a group of characters.
    c. only numbers.
    d. only alphabetic characters.

11. The ? wildcard is used to specify:
    a. a single character position.
    b. a group of characters.
    c. only numbers.
    d. only alphabetic characters.

12. The optional switches that can be used with the DIR command include:
    a. /w to cause the directory to be displayed in several columns across the screen.
    b. /p to cause DIR to pause each time the directory fills up the screen.
    c. both a and b.
    d. none of the above.

13. The FORMAT command, used to establish the necessary data storage characteristics on a disk, is used:
    a. to format new diskettes.
    b. to reformat existing diskettes only when necessary.

c. to reformat the screen.
d. both a and b.
e. both b and c.
f. both a and c.
g. a, b, and c.

14. Does the FORMAT command followed by the /s switch perform the same function as the SYS command insofar as copying the MS-DOS operating system to a new disk?
    a. Yes, except that SYS does not copy COMMAND.COM.
    b. Always.
    c. Sometimes.
    d. Never.

15. The CHKDSK command performs two basic functions:
    a. It checks for and displays the status of a disk and reports any errors it encounters.
    b. It corrects some types of errors if instructed to do so.
    c. It ignores any kind of errors it detects.
    d. It automatically corrects errors as they are detected.

16. MODE is a multifunction command used to set the operations of various devices, including:
    a. the monitor.
    b. the parallel ports.
    c. the serial ports.
    d. all of the above.
    e. none of the above.

Batch Processing

ABOUT THIS CHAPTER

As you become more familiar with MS-DOS commands, you gain an understanding of how, when, and why to use specific commands. In fact, what you may have found at first difficult becomes increasingly routine as you employ these commands more often.

The fact is that many of the operations you perform with the computer are repetitive. You probably find yourself using certain sequences of commands, in the same pattern, over and over again. Just as the editing keys gave you one shortcut to avoid useless repetitiveness, MS-DOS has another helpmate to save you time and frustration. This new tool is called a batch file, and in this chapter we are going to see how batch files can make your computing more efficient.

WHAT ARE BATCH FILES?

A batch file is a special type of file that contains a series of commands that can be automatically executed by MS-DOS. As viewed by MS-DOS, a batch file is in fact a command that contains a series of other commands in text form.

Batch files are something like a cookbook for commands. They contain lists of steps in the form of MS-DOS commands that combine to produce one result. After this recipe is established, the batch file gives you the same result every time you run it. The ingredients in a batch file are data files. These may change from time to time, but the product of the batch file is still the same. An example may explain this further.

There is a standard commodity in everyone's life called "bread." Bread is really a combination of wheat, liquid, and flavoring. When you make bread, the ingredients may vary. You can use whole wheat or white flour; you may include water or milk; you may add raisins or caraway seeds. The steps, however, in making bread always follow a specific pattern. First you measure, then you combine, then you knead, and finally you bake. The result is bread. A recipe for bread is a shortcut most cooks use because it defines what and how much and in what order. Not only does this reduce mistakes, it makes the process go faster because the procedure is already laid out; you just follow the instructions. When you want to eat a piece of bread, you just cut off a slice; you don't have to go out and cut the wheat, grind the flour, and so on.

Batch files perform a similar service for MS-DOS users. You enter a series of commands that, when executed in order, provide specific results. The product is always the same because you follow the same steps each time. Even if you enter different filenames, the commands still perform in the same order. And because all of these commands are stored in one file, identified by a batch filename, you can use this formula over and over again, simply by entering the batch filename. This is faster than entering each of the commands separately and eliminates mistakes, since the commands are already correctly entered in the batch file. The batch file is already made up.

Batch files are ASCII text files, just like the files you use when you work with typical MS-DOS commands such as DIR, COPY, and TYPE. The files you use most frequently hold various kinds of information, data, programs, or operating system commands. Batch files contain commands and some explanatory statements. How much a batch file can do is dependent on how many commands you enter. Batch files are most useful when they perform a sequence of commands that you use very frequently.

Here is one example of the convenience of batch files. You may find that you frequently perform the following sequence of events. First you format a diskette, then you copy files to it, then you ask for a directory of the diskette, and finally you look at one or more of the files to check the contents. This procedure can be done by entering four commands: FORMAT, COPY, DIR, and TYPE. You can enter each of these commands separately, repeating the drive designations and filenames each time. But you can save yourself time and eliminate the inevitable typing errors by putting all these commands in one batch file. To execute this batch file all you do is enter one command, the name of the batch file. Does this sound confusing? Let's review your normal procedure.

First you enter the FORMAT command.

    format b:

After the diskette is formatted you enter a second command.

    copy a:datafile b:

When the copy is completed you ask for a directory.

    dir b:

And finally, you list the contents of the file.

    type b:datafile

Now let's see how you can put all these commands in one batch file.

CREATING A BATCH FILE

Batch files can be easily created by using any text editor, such as EDLIN, or a word processor.

Before you can follow a recipe it has to be written down. Putting a series of commands in a batch file is simple. The rules for a batch filename are the same as for other filenames, but in a batch file you must include the extension .BAT.

To run through this exercise on batch files, you are going to create a practice file called "datafile." For brevity's sake, this file will contain only one line: "This is a demonstration batch file." Because this is an ASCII file, you can use EDLIN to create this data file.

EDLIN is on your system diskette as the file "EDLIN.COM." Your "datafile" will also be on the system diskette. Put this diskette in drive A and call up EDLIN.

```
A > edlin datafile < ENTER >
New file
*i < ENTER >
        1:*This is a demonstration batch file. < ENTER >
        2:*^C

*e < ENTER >
```

This file is going to be the generic data file in our example. It stands for any files you might want to use in the batch file.

A Choice of Methods

Up until now, using EDLIN was the only method you knew for creating a file. But there is an alternative way to create files, using the COPY commands. You are going to use both methods to create your batch file. The two methods are summarized in *Table 8-1.*

<u>Edlin</u>

As is true whenever you use EDLIN, you must be sure the system diskette you are using contains the EDLIN.COM file. This diskette is probably still in drive A from the creation of "datafile" in the previous example. Use it now to combine the ingredients in your master batch file "copydata.bat." The filename must contain the .BAT extension.

```
A > edlin copydata.bat < ENTER >
```

Table 8-1.
Two Ways To Create a
Batch File

Using EDLIN	Using COPY CON:
External command (you need the system diskette).	Internal command (you don't need the system diskette).
You can edit lines within the file.	You can't edit a line in the file if you've already pressed <ENTER>.

Enter one command per line.

```
New file
*i <ENTER>
        1:*format b: <ENTER>
        2:*copy a:datafile b: <ENTER>
        3:*dir b: <ENTER>
        4:*type b:datafile <ENTER>
        5:*^C

*e <ENTER>
```

Each command contained in a batch file must be on a line of its own.

Each command is entered on a separate line. This is the standard EDLIN procedure. The only difference is that your filename contains the .BAT extension. This batch file assumes that the diskette in drive B is unformatted (line number 1). It "believes" that the data you want to copy ("datafile") is on the diskette in drive A, and that you want to copy this file to the diskette on drive B (line number 2). You then want to check the directory for the existence of the file (line number 3) and type out the contents of the file (line number 4).

Copy

Another way to create a file is to type the information directly into a file using the COPY commands. To do this you use COPY in conjunction with the CON: device name. CON: is one of those reserved device names that MS-DOS uses to recognize parts of the computer system. CON: stands for console (your keyboard). When you use COPY CON:, you tell MS-DOS to copy all the information you are typing in on your keyboard and put it directly into a file. The advantage of using COPY CON: is that you do not have to have EDLIN on the diskette to create the file. The disadvantage is that you cannot edit a line in a COPY CON: file after you have pressed <ENTER>.

An alternative method (and often the quickest way) of creating a batch file is to use the COPY command to copy what is typed on the keyboard to the batch file. A special device name, CON: is used to represent the console (the console always means the "keyboard for input" and "monitor screen for output").

To create "copydata.bat" using COPY CON:, enter the commands in sequence. There are no line numbers when using COPY CON:. Again, enter one command per line.

```
A> copy con: copydata.bat <ENTER>
format b: <ENTER>
copy a:datafile b: <ENTER>
dir b: <ENTER>
type b:datafile <ENTER>
^Z <ENTER>
```

^Z (Ctrl Z) is the end of file marker.

After you enter the end of file marker, MS-DOS responds.

```
1 File[s] copied
```

The file has been copied onto the diskette in drive A. This is indicated by the fact that A > is the current drive. Creating a batch file using COPY does not cause any of the commands within the file to be executed. To MS-DOS they are just like any other text. The "1 File(s) copied" message means that this created file is now stored on the diskette in drive A.

USING A BATCH FILE

Starting a Batch File

Because a batch file is considered to be a command to MS-DOS, it is executed by simply entering the batch file's name without the .BAT extension. Once a batch file has started execution, all text normally displayed by the commands within the batch file will be displayed as normal, just as if the commands had been entered individually.

From now on, anytime you want to perform the FORMAT-COPY-DIR-TYPE sequence, you simply type in the name of the batch file in response to the MS-DOS prompt. Of course, you must have the diskette containing the batch file and any files to be copied in the correct drive. The sequence of commands is executed automatically. MS-DOS shows you each command as it is processed. The appearance is the same as if you were entering each command separately. Enter the batch filename. You do not need to include the extension.

```
A> copydata <ENTER>
```

The batch file begins executing.

```
A> format B:
```

(This is the first command in your batch file.)

```
Insert new diskette for drive b:
and strike any key when ready
```

(All messages associated with the FORMAT command appear automatically. You must strike a key here for the file to continue processing.)

```
Formatting....Format complete

362496 bytes total disk space
```

362496 bytes available on disk
Format another [Y/N]?n

(Again, you must respond to all command requests for input. Next, MS-DOS copies the file.)

A>copy a:datafile b:
1 File[s] copied

(MS-DOS automatically continues with the third command in the batch file.)

A>dir b:

(The normal messages associated with DIR are displayed.)

Volume in drive B has no label
Directory of B:\

DATAFILE   38   12-17-84   11:35a
              1 File[s]   361472 bytes free

(MS-DOS now executes the fourth command in the batch file.)

A>type b:datafile

(Here are the contents of "datafile.")

This is a demonstration batch file.

(When the batch file is finished, MS-DOS returns to the prompt.)

A>

Running a Batch File

When you run your first batch file you will be amazed at how quickly the commands happen. You may even feel a lack of control watching messages and commands appear on the screen. But MS-DOS keeps you informed of what it is doing each step of the way. Each command is displayed as the batch file reaches it, and all messages and queries associated with the command are displayed during processing. The difference is that you can just sit back and observe.

This is the wonder of batch processing. With the simple input of one filename and a response to the "strike key" and "FORMAT another" queries, you have formatted a disk, copied a file, displayed a directory, and typed out the contents of a file. And MS-DOS has returned to await your next command.

You can execute several batch files in a row. To do this, simply make the last command in a batch file the name of another batch file. For example, suppose we had two batch files: "copydata" and "erasedat." "Erasedat" might be a batch file to clean up a diskette after all the needed files had been copied. The last command line of "copydata" would contain the name "erasedat."

```
format b:
copy a:datafile b:
dir b:
type b:datafile
erasedat.bat
```

When you call another batch file from within a file, the processing continues with the first command in the new file, as depicted in *Figure 8-1*. This is a one-way street, however. You can't return to "copydata" once you begin processing "erasedat." These files are chained one to the other.

**Figure 8-1.
Superbatch**

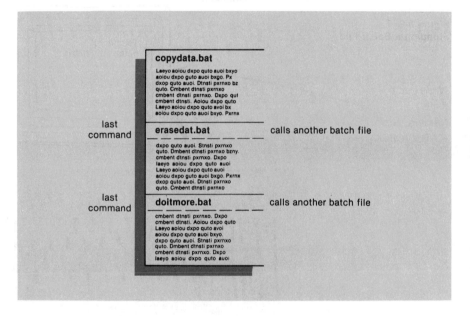

This example is a simple illustration of how useful batch files can be. You are probably already beginning to fashion your own batch files to eliminate the drudgery of certain sequences of operations you perform quite frequently.

Stopping a Batch File

To stop a batch file before it finishes normally, use the <Ctrl> C or <Ctrl> <Break> functions. MS-DOS will subsequently display a prompt asking you if you indeed want to stop the batch process or whether it should continue.

Occasionally you may find yourself in the middle of a batch file, and you want to stop the processing. Perhaps you realize that you don't have time to complete the batch file, you want to use different data diskettes, or you don't want a series of chained batch files to execute. Whatever the reason, MS-DOS allows you the option of stopping batch files in the middle of an operation. You stop batch processing just like you interrupt any on-going operation on the computer: you press ^C or <Ctrl> <Break>. When a batch file is processing and you press ^C, MS-DOS displays a message.

Terminate batch job [Y/N]?

A Y answer tells DOS to ignore the rest of the commands in the batch file and return you to the DOS prompt. An N answer tells DOS to terminate processing of the current command but to continue processing with the next command in the batch file. Guidelines for this procedure appear in *Figure 8-2.*

For example, while processing the "copydata" file, you may not want to see the entire directory of the diskette. Therefore, you would press <Ctrl> <Break> while the DIR command was processing and then type N in response to the terminate question. Processing would continue with the TYPE command.

Figure 8-2.
Stopping a Batch File

While batch file is running, press ⟨Ctrl⟩ ⟨Break⟩.

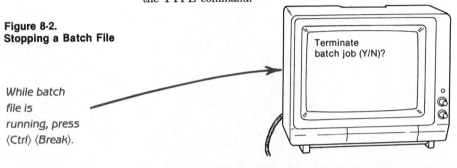

REPLACEABLE PARAMETERS

Often you may want to perform the same sequence of commands on different sets of files. In the initial version of "copydata," you were able to copy only one file, "datafile." But this situation is very limiting. It means that whenever you want to copy some other file besides "datafile," you need to create a new batch file containing the new filename. Obviously this limits the timesaving capabilities of batch files.

A parameter is the part of a command that indicates what the command is to be performed on. Usually this is the name of the file that will be affected by the command. The command "copy a:datafile b:" consists of the actual command name "copy" and the parameters that identify on what, that is, on the file in drive A called "datafile." "Datafile" is a parameter of this command.

Replaceable parameters are "dummies," which means that they are symbols that stand for the actual names of real files. In batch files, replaceable parameters are indicated by the percent sign (%) followed by a number, for example, %1 or %2. The actual files that replace these symbols are specified when you call the batch file. The name of the file to replace %1 follows the batch filename; the file to replace %2 comes next on the command line.

A batch file can be written in such a way that when it is typed at the MS-DOS prompt you can specify optional parameters that are subsequently used as parameters to any of the MS-DOS commands contained within the batch file. These optional parameters are called replaceable parameters.

Imagine that you have created a batch file to display the contents of several files. You want to use this file over and over again, but you will type out different files each time, so you create the batch file using replaceable parameters. The name of this file is "typeit.bat." Within the file are three commands.

```
type %1
type %2
type %3
```

When you call the file you indicate the files to be substituted for the %1, %2, and %3 parameters by listing them in order on the command line. Leave a space between parameters.

```
typeit chap1 chap2 chap3
```

When MS-DOS encounters the first dummy parameter, %1, it substitutes chap1 for this parameter. Then chap2 is substituted for %2, and chap3 for %3. If the file also contained another command using these parameters, then chap1, chap2, and chap3 would again be substituted.

```
copy %1
copy %2
copy %3
```

The replaceable parameters will have the same values throughout the batch file.

The parameters listed after the filename are substituted whenever %1, %2, or %3 are called for in the batch file.

```
type %1
type %2
type %3
copy %1
copy %2
copy %3
```

You can have up to ten replaceable parameters (%0-%9) in a batch file. It is possible to have more; see the SHIFT command later in this chapter for ways to get around this limitation. %0 is reserved for the name of the batch file itself. Thus, typing %0 in the file above would cause MS-DOS to type out the "typeit" file itself.

Replaceable parameters can be used in any batch file. Just remember that you must specify what files are to be substituted for the dummy parameters when you call the file.

You can use all of the MS-DOS commands in a batch file. But, in addition, there are specific batch commands (or subcommands) that are only used in batch files.

COMMANDS IN BATCH PROCESSING

The ECHO Command

The ECHO command is a special command used to turn on or off the echoing (display) of the individual commands contained in a batch file as they are being executed.

The concept of echoing is not new to you. We discussed echoing in a different context earlier when we used the editing keys ^P and ^N to control the echoing of the screen to the printer. Here the same type of echoing is meant, but we are talking about echoing the commands within a batch file to the screen.

Normally, the ECHO command is in the ON mode. In the ON mode, each command is echoed (displayed) on the screen as that command is processing. The display of each command can be useful when you want to keep close track of what is happening inside a batch file. But this echoing feature can also be bothersome when you don't need it, cluttering up the screen with useless information.

If you don't want to see each command displayed on the screen, you can set ECHO to the OFF mode. When ECHO is OFF, the commands themselves do not appear on the screen, but all messages associated with the commands are still displayed. To eliminate echoing, enter this command before any commands you don't want to see. For example, if we wanted to include ECHO OFF in our "copydata" file, we would enter it first.

```
A>copy con: copydata.bat <ENTER>
echo off <ENTER>
format b: <ENTER>
copy a:datafile b: <ENTER>
dir b: <ENTER>
type b:datafile <ENTER>
^Z <ENTER>


                 1 File[s] copied
```

When you run this version of "copydata" you will not see any command lines on the screen after the initial ECHO OFF command.

```
A>copydata <ENTER>
A>echo off
```

(This first command tells you ECHO is OFF. Command messages still appear.)

```
Insert new diskette for drive B:
and strike any key when ready
```

(Press a key to continue.)

Formatting....Format complete

362496 bytes total disk space
362496 bytes available on disk

Format another [Y/N]?n

(You answer N.)

1 File[s] copied
Volume in drive B has no label
Directory of B: \

(DIR output is displayed.)

DATAFILE   38   11-20-84   11:49a
                  1 File[s]   361472 bytes free
This is a demonstration batch file.

A>

If at some point in the batch file you again wanted to see the echoing of each command as it was processed, you would enter a new ECHO command, ECHO ON. All subsequent commands would then appear on the screen.

ECHO has another option that allows you to put messages on the screen, even when ECHO is in the OFF mode. Although you will not see the commands, you will see the message. Let's set the ECHO OFF in our "copydata" batch file, but include a message we do want to see displayed.

The ECHO command can also be used to cause any text you desire to be displayed on the screen while echoing has been turned off (by a previous ECHO OFF command). To echo text to the screen, simply insert ECHO followed by the text to be displayed at the point in the batch file where you want the text displaying to occur.

```
A> copy con: copydata.bat <ENTER>
echo off <ENTER>
format b: <ENTER>
copy a:datafile b: <ENTER>
dir b: <ENTER>
echo Here are the contents of datafile: <ENTER>
type b:datafile <ENTER>
^Z <ENTER>
```

The results of this batch file are exactly the same as those of the last example until the DIR listing has been displayed. Then our message is echoed.

DATAFILE   38   11-20-84   11:49a
                  1 File[s]   361472 bytes free
Here are the contents of datafile:
This is a demonstration batch file.

A>

If you enter ECHO with no parameters, MS-DOS displays the current status of ECHO (ON or OFF). Use ECHO to decide which commands you want to see during batch file processing and to give yourself helpful messages regardless of the status of the ECHO command.

The REM Command

The REM command is used in batch files to insert text that is not to be treated as a command by MS-DOS. REM is useful for inserting text that describes the function of a batch file or that describes a specific batch command line. If an ECHO OFF command has been previously executed, the line containing the REM command will not be displayed when the batch file executes.

The REM (REMark) command is used, like the ECHO command, to put comments into a batch file. These can be statements to you (or any user of the batch file) that explain what the file does or what is happening at a specific moment. REM statements are affected by the status of ECHO. When ECHO is in the OFF mode, REM statements are not displayed in the same way that commands are not displayed. A comparison of the ECHO and REM commands is given in *Table 8-2*.

REM commands can contain any information you think will help you understand the batch file better. You can also use REM to insert blank lines in a file. The following batch file, "newdisk," formats and puts the system on new diskettes. It then checks the condition of the diskette.

```
A> copy con: newdisk.bat <ENTER>
rem This file formats and checks new disks. <ENTER>
rem The system will be put on the diskette. <ENTER>
format b:/s <ENTER>
dir b: <ENTER>
rem Here is the condition of this diskette. <ENTER>
chkdsk b: <ENTER>
rem This diskette is ready to use, don't forget to label it! <ENTER>
^Z <ENTER>
         1 File[s] copied
```

To run "newdisk," enter the filename.

```
A>newdisk <ENTER>
```

This is what you will see on the screen:

```
A>rem This file formats and checks new disks.

A>rem The system will be put on the diskette.

A>format b:/s
Insert new diskette for drive B:
and strike any key when ready
```

(You press a key.)

```
Formatting....Format complete
System transferred

    362496 bytes total disk space
     40960 bytes used by system
    321536 bytes available on disk
```

Format another [Y/N]?n
A>dir b:

(You answer N.)

Volume in drive B has no label
Directory of B:\

COMMAND   COM: 17664   3-08-83   12:00p
             1 File[s]   321536 bytes free

A>rem Here is the condition of this diskette.

A>chkdsk b:
  362496 bytes total disk space
   22528 bytes in 2 hidden files
   18432 bytes in 1 user files
  321536 bytes available on disk

  262144 bytes total memory
  237456 bytes free

A>rem This diskette is ready to use, don't forget to label it!
A>

You can see from this example how the addition of REM statements can help clarify the contents and operations of a batch file. If you wish, you can use the ECHO OFF mode to eliminate the display of all command lines, but remember this will also eliminate the display of all REM statements.

Table 8-2.
Comparison of ECHO
and REMark

	ECHO		REMark
ON	Commands are displayed.	ECHO ON	REM statements are displayed.
OFF	Commands are not displayed but messages still appear.	ECHO OFF	REM statements are not displayed.

The PAUSE Command

The PAUSE command is used to cause a batch file to pause at a specific point in a batch file while it is executing. When any key is pressed after a batch file has paused as a result of a PAUSE command, MS-DOS resumes executing the BATCH file where it left off. Alternatively, the <Ctrl> C or <Ctrl> <Break> keys can be pressed to abort the batch file while it has paused.

The PAUSE command puts a built-in stop into a batch file. You use this command when you need to do something before the next command is executed, such as change a diskette or turn on the printer. You might also use PAUSE to allow a full screen to be read before proceeding to the next screen.

Because you stop processing with the PAUSE command, you must then press a key to continue the batch file. As part of the PAUSE command, MS-DOS has an automatic message that appears after the PAUSE command—"Strike any key when ready." You don't need to add this message, it will always appear after a PAUSE command. PAUSE could be incorporated into our "newdisk" batch file.

```
A> copy con: newdisk.bat <ENTER>
rem This file formats and checks new disks. <ENTER>
pause Remove the diskette currently in drive B. <ENTER>
rem The system will be put on the diskette. <ENTER>
format b:/s <ENTER>
dir b: <ENTER>
rem Here is the condition of this diskette. <ENTER>
chkdsk b: <ENTER>
rem This diskette is ready to use, don't forget to label it! <ENTER>
^Z <ENTER>

        1 File[s] copied
```

A new version of "newdisk" would be created.

```
A>rem This file formats and checks new disks.

A>pause Remove the diskette currently in drive B.
Strike a key when ready....
```

(You press a key.)

```
A>rem The system will be put on the diskette.

A>format b:/s
Insert new diskette for drive B:
and strike any key when ready

Formatting....Format complete
System transferred

    362496 bytes total disk space
     40960 bytes used by system
    321536 bytes available on disk

Format another [Y/N]?n
```

(You answer N.)

```
A>dir b:

A>dir b:

    Volume in drive B has no label
    Directory of B: \

    COMMAND      COM:      17664     3-08-83     12:00p
                 1 File[s]           321536 bytes free

A>rem Here is the condition of this diskette.

A>chkdsk b:
    362496 bytes total disk space
     22528 bytes in 2 hidden files
     18432 bytes in 1 user files
    321536 bytes available on disk

    262144 bytes total memory
    237456 bytes free

A>rem This diskette is ready to use, don't forget to label it!
A>
```

PAUSE is useful as a safety device within a batch file. In this case you use it as a warning, so you will be sure not to format over a diskette that contains data. This warning can be very effective in helping you avoid those errors that we all make at one time or another. For example, you might have included in a batch file the command to erase all old files. Inserting a pause command could save you from a frustrating mistake.

```
dir b:
pause Make sure all desired files have been copied, or BREAK.
del oldfiles
```

The GOTO Command

A batch file can be constructed in such a way so that it behaves like a program written in BASIC or another programming language by using GOTO commands to branch to specific parts within a batch file or to create repeating loops.

The GOTO command works in conjunction with a label. The label is any name you choose that identifies a location in a batch file, rather like the way a line number in EDLIN indicates a location. The label is preceded by a colon (:). GOTO transfers control of the processing to the line after the label.

GOTO is a convenient command when you want to keep repeating a certain activity without changing any parameters. Suppose you had a letter and needed several duplicates made. Using GOTO, you could set up a batch file to type out as many duplicates as you needed.

When you use GOTO with a label designation, you create a loop. A loop is an operation that will keep repeating until you stop it. To escape from a loop in a batch file, use ^C or <Ctrl> <Break> to terminate the job. The loop itself is not displayed on the screen. A GOTO loop is illustrated in *Figure 8-3*.

Figure 8-3.
The GOTO Command

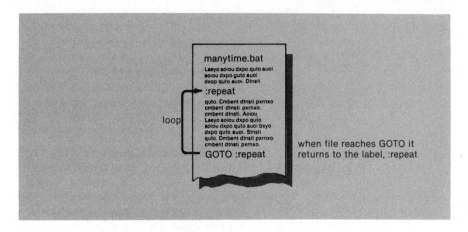

The name of this batch file is "manytime.bat." The label that defines where the command returns is called ":repeat."

```
A> copy con:manytime.bat <ENTER>
rem This file makes duplicate copies of a letter. <ENTER>
echo off <ENTER>
copy a:letter b: <ENTER>
:repeat <ENTER>
type b:letter <ENTER>
echo Press CTRL BREAK to stop this batch file. <ENTER>
goto :repeat <ENTER>
^Z <ENTER>

        1 File[s] copied
```

To run this batch file you must have the file "letter" on the diskette in drive A, along with the "manytime.bat" file. For our example, the file "letter" contains one line, "This is a sample for the goto command." To execute "manytime," enter the name of the batch file.

```
a> manytime <ENTER>
```

"Manytime" results in this display:

```
A>rem This file makes duplicate copies of a letter.
A> echo off
        1 File[s] copied
This is a sample for the goto command.
Press CTRL BREAK to stop this batch file.
This is a sample for the goto command.
Press CTRL BREAK to stop this batch file.
This is a sample for the goto command.
```

Press CTRL BREAK to stop this batch file.

.

.

.

These messages continue to be displayed until you stop processing by pressing <Ctrl> <Break>.

The IF Command

The IF command is provided so that within a batch file, you can check and compare strings of text, check for the existence of specified files, or check for errors and cause the batch file to behave in certain ways according to the results.

The IF command tells the batch file to continue processing the next command if a certain condition is true. As illustrated in *Figure 8-4*, the condition can be one of three options: IF exist, IF string, and IF ERRORLEVEL.

IF Exist

IF exist uses a file specification as the test. If the file exists (the condition is true), then processing passes to the specified GOTO location. If the file does not exist (the condition is false), then batch processing continues with the next command.

For our IF exist example, let's create a batch file that duplicates a letter until it is instructed to stop, just like our "manytime" batch file. But this batch file contains another instruction. It tells MS-DOS to check first to see if the letter has been copied from A to B. If the letter does not exist on B, the batch file formats the diskette in B, copies the file to B, makes sure the file is on B by listing a directory, and then starts the duplication process. If the file already exists on B, the letter has been copied and duplication begins immediately. Here are the contents of the "copylet" batch file:

```
A> copy con: copylet.bat <ENTER>
echo off <ENTER>
if exist b:letter goto :exists <ENTER>
format b: <ENTER>
copy a:letter b: <ENTER>
dir b: <ENTER>
:exists <ENTER>
type b:letter <ENTER>
echo Press CTRL BREAK to stop this batch file. <ENTER>
goto :exists <ENTER>
^Z <ENTER>
```

        1 File[s] copied

Here are the results of the first run of "copylet":

A> copylet <ENTER>

A> echo off
Insert new diskette for drive B:
and strike any key when ready

(The "letter" file was not found on the B diskette so formatting begins.)

     Formatting....Format complete

       362496 bytes total disk space
       362496 bytes available on disk

     Format another [Y/N]?n   1 File[s] copied

(You answer N; MS-DOS proceeds to copy the file to B.)

     Volume in drive B has no label
     Directory of B: \

(MS-DOS lists the directory.)

     LETTER   40   11-20-84   12:54p
              1 File[s]   361472 bytes free

(TYPE command executes ECHO message.)

     This is a sample for the goto command.
     Press CTRL BREAK to stop this batch file.
     This is a sample for the goto command.
     Press CTRL BREAK to stop this batch file.
     This is a sample for the goto command.
     Press CTRL BREAK to stop this batch file.
     This is a sample for the goto command.
     Press CTRL BREAK to stop this batch file.
     This is a sample for the goto command.
     Press CTRL BREAK to stop this batch file.
     This is a sample ....

The file is now in the :exists loop.

     The first time you run "copylet," the "letter" file will not be found on the B diskette unless it had been copied previously. The batch file checks for this condition. Not finding the file on the indicated diskette, it proceeds to format the diskette, copy the file, and give you a directory. Duplication then continues until you halt the batch file.

     Provided you use the same diskette in drive B, the results will be different the second time you run "copylet."

     A>copylet <ENTER>

     A>echo off
     This is a sample for the goto command.
     Press CTRL BREAK to stop this batch file.
     This is a sample for the goto command.
     Press CTRL BREAK to stop this batch file.
     This is ....

On all consequent runs of "copylet," the condition is true (the "letter" file already exists on drive B). Therefore, the batch file skips directly to the :exists loop and begins duplicating the letter. This continues until you terminate the batch file.

IF String

The IF command can also be used to check and compare any replaceable parameters that are specified against specific text strings or other parameters.

The second IF option uses a string as a test. A string is simply computereze for a group of characters. In this IF command you tell DOS to go to a specific location or perform a certain operation when the strings match (the condition is true). When you enter the strings into the command, they are separated by two equal signs (==). For example, we might have a batch file with replaceable parameters. It contains this command:

IF %1 == Seamus echo Seamus is ready.

Whenever Seamus was entered as the %1 parameter, this condition would be true, and the echo command "Seamus is ready" would be displayed. However, if Matt was entered as the %1 parameter, then the condition would be false and the echo message would not appear.

Figure 8-4.
The IF Command

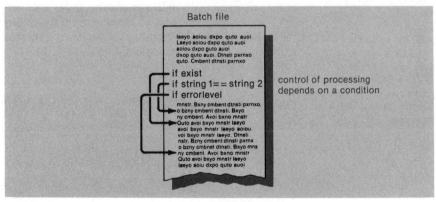

Batch file

laeyo aoiou dxpo quto auoi
Laeyo aoiou dxpo quto auoi
aoiou dxpo quto auoi
dxop quto auoi. Dtnsti pxrnxo
quto. Cmbent dtnsti pxrnxo

if exist
if string 1== string 2
if errorlevel

mnstr. Bxny cmbent dtnsti pxrnxo.
o bzny cmbent dtnsti. Bxyo
ny cmbent. Avoi bxno mnstr
Quto avoi bxyo mnstr laeyo
avoi bxyo mnstr laeyo aoiou.
voi bxyo mnstr laeyo. Dtnsti
nstr. Bzny cmbent dtnsti pxrnx
o bzny cmbnet dtnsti. Bxyo mns
ny cmbent. Avoi bxno mnstr
Quto avoi bxyo mnstr laeyo
laeyo aoiu dxpo quto auoi

control of processing depends on a condition

IF ERRORLEVEL

The third IF option uses ERRORLEVEL as the test. ERRORLEVEL is an indicator (sometimes called a flag) that signals the status of a certain condition. ERRORLEVEL is internally set as a part of certain MS-DOS commands. It indicates whether an operation was successfully performed. ERRORLEVEL 1 indicates failure of the operation; ERRORLEVEL 0 indicates successful completion of the command.

Imagine that you had a program that copied all files from one diskette to another. This "copyall" file includes three commands.

```
copy a:*.* b:
if errorlevel 1 echo copyall failure
dir b:
```

The message "copyall failure" appears on the screen whenever all the files are not successfully copied. Non-completion of the operation in this case makes the condition true. The message does not appear when all the files are copied, because this results in an ERRORLEVEL of 0 and the IF condition is false.

These IF commands may seem a bit complicated at first. Take your time and go slowly as you begin to use this command. A few practice sessions will increase your confidence. You will quickly discover how useful the IF command can be in making your batch commands do exactly what you need them to do.

The SHIFT Command

The SHIFT command is used to shift the contents of any specific replaceable parameters downward: parameter %1 is transferred to %0, %2 to %1, %3 to %2, and so on. This command allows you not only to check all parameters initially specified with the batch file by doing continual shifts so that only %0 need be checked but also to specify more than ten parameters on the batch file's command line.

After you have developed some of your own batch files and have seen just how timesaving they can be, you may eventually run into the problem of wanting to use more than ten replaceable parameters. You may want to type out twelve files or copy fifteen files. The SHIFT command solves this dilemma by allowing you to exceed ten replaceable parameters. You can't just add %11, %12, and so on. Instead, after you have substituted the first ten parameters, your %1 parameter drops off the list and all the remaining parameters shift one position to the left.

Suppose you want to create a batch file to display the letters of the alphabet up to and including the letter L. This means there are twelve parameters you want substituted into the file. This is how the contents of "alphabet" appear:

```
echo off
echo %0 %1 %2 %3 %4 %5 %6 %7 %8 %9
SHIFT
echo %0 %1 %2 %3 %4 %5 %6 %7 %8 %9
SHIFT
echo %0 %1 %2 %3 %4 %5 %6 %7 %8 %9
SHIFT
echo %0 %1 %2 %3 %4 %5 %6 %7 %8 %9
SHIFT
```

You execute this file by calling the batch file.

A>alphabet A B C D E F G H I J K L <ENTER>

The first time you use parameters in your batch file, the first ten parameters are substituted just as they were entered. But after the SHIFT command, all the parameters would move over one space to the left. The leftmost parameter is dropped, and the new parameter (number 10 in the list) is moved into the %9 position. This move to the left continues each time you issue the SHIFT command.

The output of "alphabet" looks like this:

```
A>echo off
alphabet A B C D E F G H I
A B C D E F G H I J
```

```
B C D E F G H I J K
C D E F G H I J K L
```

You can easily see how you could continue substituting parameters until all that you included have been displayed. Once there are fewer than ten parameters left, the spaces to the right will be left blank.

The FOR Command

The FOR command provides a function called FOR-LOOP, frequently found in programming languages. The FOR command allows you to examine a series of parameters to a specific MS-DOS command and cause that command to execute repeatedly, each time with a different parameter, until all parameters have been covered.

As illustrated in *Figure 8-5*, this batch command allows repetition of the same command on a series of files and uses a few new concepts. The first is the concept of a set. A set is a group of files that follow the "in" portion of the FOR command. Thus, the set in the following example is chap1.txt, chap2.txt, and chap3.txt. Immediately following the FOR command is a variable, designated by two percent signs (%%) and a name. This variable also follows the "do" section of the command. The FOR command allows you to repeat an action or operation for each of the files contained in the set.

Suppose you want to create a batch file to check for the existence of files on a diskette, in this case, three files named chap1, chap2, and chap3. The FOR command can accomplish this.

    for %%A in [chap1.txt chap2.txt chap3.txt] do dir %%A

If the files are found, three results are displayed.

    dir chap1.txt
    dir chap2.txt
    dir chap3.txt

You can make this command even more powerful by using wildcards for the set. Here is an easy, fast way to copy all the files on a diskette:

    for %%B in [*.*] do copy %%B

**Figure 8-5.
The FOR Command**

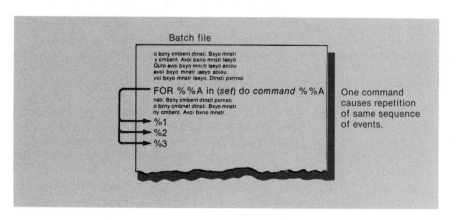

AUTOEXEC.BAT

So far when you created batch files, each has been given a unique name. There is one type of batch file that comes named and performs one specific and very useful function. This is the AUTOEXEC.BAT file.

AUTOEXEC.BAT is designed to make starting up the computer more efficient. When you boot the system, MS-DOS automatically examines the contents of the boot diskette. If it finds an AUTOEXEC.BAT file on the diskette, it immediately executes this command first. Thus, by putting an AUTOEXEC.BAT file on your boot diskette, you can go directly to the program you want. Suppose you want to use your word-processing program. If you boot normally, these are the steps you take to arrive at the opening menu of a word-processing program, called, let's say, with the letters ws.

First you turn on the computer (or press <Ctrl> <Alt> <Del> if it is a warm boot) and let the computer start up. The first messages after the boot are the time and date requests.

AUTOEXEC.BAT is reserved for use by MS-DOS. When the system is powered up or reset and the MS-DOS operating system is loaded, MS-DOS automatically searches for the file AUTOEXEC.BAT on the default drive. If found, MS-DOS executes its contents just as it would any other batch file. This function is very useful if you want certain commands automatically executed whenever you start up the system.

```
Current date is Tue 1 01-1980
Enter new date:
Current time is 0:00:00
Enter new time:
```

After responding to these requests, the opening screen is shown.

```
The XYZ Personal Computer DOS
Version 2.0 (C) Copyright XYZ Company, 1981, 1982

A>
```

At this point, you must remove the system diskette, insert the word-processing diskette, and call the file you want: ws.

But by using AUTOEXEC.BAT you can arrive at this same point with only one entry. An AUTOEXEC.BAT can contain only two lines, the ECHO OFF command and the name of the file you want to go to.

```
A>copy con: autoexec.bat <ENTER>
echo off <ENTER>
ws <ENTER>
^Z <ENTER>
```

Of course, to make this work, you have to first put the system on your word-processing diskette so that you can boot using this diskette. The AUTOEXEC.BAT file must also be on this diskette.

Now to get the word-processing program, simply start the system. The opening menu appears with no further input.

AUTOEXEC.BAT could be used to move you right into a BASIC program.

```
A>copy con: autoexec.bat <ENTER>
echo off <ENTER>
```

basica b:begin <ENTER>
^Z <ENTER>

When you boot, the BASICA interpreter on drive A is loaded into
the computer, followed by the "begin.bas" program on drive B, which
would then begin to run. All you have to do is be sure the correct diskettes
are in the correct drives.

AUTOEXEC.BAT files skip over the time and date requests. If
you want to use AUTOEXEC.BAT and still enter this information, just
include the TIME and DATE commands in your AUTOEXEC.BAT file.

One note of caution: you can have only one AUTOEXEC.BAT file
on a diskette. Because each file must have a unique name, you are limited
to one AUTOEXEC.BAT. If you try to create more than one
AUTOEXEC.BAT file, the previous AUTOEXEC.BAT will be erased as
you enter the new data.

SUMMARY

In this chapter you were introduced to batch files and batch
processing. You learned that you can create files using both the EDLIN
program and the COPY CON: command. Each of the batch commands,
ECHO, REM, PAUSE, GOTO, IF, SHIFT, and FOR, was explained. The
creation of an AUTOEXEC.BAT file and some common uses of this type of
file were explored. Batch processing is an area that you will continue to
develop as you find your own uses for this special feature of MS-DOS.

Of course, the more you work with your computer, the more files
you create and need to store and retrieve. Some of your diskettes may be
pretty confusing by now, and your directories are probably becoming a
maze of names. In the next chapter you are going to learn how to organize
those directories so that you can find what you want, when you want it.

WHAT HAVE WE LEARNED?

1. Batch files contain MS-DOS commands, filenames, and a few special
   commands; names of batch files always end with the extension .bat. To
   create a batch file, use EDLIN or use the command COPY CON: and end by
   entering control-z alone on the last line.
2. To run a batch file, type its name at the prompt. To interrupt the operation
   of a batch file, type control-c or shift-break.
3. You can include replaceable parameters (%1 or %2 and so on) in a batch file;
   to invoke the batch file, type in the names of the files you wish the batch file
   to operate on.
4. The ECHO command can be set to ECHO ON or ECHO OFF and print or
   inhibit printing the batch file commands to screen as the file executes.
5. The REM command is used to begin a line of explanatory comments.
6. Place the PAUSE command in a batch file at a point where you intend the
   operation to pause for you to do something, such as swap disks.
7. The GOTO command repeats the batch file instruction sequence from
   whatever label, preceded by a colon, you specify.
8. The IF command allows GOTO branching to a label depending on the
   existence of a file or a complete match of two strings or an error indication.

9. The SHIFT command allows re-use of replaceable parameters %0 to %9 to extend the total number of substitutions.
10. The FOR command allows us to execute a DOS command on a group of files.
11. The AUTOEXEC.BAT file contains the same instructions as other batch files and is automatically executed after the system boots itself.

Quiz for Chapter 8

1. The MS-DOS batch function is used to:
   a. automatically execute a series of MS-DOS commands contained within a batch file.
   b. execute a file that is somewhat like a cookbook of commands.
   c. execute a file that has the extension .BAT.
   d. all of the above.

2. Batch files always contain:
   a. binary-coded data.
   b. ASCII text.
   c. encrypted data.
   d. none of the above.

3. A batch file can be created using:
   a. a text editor such as EDLIN.
   b. a word processing program.
   c. the "COPY CON: filename" command sequence, where "filename" is the name of the batch file.
   d. any of the above.
   e. none of the above.

4. A batch filename must contain:
   a. the extension .BAT.
   b. any extension.
   c. no extension.

5. A batch file is executed by MS-DOS by entering the filename:
   a. with the extension .BAT.
   b. without the extension .BAT.
   c. either of the above.
   d. none of the above.

6. The execution of a batch file can be prematurely stopped by:
   a. pressing <Ctrl> B.
   b. pressing <Ctrl> C.
   c. pressing <Ctrl> D.
   d. pressing <Ctrl> G.

7. Up to how many replaceable parameters may be checked within a batch file when it is executed?
   a. 2
   b. 5
   c. 10
   d. 20

8. The special batch ECHO command is used for:
   a. turning off echoing of text to the display.
   b. turning on echoing of text to the display.
   c. echoing specified text to the display.
   d. any of the above.
   e. none of the above.

9. The REM command is used to:
   a. insert commands in a batch file.
   b. remove text from a batch file.
   c. insert in a batch file remarks or comments that are not to be treated as commands by MS-DOS.
   d. none of the above.

10. To cause the batch file to pause at a specific point while it is executing, you should insert what command in the batch file at the point where you want the pause to occur:
    a. STOP command.
    b. PAUSE command.
    c. <Ctrl> S command.
    d. <Ctrl> Z command.

11. The GOTO command is used in batch files to:
    a. cause a branch to another part of the batch file.
    b. branch so that a repetitive loop occurs.
    c. either a or b.
    d. none of the above.

12. The IF command is used to:
   a. check the existence of a specified file on a disk.
   b. check and compare two text strings.
   c. check for an error condition.
   d. any of the above.
   e. none of the above.

13. The SHIFT command is used to:
   a. shift the contents of each replaceable parameter downward.
   b. allow the use of more than ten replaceable parameters.
   c. shift the screen sideways.
   d. shift the definition of the keys on the keyboard over by one position.

14. The FOR command is used to execute repeatedly the same command, each time with a different parameter, until:

   a. some of the specified parameters have been covered.
   b. the second parameter has been covered.
   c. all specified parameters have been covered.
   d. any of the above.
   e. none of the above.

15. When the system is first powered up or is reset and the operating system is loaded, MS-DOS automatically searches for a specific batch file. If the file is found, MS-DOS immediately executes it. This batch file is called:
   a. NORMAL.BAT
   b. SPECIAL.BAT
   c. AUTOEXEC.BAT
   d. OK.BAT.

Tree-Structured Directories

ABOUT THIS CHAPTER

By now you are well acquainted with the use of directories. Directories are a quick reference index to the contents of each floppy diskette. When listed with the DIR command, directories give the names and sizes of files and a date-time reference indicating when they were created or last modified.

Directories, of course, are not unique to the computer world. A frequently used directory is a phone book. The phone book is a simple directory. The entries are alphabetized by last name. An entry is listed in one location only, according to surname. When you know exactly the name you are looking for, the correct spelling, the first initial or name and the address, you can find a number quickly.

But a phone directory also illustrates a problem with simple directories. When you have too much information, as when there are pages and pages of the same last name and that's all the information you have, phone books lose their effectiveness. Instead of being a shortcut to information, they become a burden.

This same situation can occur in your information-retrieval system. When you accumulate too many files, you may actually dread the output of the DIR command. A double-sided diskette can hold up to 112 files, and listing the directory can involve several screens. Each screen must be stopped from scrolling and examined. This can take a lot of time. In this chapter you will learn a new method of structuring directories.

FILE STORAGE

Tree-structured directories, introduced under MS-DOS Version 2.0, is a concept borrowed from mainframes and minicomputers. Tree-structured directories, especially on hard disks, provide considerable flexibility in the way you can store files.

The difficulty of accessing and storing many files demands a solution in two different areas. First, a tool is needed that can store many files in a small space. This tool, the hard or, fixed, disk, is borrowed from larger mainframe computer systems, which have always had a great deal of information to process. Now, 10-megabyte fixed disks are available for personal computers. A 10-megabyte fixed disk stores approximately 10 million characters. As you can imagine, that is either one incredibly long file, which might be impossible to use, or several hundred smaller files. A typical number of files on hard disk might be anywhere from 500 to 800.

The hard disk necessitates a new method of directory structuring. MS-DOS, again borrowing from mainframe computers and minicomputers, has provided the answer with the use of tree-structured directories.

In this type of structure, a main, or root, directory branches into several subdirectories, which in turn can generate other subdirectories. To move around from root to subdirectory or from subdirectory to subdirectory, you use a path that is included in a command as a pathname.

PREPARING YOUR DISKETTE

Arranging the storage of files on a floppy or hard disk using tree-structured directories is especially useful when you have a large number of files and you want them organized into groups of files.

Tree-structured directories are designed to help you create order from the confusion of many, many files. But their use is not limited to the larger capacity of fixed-disk systems. You can use this structure on your floppy-disk systems as well.

This discussion centers on the use of tree-structured directories for floppy-disk users. If you do have a fixed-disk system, this discussion as well as Chapter 11 will be of interest.

First you will need an example diskette. Preparing this diskette is going to do two useful things for you. First, it will show you just how much you have learned. Second, it will provide you with the tools necessary for greater directory control.

You will need your system diskette to format a new diskette in this example. In addition, you will be copying an external command, TREE.COM, from the system diskette. Be sure your system diskette contains this file. To create the files on your example diskette, use the COPY CON: method described in Chapter 8. Enter the commands listed below, and follow the instructions and explanations.

Put your system diskette in drive A and a new diskette in drive B. Format the diskette (include the system). When "Format another (Y/N)?" appears, press N.

A>format b:/s <ENTER>

Copy TREE.COM is a command file you'll need on the diskette.

A>copy tree.com b: <ENTER>
    1 File(s) copied

Change the current drive to B.

A>b: <ENTER>

Now we are going to create some "dummy" files. You can use EDLIN instead of COPY CON: if you prefer.

B>copy con: weather <ENTER>

The contents of the files do not matter. We are making them short and to the point.

File contains weather information. <ENTER>
^Z <ENTER>
    1 File(s) copied
B>copy con: soil <ENTER>
File contains soil information. <ENTER>
^Z <ENTER>
    1 File(s) copied

```
B>copy con: yields <ENTER>
Record of last year's yields. <ENTER>
^Z <ENTER>
  1 File[s] copied

B>copy con: texture <ENTER>
Notes on fruit texture. <ENTER>
^Z <ENTER>
  1 File[s] copied

B>copy con: color <ENTER>
Notes on fruit color. <ENTER>
^Z <ENTER>
  1 File[s] copied
```

That's all there is to it. Five files created, just like that. You can take a look at your example diskette with DIR.

```
B>dir <ENTER>
```

```
COMMAND   COM      17664    3-08-83   12:00p
TREE      COM       1513    3-08-83   12:00p
WEATHER                36   12-17-84    1:04p
SOIL                   33   12-17-84    1:04p
YIELDS                 31   12-17-84    1:05p
TEXTURE                25   12-17-84    1:05p
COLOR                  23   12-17-84    1:06p
          7 File[s]        314368 bytes free
```

SUBDIRECTORIES

When the FORMAT command is used to format a disk, it automatically creates what is called the root directory. It is in the root directory that all the files previously described in this book reside. Under MS-DOS 2.0, the root directory can also contain what are called subdirectories.

Creating a root directory is easy. You have done it many times already; FORMAT automatically creates a root directory every time it formats a diskette. The directory, which can hold up to 112 files, is the root directory of the tree-structured system. In MS-DOS Version 2.0 and all later versions, this root directory can also hold subdirectories.

A subdirectory is used to contain files separate from the root directory or other subdirectories. A subdirectory stems from the root directory much like the trunk and branches stem from the roots of a tree. Therefore, a subdirectory that originates in the root directory can also contain other subdirectories, and those subdirectories can contain more subdirectories.

Subdirectories hold files. These files may contain groups of related data, or they may contain other subdirectories. MS-DOS treats all files the same. The only difference is that you can use subdirectories to get to other subdirectories. Once you are in a file, however, all you can do is go back to a directory.

Think about the maps you use when you go into the forest. These maps contain a maze of trails, as illustrated in *Figure 9-1*. Suppose a group of hikers starts out from the same point. This starting point, the "straight and narrow" trail, is like the root directory. It is the source of all other paths.

Some hikers follow the "straight and narrow" to "dead end" or "direct." These are their final destinations. Like a root directory, "straight and narrow" contains final destinations (locations where files are stored).

**Figure 9-1.
The Map**

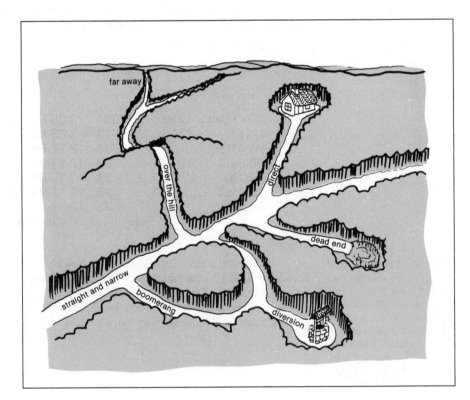

A subdirectory is actually viewed by MS-DOS as a special type of file containing information about the files (normal files and other subdirectories) stored within the subdirectory.

For other hikers, the "straight and narrow" is just the first step on a journey to "boomerang" or "over the hill." In this case, the root is the path to other subdirectories. The subdirectories "boomerang" and "over the hill" may contain final destinations of their own, where files are stored, or they may be links to other subdirectories such as "far away" and "diversion."

The important thing to realize about directories and subdirectories is that they contain files. Any of these files (locations) can also be subdirectories, paths to other files.

PATHNAMES

A file stored anywhere in the directory tree-structure of a disk can be referenced or accessed from any other location by using a pathname.

The only function of a subdirectory is to group files. Like filenames, the names of subdirectories may contain up to eight characters plus an optional three-character extension. Each subdirectory must have a unique name and it cannot be a name of a file already contained in the root directory. Subdirectory names follow all the other rules for filenames.

You find your way around in the directory by specifying a pathname. This is simply a list of names that tells MS-DOS where to start and which subdirectories to use to get to a final destination. Each subdirectory is separated from the next with a backslash (\ ). In *Figure 9-1*, the path to the "edge of the forest" would be

$$\setminus boomerang \setminus diversion \setminus edge\ of\ the\ forest$$

Notice that the root directory, "straight and narrow," is not mentioned in this pathname. That is because the root directory is indicated by the initial backslash in the pathname. You never actually enter the directory name root, instead you use an initial backslash as a shorthand for this directory.

Assume you are an agriculturist anxious to begin organizing your files. You files are now on a diskette (the one you created earlier), and they are stored in the root directory. Files are always stored in the root directory until you tell MS-DOS to put them somewhere else. First, you are going to create a subdirectory called FRUITS. Within FRUITS you are going to have a subdirectory called CHERRIES. The CHERRIES subdirectory will contain a file named "yields." To clear a path to this file, tell MS-DOS where to start and then you give clear directions.

$$ROOTS \rightarrow FRUITS \rightarrow CHERRIES \rightarrow YIELDS \rightarrow$$

$$\setminus fruits \setminus cherries \setminus yields$$

This path translates into: starting from the root (indicated by the initial backslash), go to the file FRUITS (which is a subdirectory), go to the file CHERRIES (which is a subdirectory), and then find the file "yields."

Almost all the commands in MS-DOS can be performed on specific files in different subdirectories. All you need to do is to tell MS-DOS which path to take to get to the file.

Pathnames are the organizing tools for sophisticated use of your disks. Subdirectories can save you lots of time and help you keep your files better organized. Pathnames are a quick way to create, copy, delete, and reorganize files. But don't get carried away. The best tree-structured directory is on that is simple.

If you make your structure too complicated, you will get lost on the path, and MS-DOS will spend a lot of time getting to the specified destination. One good idea, until you are more familiar with subdirectories and pathnames, is to limit your subdirectories to the root file.

SPECIAL COMMANDS

> The internal command MKDIR (or MD) creates a subdirectory. After creating a subdirectory, use the external command TREE to display the updated directory structure of your disk.

There are some special commands MS-DOS reserves for creating and maintaining tree-structured directories: MKDIR, CHDIR, RMDIR, TREE, and PATH. Let's look at each of these commands. Be sure the diskette you are using with these examples is in drive A. For safety's sake, remove any diskette in drive B.

The MKDIR Command

When you format a diskette it contains one directory, the original root directory. To create subdirectories on the disk, use the MKDIR (MaKe DIRectory) command. (The process is illustrated in *Figure 9-2.*) Let's use MKDIR to create the subdirectory FRUITS. When using this command you may enter MKDIR or the shorter abbreviation MD. Put your example diskette in drive A.

Cartoon 9-1

Figure 9-2.
The MKDIR Command

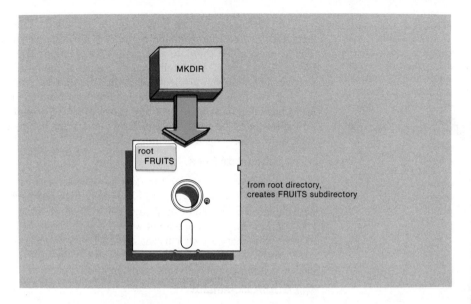

MKDIR

root
FRUITS

from root directory,
creates FRUITS subdirectory

MKDIR is an internal command. This means you can create a new
directory whenever you are operating in MS-DOS (A or B prompt). This
directory is being created from the root directory. Type in the command,
followed by the symbol for the root (\) and then the subdirectory name.

A> mkdir \ fruits <ENTER>

The computer makes those whirring sounds familiar to you from
using the FORMAT and COPY commands. Then the MS-DOS prompt
reappears. Your new subdirectory now exits in the root directory on the
diskette in the current drive.

To verify the creation of FRUITS, use DIR to list the contents of
the root directory. Nothing special is needed to do this; it is the same DIR
command you have used before.

A> dir <ENTER>

```
Volume in drive A has no label
Directory of A: \


COMMAND   COM     17664    3-08-83    12:00p
TREE      COM      1513    3-08-83    12:00p
WEATHER             36    11-21-84    2:19p
SOIL                33    11-21-84    2:20p
YIELDS              31    11-21-84    2:22p
TEXTURE             25    11-21-84    3:27p
COLOR               23    11-21-84    3:32p
FRUITS          <DIR>      11-21-84    3:45p
           8 File[s]       313344 bytes free
```

In addition to the TREE command, the DIR command can be used to list all subdirectories created in the current directory. A subdirectory is always shown with the symbol <DIR>. Although a subdirectory is in fact a file, it cannot be copied, renamed, or deleted. Only the files stored within a subdirectory can be treated as normal files.

Right there at the bottom of the list is FRUITS. MS-DOS nicely reminds you that this is a subdirectory by including the <DIR> extension. You are also given the date and time of its creation. The second line of this listing (Directory of A:\) tells you by means of the backslash, which is the root symbol, that you are looking at the root directory of A.

Because you created this subdirectory from the root directory, you could have eliminated the first backslash. MS-DOS will always begin a directory operation from the directory you are in. In this case you are in root, so you don't need to include the initial \.

A>mkdir fruits

Suppose you wanted to do a lot of work with the FRUITS subdirectory. You were going to copy many files and perhaps create a few new subdirectories. You can always get to a subdirectory by starting at the root and moving down one level with the pathname \FRUITS. But, just as you often change your current drive when you want to use drive B extensively, you can also change your current directory. This makes it easier to issue commands that refer only to a specified subdirectory.

The CHDIR Command

The internal CHDIR command (or CD) changes the default directory. After you start up the system, the root directory is the default directory. The CHDIR command can be used to make a subdirectory the default directory or to change the default directory back to the root.

Changing directories is as easy as making them, simply give the CHDIR (CHange DIRectory) command. The command is followed by the name of the directory that you want as your base of operations. You may use the abbreviation CD if you wish. Because you are currently in the root directory, you don't need to include the opening \ in this command.

A>chdir fruits <ENTER>

This command instructs MS-DOS to change from the current directory to the subdirectory FRUITS. You will hear the disk drive whirring. And then there is silence. MS-DOS does not indicate that the directories have changed; it simply returns the A prompt. You can check which directory you are in by using DIR. No beginning slash is necessary, because you believe you are currently in the FRUITS subdirectory.

A>dir <ENTER>

What you are requesting is a directory listing of the current directory.

```
Volume in drive A has no label
Directory of A:\fruits

.        <DIR>        12-17-84      1:29p
..       <DIR>        12-17-84      1:29p
                   2 File[s]      313344 bytes free
```

(Your numbers may be different.)

The second line of the directory message tells you what you want to know. It indicates that this is a directory of the diskette in drive A:\fruits. Because the directory name is preceded by one slash, indicating the root directory, you know that this directory is a first-level subdirectory.

The next two lines of the directory listing are something you have not seen before. The single period and the double period stand for the directory itself and its parent directory. You'll explore these directory symbols a bit later. The final line of the directory listing puts you back on familiar turf. It says there are two files in this directory and gives the amount of bytes still available on the diskette.

While you are in this directory, you can do all the normal file operations—as long as the files exist in this directory. If you try to do something with files in the root directory or in another subdirectory, MS-DOS will respond with a "File not found" error message. You are currently stuck in this subdirectory. You must issue another CHDIR command to get out of the subdirectory.

A review of the CHDIR command appears in *Figure 9-3.*

Figure 9-3.
The CHDIR Command

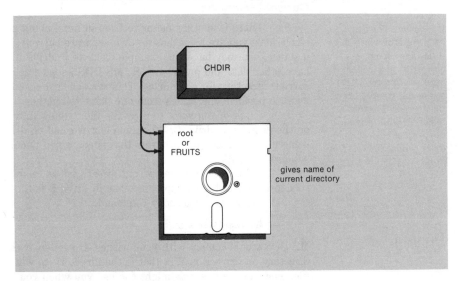

Returning to the Root Directory

When a pathname contains only a single backslash it means "reference the root directory," regardless of which directory is the default.

There is a quick and easy way to get back to the root directory no matter where you are within the subdirectory structure. Issue the CHDIR command with the root symbol, the single backslash (\ ). This changes the default directory to the root.

A>chdir \ <ENTER>

Use DIR to verify that you have returned to the root directory.

A>dir <ENTER>

Volume in drive A has no label
Directory of A: \

COMMAND   COM   17664   3-08-83   12:00p
TREE   COM   1513   3-08-83   12:00p

WEATHER	36	11-21-84	2:19p
SOIL	33	11-21-84	2:20p
YIELDS	31	11-21-84	2:22p
TEXTURE	25	11-21-84	3:27p
COLOR	23	11-21-84	3:32p
FRUITS	<DIR>	11-21-84	3:45p
	8 File[s]	313344 bytes free	

You can tell you are in the root directory by the second line of the display, the directory message with a single backslash. Of course, you probably know that you are in the root because of the files listed. But when you have many files and diskettes, this second line will be helpful in identifying your current directory.

Current Directories

It is always important to keep track of which directories are current in each disk drive in a system. By quickly using the DIR command, you can check the current directory status of any disk drive in the system before issuing other commands.

There is another factor to keep in mind about current directories. Each drive you are using has its own separate current directory. For instance, you may have the example diskette in drive A. In drive B you have other data and program files. MS-DOS keeps track of a separate current directory for each drive. This can cause some confusion when you want to perform operations from one drive to another.

Suppose you want to copy the file "yields" into the root directory on the diskette in drive B. When you last worked on drive B you were using a word-processing program that is contained under its own subdirectory, WP.

MS-DOS views the current directories as follows: in drive A is the root directory of the example diskette; in drive B is the WP subdirectory.

If you issue this copy command,

A>copy yields b:

MS-DOS would comply with your wishes. However, because the current directory on drive B is WP, that is the directory to which it would copy the file. You can see how this might confuse you when you went searching for "yields" in the root on B. (It is very simple to get the file to the right directory, but you must be sure to include the correct path.) For safety's sake, it is always a good idea to check on your current directories before you perform any operation.

To find out the current directory, just enter CHDIR by itself.

A> chdir <ENTER>

In this case, the change directory command really becomes the check (or identify) the current directory command. If you were in the root directory, you would see this listing:

A: \

If you were in a subdirectory, the current directory would look like this:

A: \ fruits

You can see that CHDIR is a versatile command, one that you will use a great deal. It allows you to change directories easily and return to quickly to the root directory, and it provides quick identification of the current directory. The operation of this command is outlined in *Figure 9-4*.

Figure 9-4.
Current Directory

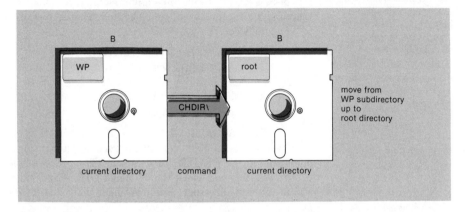

COPYING FILES TO A SUBDIRECTORY

When you listed the contents of the FRUITS subdirectory, you noticed that the directory listed only the . and .. files; the rest of the subdirectory was empty. How do you get files into a subdirectory? The same way you always move files, with the COPY command.

On the diskette in drive A you have two files, "weather" and "soil," along with some other files. Because the "weather" file contains weather data on all fruit crops and the "soil" file contains soil data on all fruit crops, we would like to have these files in the FRUITS subdirectory.

Make sure that root is your current directory. Enter CHDIR to check the current directory status; if necessary, enter CHDIR \ to get to the root directory. "Weather" and "soil" are now part of the root directory. To be sure that everything is according to plan, use DIR to check the directory.

A>dir <ENTER>

Volume in drive A has no label
Directory of A: \

COMMAND	COM	17664	3-08-83	12:00p
TREE	COM	1513	3-08-83	12:00p
WEATHER		36	11-21-84	2:19p
SOIL		33	11-21-84	2:20p
YIELDS		31	11-21-84	2:22p
TEXTURE		25	11-21-84	3:27p
COLOR		23	11-21-84	3.32p
FRUITS		<DIR>	11-21-84	3:45p
		8 File[s]	313344 bytes free	

When you are copying files between directories, the destination directory name need be specified only with the command, much like a disk-drive identifier is used. Likewise, when you display the contents of a subdirectory that isn't the default, only the subdirectory's name need be specified.

Because this is the same procedure you use to copy files from one diskette to another, think of the transfer in terms of source and target. The directory that currently holds the files is the source directory. The subdirectory to which the files will be copied is the target directory. To MS-DOS, FRUITS is just like any other file. As long as you specify a source and a target, it will copy the files, even if one of those files happens to be a subdirectory.

```
A>copy weather fruits <ENTER>
        1 File[s] copied

A>copy soil fruits <ENTER>
        1 File[s] copied
```

You now have two new files in your FRUITS subdirectory. The files have not been deleted from the root directory; they have simply been duplicated in the FRUITS subdirectory. The procedure is reviewed in *Figure 9-5*. You can check this by using DIR. First make sure the files are still in the root directory. Because this is your current directory, just enter DIR.

```
A>dir <ENTER>


    Volume in drive A has no label
    Directory of A:\

    COMMAND   COM      17664    3-08-83    12:00p
    TREE      COM       1513    8-30-83    12:00p
    WEATHER              36    12-17-84     1:04p
    SOIL                 33    12-17-84     1:04p
    YIELDS               31    12-17-84     1:05p
    TEXTURE              25    12-17-84     1:05p
    COLOR                23    12-17-84     1:06p
    FRUITS          <DIR>      12-17-84     1:29p
                 8 File[s]      311296 bytes free
```

You can see that both "weather" and "soil" are still in this directory.

One way to verify that "weather" and "soil" are also part of the FRUITS subdirectory is to change the current directory to FRUITS and then use the DIR command.

```
A>chdir fruits <ENTER>
A>dir <ENTER>
```

**Figure 9-5.
Copying Files to a
Subdirectory**

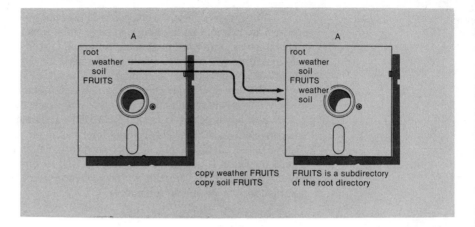

copy weather FRUITS
copy soil FRUITS

FRUITS is a subdirectory
of the root directory

You can also check on FRUITS without leaving the root directory, that is, without changing the current directory. Just ask for a directory listing with a pathname.

A> dir \ fruits <ENTER>

Volume in drive A has no label
Directory of A: \ fruits

.	<DIR>	12-17-84	1:29p
..	<DIR>	12-17-84	1:29p
WEATHER	36	12-17-84	1:04p
SOIL	33	12-17-84	1:04p

4 File[s]   311296 bytes free

You can see that the two files have been added to the directory of the FRUITS directory. A comparison of the amount of bytes still free will show you that the space on the diskette has been reduced by the number of bytes in these two files.

Both root and FRUITS exist on the same diskette. More important, two copies of "weather" and "soil" exist on the same diskette, and they both have the same name. This violates one of our cardinal rules of filenaming: every file *on a diskette* must have a unique name.

We have to make a slight modification of the rule. From now on, every file *in a directory* must have a unique name.

This capability of having duplicate files has many advantages. With tree-structured directories, you cannot perform an operation on a file unless it is located in the subdirectory in which you are working. So sometimes, if files are not very long, it is convenient to have duplicates of certain files in a subdirectory.

For instance, if you were going to do some word processing on specific files, it would be necessary to have these files in the same subdirectory as your word-processing program. (Later we will give you some hints that will help you minimize the need for duplicate files, but for now let's carry on with the example.)

You are now ready to create a new subdirectory on this diskette. Not only do you grow fruits, but you also have extensive lumber holdings. So your new subdirectory is named LUMBER. It so happens that your "weather" and "soil" files also contain information on conditions related to effective forest management. So you want these files in this new subdirectory also. If you are still in the \FRUITS directory change back to root with CHDIR \. Starting in the root directory, you can perform this operation with three simple commands.

```
A>mkdir lumber <ENTER>

A>copy weather lumber <ENTER>
      1 File[s] copied

A>copy soil lumber <ENTER>
      1 File[s] copied
```

To check on the creation of this subdirectory, ask for a directory of root, your current directory.

```
A>dir <ENTER>

    Volume in drive A has no label
    Directory of A: \

    COMMAND   COM     17664    3-08-83   12:00p
    TREE      COM      1513    8-30-83   12:00p
    WEATHER             36    12-17-84    1:04p
    SOIL                33    12-17-84    1:04p
    YIELDS              31    12-17-84    1:05p
    TEXTURE             25    12-17-84    1:05p
    COLOR               23    12-17-84    1:06p
    FRUITS           <DIR>    12-17-84    1:29p
    LUMBER           <DIR>    12-17-84    1:42p
            9 File[s]       308224 bytes free
```

The new subdirectory LUMBER is part of your root directory.

Now make sure that the two files have been copied to the new subdirectory.

```
A>dir \lumber <ENTER>

    Volume in drive A has no label
    Directory of A: \lumber

    .              <DIR>       12-17-84   1:42p
```

```
    ..                    <DIR>          12-17-84   1:42p
    WEATHER                     36    12-17-84   1:04p
    SOIL                        33    12-17-84   1:04p
                 4 File[s]           308224 bytes free
```

You can now create new directories and modify their contents to fit your needs.

ACCESSING FILES

Your tree-structured directory currently has two levels. The home base is the parent, or root, directory. This is level 0, or the starting point. Beneath this level there are two first-level subdirectories, FRUIT and LUMBER. But what about the files contained in these directories? How do we get to a specific file within a specific subdirectory?

With the correct use of pathnames, you can easily move around in or reference any part of a directory structure.

To find a file, MS-DOS must have two pieces of information, the name of the file and the name of the directory that contains that file. Because subdirectories can contain other subdirectories, you need to specify the exact path that leads to the file you want.

You can get to a file in two different ways. The first is to start in the root directory and then list all of the subdirectories that intervene between the root and the directory holding the file. The second is to change to the desired subdirectory with CHDIR and then call the file.

Suppose you want a listing of a file in the FRUITS directory called "weather." You are now in the root directory. Ask for the listing using the correct pathname.

A>type fruits \ weather <ENTER>

Or use CHDIR to change the current directory.

A>chdir fruits <ENTER>

Then use the TYPE command.

A>type weather <ENTER>

Your FRUITS subdirectory contains files that pertain to all your fruit crops. But now you want to create within FRUITS another subdirectory, CHERRIES. CHERRIES will be a second-level subdirectory; that is, it will be two levels down from the root directory. Get back to the root directory by using CHDIR \ (you might still be in LUMBER). To create subdirectories in subdirectories you use the MKDIR (or simply MD) command.

A>md \ fruits \ cherries <ENTER>

In this pathname you specified two directory names, the subdirectory that already exists and the new subdirectory you are creating. All directories must be separated by slashes. The actual message received by MS-DOS from this command translates as, "Starting from the root directory (indicated by the initial backslash), go down to the first-level subdirectory FRUITS and create a new second-level subdirectory named CHERRIES."

As usual, MS-DOS does not inform you that the directory was created; it simply returns to the prompt. You can confirm that this subdirectory now exists directly from your current position in the root directory.

A>dir fruits <ENTER>

Here is how the display looks:

Volume in drive A has no label
Directory of A:\fruits

.	<DIR>		12-17-84	1:29p
..	<DIR>		12-17-84	1:29p
WEATHER		36	12-17-84	1:04p
SOIL		33	12-17-84	1:04p
CHERRIES	<DIR>		12-17-84	1:45p
	5 file[s]		307200 bytes free	

You can see that the CHERRIES subdirectory is now part of FRUITS.

If you want to check on the contents of CHERRIES, you must give the correct path.

A>dir \fruits\cherries <ENTER>

The first backslash tells MS-DOS that FRUITS is a subdirectory of root; the next slash indicates that CHERRIES is a subdirectory of FRUITS. If you wish, you can eliminate the first slash because root is your current directory, and MS-DOS always begins its search with the current directory. Here is the listing for the previous command:

Volume in drive A has no label
Directory of A:\fruits\cherries

.	<DIR>	12-17-84	1:45p
..	<DIR>	12-17-84	1:45p
	2 File[s]	307200 bytes free	

The second line in the listing confirms that this is a second-level directory, a subdirectory of a subdirectory. Our entire directory structure is shown in *Figure 9-6*. Of course, the subdirectories can contain many other files, but for simplicity we show only the ones we are using in our examples.

Establishing Paths

Almost any MS-DOS command can be used on any file in a subdirectory. The only secret is to establish the correct path to the file. The CHERRIES subdirectory in our FRUITS subdirectory is empty. Let's copy the "yields" file, currently in the root directory, into this new subdirectory. Make sure root is your current directory before attempting this.

A>copy yields fruits\cherries <ENTER>

If you want, check the contents of this subdirectory with DIR.

A > dir fruits \ cherries < ENTER >

Volume in drive A has no label
Directory of A: \ fruits \ cherries

.	<DIR>	12-17-84	1:45p
..	<DIR>	12-17-84	1:45p
YIELDS	31	12-17-84	1:05p
	3 File[s]	306176 bytes free	

Or you can call the file itself.

A > dir fruits \ cherries \ yields < ENTER >

Volume in drive A has no label
Directory of A: \ fruits \ cherries

YIELDS	31	12-17-84	1:05p
	1 File[s]	306176 bytes free	

When you are tracing a path to a file, first list the intervening subdirectories (separated by slashes). The filename comes last. This illustrates how you move down through a directory. But you can also move up in the tree structure. To move up one level, just change the directory to the parent directory.

A > cd fruits \ cherries < ENTER >

**Figure 9-6.
A Sample Directory
Structure**

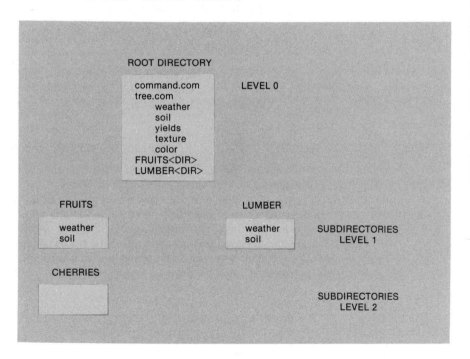

Your current directory is now the subdirectory CHERRIES. Use DIR to be sure you are in the correct subdirectory.

A> dir <ENTER>

Volume in drive A has no label
Directory of A: \ fruits \ cherries

.	<DIR>	12-17-84	1:45p
..	<DIR>	12-17-84	1:45p
YIELDS	31	12-17-84	1:05p
	3 File[s]	306176 bytes free	

A Shortcut

The special symbols . and .. shown in subdirectories represent special instructions for moving around in the directory structure.

Now you are finally going to find out the meaning of these directory entries— . (period) and .. (double period).

In the preceding example, you moved up in the directory structure by using the CHDIR command and listing the name of the parent directory. This is a valid way to move up in a directory; however, MS-DOS has given us a shortcut for moving up one level but still not affecting the current directory.

Be sure your current directory is still CHERRIES. Enter this command, leaving a space between DIR and the periods.

A> dir .. <ENTER>

MS-DOS will respond with a display.

Volume in drive A has no label
Directory of A: \ fruits

.	<DIR>	12-17-84	1:29p
..	<DIR>	12-17-84	1:29p
WEATHER	36	12-17-84	1:04p
SOIL	31	12-17-84	1:04p
CHERRIES	<DIR>	12-17-84	1:45p
	5 File[s]	306176 bytes free	

How did you get back to FRUITS? What happened is that you moved up one level.

The double period symbol tells MS-DOS: "Move me to the current directory's parent directory." As long as you are not in the root directory, you can use this .. convention to move one level up without specifying the directory's name. This does not affect the status of your current directory.

Now issue the DIR command with a single period, leaving a space between DIR and the period.

A> dir . <ENTER>

Volume in drive A has no label
Directory of A: \ fruits

.	\<DIR\>	12-17-84	1:29p
..	\<DIR\>	12-17-84	1:29p
YIELDS	31	12-17-84	1:05p
	3 File[s]	306176 bytes free	

The CHERRIES subdirectory is listed. The single period tells MS-DOS: "Apply this command to me, the current directory." Notice that using the period conventions does not change the current directory. These conventions are used only in subdirectories. They do not appear in root directories. You don't have to use these symbols, and don't do so at first if they confuse you. But gradually, as you become more familiar with tree-structured directories, try experimenting with their use again. They may save you a lot of time.

MOVING AROUND IN A TREE-STRUCTURED DIRECTORY

To understand the usefulness of the tree-structured directory system, you need to practice a bit with moving around in the structure. To do this we are going to use the COPY command.

First, let's add a little complexity to our tree. You now want to enter your records on a second crop, peaches. The logical place for this new data is a subdirectory under FRUITS. Move back to the root directory using CHDIR \ (assuming you are still in the FRUITS/CHERRIES subdirectory).

A\> mkdir \ fruits \ peaches \<ENTER\>

The information that you want to store in this subdirectory is in the file "color" ("color" is currently in the root directory).

A\> copy color fruits \ peaches \<ENTER\>

The system replies.

1 File[s] copied

To illustrate a point, let's assume that the file you want to include in this directory is on another diskette. You would have to use a different command.

A\> copy b:color fruits \ peaches \<ENTER\>

MS-DOS allows you to copy information from a file on one diskette to a directory or subdirectory on a diskette in another drive. All you need to do is include the drive indicator.

There is one more file in the root directory that you want to include in this PEACHES subdirectory. It is called "texture."

A\> copy texture fruits \ peaches \<ENTER\>

If you want to, use the DIR command now to verify the new subdirectory and its contents.

A\> dir fruits \ peaches \<ENTER\>

Volume in drive A has no label
Directory of A: \ fruits \ peaches

.	<DIR>		12-17-84	1:53p
..	<DIR>		12-17-84	1:53p
COLOR		23	12-17-84	1:06p
TEXTURE		25	12-17-84	1:05p
	4 File[s]		303104 bytes free	

As a final step, we are going to create a new subdirectory in
LUMBER. This is called REDWOOD.

A>mkdir lumber \ redwood <ENTER>

Figure 9-7 is a map of our complete, tree-structured directory.

**Figure 9-7.
The Completed
Directory Structure**

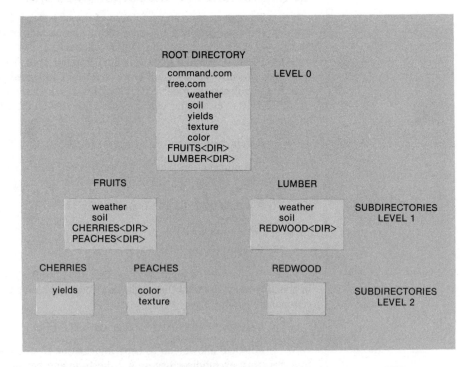

Within the CHERRIES subdirectory is a file called "yields." You
have spent a lot of time setting up this file and now want to use the same
general contents in your REDWOOD subdirectory. Here are the steps you
take to transfer "yields" from one subdirectory to another. The path is
illustrated in *Figure 9-8*.

First, make sure you are in the root directory. Because you are
dealing with second-level directories, you must go up to the root and then
down into the subdirectories. You can't go across to level one or level two
subdirectories; the path must go through the common link, the root.

**Figure 9-8.
Moving Around
Subdirectories**

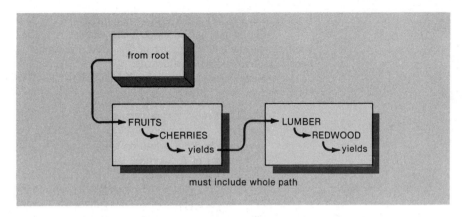

A>copy fruits \ cherries \ yields lumber \ redwood <ENTER>
   1 File[s] copied

A DIR command confirms the copy.

A>dir lumber \ redwood <ENTER>

   Volume in drive A has no label
   Directory of A: \ lumber \ redwood

.		<DIR>		12-17-84	1:56p
..		<DIR>		12-17-84	1:56p
YIELDS			31	12-17-84	1:05p
	3 File[s]		301056 bytes free		

With tree-structured directories, you can move quickly within a complex structure. This is essential when you are dealing with a large number of files on a fixed disk. But this COPY command also demonstrates the importance of clear, easily defined paths. You can see that if you create too many subdirectories within subdirectories, you could easily get lost in the resulting maze. Keep the paths simple.

MAINTAINING YOUR FILES

All of the normal rules associated with the COPY command are in effect when you are working with subdirectories. Suppose, for instance, that you want to copy the contents of the subdirectory PEACHES into REDWOOD. You want to copy all the files in the subdirectory, so the easiest method is to use a wildcard with the COPY command. PEACHES contains two files, "color" and "texture."

A>copy \ fruits \ peaches \ *.* \ lumber \ redwood <ENTER>

MS-DOS will tell you what is going on.

A: \ FRUITS \ PEACHES \ COLOR
A: \ FRUITS \ PEACHES \ TEXTURE
   2 File[s] copied

Both files in PEACHES are now also in REDWOOD.

The usual caution when using wildcards applies: make sure you want all the files, or a number of files that are similar, to be copied before becoming involved with wildcards.

Now check the contents of LUMBER/REDWOOD with the DIR command.

A>dir \lumber\redwood <ENTER>

Volume in drive A has no label
Directory of A:\lumber\redwood

.	<DIR>		12-17-84	1:56p
..	<DIR>		12-17-84	1:56p
YIELDS		31	12-17-84	1:05p
COLOR		23	12-17-84	1:06p
TEXTURE		25	12-17-84	1:05p
	5 File(s)		299008 bytes free	

After you have worked to build a beautiful, well-designed tree-structured directory, you have reason to be proud. But some of your directories will become obsolete. If you just go on building bigger and better directories, you will make path-finding both confusing and time consuming.

Just as MS-DOS provides DEL (or ERASE) to eliminate no-longer-needed files, it also has a command to rid you of unnecessary directories.

The RMDIR Command

The internal command RMDIR (or RD) is used to remove or erase a subdirectory. A subdirectory can be erased, however, only if does not contain any files or other subdirectories.

The RMDIR (ReMove DIRectory) command helps you with the housekeeping chores in your directory structure. But before you can eliminate a directory, you must first provide for the files inside it. This is a safety feature that MS-DOS builds into the directory structure. It can prevent you from accidentally erasing a file while eliminating a directory.

Suppose that halfway through the growing season there is a terrible infestation of Tasmanian peach flies. Your entire peach crop is down the drain, and you destroy all your peach trees. You no longer need your PEACHES subdirectory cluttering up your directory structure. To remove this directory you must first get to the correct subdirectory.

A>chdir fruits\peaches <ENTER>
A>dir <ENTER>

As with all erase functions, be careful. Be sure you are in the correct subdirectory.

Volume in drive A has no label
Directory of A:\fruits\peaches

.	<DIR>	12-17-84	1:53p
..	<DIR>	12-17-84	1:53p

COLOR	23	12-17-84	1:06p
TEXTURE	25	12-17-84	1:05p
4 File[s]		299008 bytes free	

Now erase the files in the subdirectory. Be sure you don't need any of the files before you erase.

A>erase *.* <ENTER>
Are you sure [Y/N]? y <ENTER>

You answer yes.

With the files gone, you can erase the subdirectory. You must be one level up from the subdirectory you want to erase. Move up to the FRUITS subdirectory.

A>cd .. <ENTER>

Now remove the subdirectory.

A>rmdir peaches <ENTER>

It is a good idea to use DIR to be sure the subdirectory is gone.

A>dir <ENTER>

Volume in drive A has no label
Directory of A: \ fruits

.	<DIR>		12-17-84	1:29p
..	<DIR>		12-17-84	1:29p
WEATHER		36	12-17-84	1:04p
SOIL		33	12-17-84	1:04p
CHERRIES	<DIR>		12-17-84	1:45p
5 File[s]			302080 bytes free	

When you modify your tree structure frequently, it is often difficult to keep track of exactly which files and subdirectories belong where. How can you quickly get an overview of the tree structure on any given diskette?

One way is to use DIR and note all the files with the <DIR> extension. Then you can use CHDIR to reach each of these subdirectories, and DIR again, while noting which files are <DIR> files here and so on. This is time-consuming and frustrating. Once again, MS-DOS has anticipated this need and provides a command to give you a guide to your overall directory.

The TREE Command

The external command TREE is used to display the entire directory structure of a disk, including all files stored in each subdirectory.

TREE is an external command that displays every pathname on a given diskette. To use it you must have your system diskette in drive A or a copy of TREE.COM on the diskette you want to examine. Of course, you must be in the directory that holds that command. Make sure you are in the root directory and issue this command. Include the /f switch to get a listing of files in each subdirectory.

A>tree /f <ENTER>

Here is the TREE display for our example diskette.

DIRECTORY PATH LISTING FOR VOLUME ???????????

Path: \ FRUITS
Sub-directories: CHERRIES
Files: WEATHER
                  SOIL

Path: \ FRUITS \ CHERRIES
Sub-directories: None
Files: YIELDS

Path: \ LUMBER
Sub-directories: REDWOOD
Files: WEATHER
                  SOIL

Path: \ LUMBER \ REDWOOD
Sub-directories: None
Files: YIELDS
                  COLOR
                  TEXTURE

When you call for a file, MS-DOS looks for it only in the current
directory. If you specify a pathname, then MS-DOS looks there. It looks for
the file in only one location. This is true whether you are using an MS-DOS
command, such as COPY, or executing a program that needs a data file.
Only one directory is searched, either the current one or the one specified
in a path. This is also true of your program files. When you call for a
program, MS-DOS immediately searches for it in the current directory. If it
is not found, it won't be executed.

But programs have an extra advantage over other files in tree-
structured directories. The search for programs can be extended to other
directories by using a special command.

The PATH Command

The internal command PATH is used to establish a search path for external commands, program files, and batch files. When a command is entered at the MS-DOS prompt, and a search path has been defined, MS-DOS will first search the current directory on the current disk drive. If the file is not found, MS-DOS will continue searching according to the guidelines established by PATH.

The PATH command does not have anything to do with the use of pathnames in general. It is only used to search for DOS commands, programs, files, and batch files not found in the current directory. The names in a PATH command must be separated by semicolons.

Because you don't have any program files or batch files in your directory, you will have to abandon the orchards for a moment. Imagine that you are in a subdirectory on drive A that is called \NEWPROGS. You are looking for a program called RUNSUM.BAS. Here is how you tell MS-DOS where to look for the program.

> A>path \ACCTING; \PROGS \MISC; \ <ENTER>

Then, when you enter the program name "RUNSUM.BAS," MS-DOS searches for the program in four places:

- The current directory (this is automatic).
- The ACCTING directory under the root.
- The MISC directory under the PROGS directory under the root.
- The root itself (indicated by \ ).

The PATH command can also search in directories on other drives. Just include the drive designator in the PATH command.

> A>path \ACCTING; \PROGS \MISC;B: \OLDPROGS <ENTER>

If you enter PATH without any other information, MS-DOS will search the last path it was given. To discontinue this extensive searching feature, enter PATH with a single semicolon.

> A>path ; <ENTER>

After this command, the search reverts to the current directory only.

SOME GUIDELINES

Although the search path established by the PATH command can be changed at any time, a standard search path can be defined in your AUTOEXEC.BAT file so that it is automatically defined when the system is powered up or is reset.

Like many tools in MS-DOS, tree-structured directories can be useful or mystifying. The idea is to start slowly and build as you go. As long as your directory structure makes sense to you and is logical for your needs, it will save you time and energy.

Don't get carried away creating a new subdirectory for every file. Obviously, if your computer spends all its time tracing down subdirectories and files, you will never get anything else done. Every time MS-DOS establishes a subdirectory, it uses up approximately 500 additional bytes of RAM. If you create too many subdirectories, you may one day find that you don't have enough room to run large programs.

When creating directories, keep in mind the mechanics of moving around inside them. While it is easy to move up and down a limb, it is impossible to swing between limbs. Make sure that your levels contain logical subdirectories and that you eliminate the need to go up and down again to get to a file you use frequently.

Remember that subdirectory files also occupy space on a disk and grow larger as more files are stored in them. It is therefore wise to keep the number of subdirectories to a minimum when using floppy diskettes. However, a complex directory structure on a hard disk does not require as much attention to disk space because of the much larger storage capacities.

On floppy-disk systems it is a good idea to keep all your subdirectories in the root. This makes it easy for you to find exactly what you need without time-consuming searches. If possible, keep data files that run with specific programs in the same directory. Then, when a program needs a data file, it can find it right in the current directory.

Keep in the root directory all utilities and command files that you use frequently. This will save you time and make them available for all files in the directories under the root.

You can even keep most of your programs in the root directory. Once you have established a home for your programs, use PATH to keep these programs readily available.

Give your subdirectories distinct names.

SUMMARY

This concludes your introduction to tree-structured directories. Using this tool, with restraint, on floppy-disk systems is a convenience. But using this tool on fixed-disks is a necessity. In this chapter you have learned about root directories and subdirectories. You have traveled along the path to better file organization. In addition to learning how to put files in a subdirectory, you have moved around inside the tree-structured directory to create pathnames to find and store your files. Finally, you have become familiar with the directory commands: MKDIR, CHDIR, RMDIR, TREE, and PATH.

WHAT HAVE WE LEARNED?

1. Tree-structured directories include a main, or root, directory and sets of subdirectories related through paths.
2. Subdirectories allow you to group files and even other subdirectories into categories.
3. A pathname specifies the straight-line path through names of upper and lower level directories, separated by backslashes, to get to a filename; MS-DOS commands will work with pathnames just as if they are extended filenames.
4. The MKDIR command lets you create a subdirectory.
5. The CHDIR command (same as CD) followed by a pathname lets you change from one directory or subdirectory to another; used by itself, it tells you the name of the current directory.
6. The period and double period (. ..) are short-cutting conventions that direct commands to operate on the current and parent directories, respectively.
7. The RMDIR command lets you remove subdirectories, but only after you move or erase all files within it.
8. The TREE command displays every pathname on the disk; the /f switch lists all files in each subdirectory.

Quiz for Chapter 9

1. Tree-structured directories, introduced under MS-DOS Version 2.00, allow you to:
   a. create structures of directories on disks that resemble the structure of a tree (root, trunk, and branches).
   b. create subdirectories.
   c. create subdirectories within subdirectories.
   d. any of the above.
   e. none of the above.

2. The directory that is always created after a disk is formatted with the FORMAT command is called the:
   a. ground.
   b. root.
   c. branch.
   d. leaf.

3. Is the root directory always the parent directory for the entire directory structure on a disk?
   a. Yes.
   b. Sometimes.
   c. No.
   d. Never.

4. A subdirectory is, in fact, a special type of:
   a. disk drive.
   b. file.
   c. key.
   d. display.

5. Can subdirectories be named following the same rules used for normal files?
   a. No.
   b. Only if the parent directory is the root.
   c. Yes.

d. Only if the subdirectory does not contain other subdirectories.

6. A subdirectory, or a file, within a subdirectory can be referenced by an MS-DOS command anywhere within the directory structure by using:
   a. pathnames.
   b. branchnames.
   c. maps.
   d. diagrams.

7. A pathname can consist of:
   a. a single \ to refer to the root directory.
   b. a single subdirectory name with or without a preceding \.
   c. a string of consecutive subdirectory names, each separated by a \.
   d. any of the above.

8. A subdirectory is created using the:
   a. EDLIN command.
   b. CHDIR (or CD) command.
   c. MKDIR (or MD) command.
   d. RMDIR (or RD) command.
   e. COPY command.

9. To change the current, or default, directory, the following command is used:
   a. COPY.
   b. CHDIR (or CD for short).
   c. MODE.
   d. EDLIN.

10. A directory pathname can be used with:
    a. any MS-DOS command that deals with files.
    b. any MS-DOS command that doesn't deal with files.
    c. either of the above.
    d. none of the above.

11. A subdirectory can be deleted (by using RMDIR or RD) only if it:
- **a.** contains files.
- **b.** contains subdirectories.
- **c.** has had all its files and subdirectories previously erased.
- **d.** none of the above.

12. The parent directory of the current subdirectory can be referenced, or accessed, by using what symbol with an MS-DOS command:
- **a.** . (one period).
- **b.** .. (two periods).
- **c.** ... (three periods).
- **d.** Any number of periods.

13. The TREE command is used to display the entire directory structure of a disk. What symbol is required if you also want TREE to display all the files contained in each subdirectory?
- **a.** None.
- **b.** /f.
- **c.** A disk drive identifier.
- **d.** A file name.

14. The search path established when using the internal command PATH can include:
- **a.** more than one disk drive identifier.
- **b.** more than one directory path.
- **c.** both a and b.
- **d.** none of the above.

Data Management Commands

ABOUT THIS CHAPTER

In this chapter, we will discuss pipes, filters, and redirection, sophisticated data management commands. These commands give you choices in determining where your information comes from (input) and where it goes after you're finished with it (output). They are the frosting on the cake in allowing you to make the most of your MS-DOS operating system.

STANDARD INPUT AND OUTPUT DEVICES

New facilities added to MS-DOS Version 2.0 provide the ability for input and output directed to and from commands to be optionally modified using special characters.

You know from your own computer use that normally you enter information from your keyboard. The keyboard is the standard input device in personal computer systems. When you want to look at your input or see the results of programs, you use your screen. The monitor, or display screen, is the standard output device in personal computer systems. These two devices are shown in *Figure 10-1*. Using MS-DOS Version 2, however, it is possible to use other devices for input and output. For example, a file can be the source of input and a second file can be the location of the output.

Figure 10-1.
Keyboard and Display

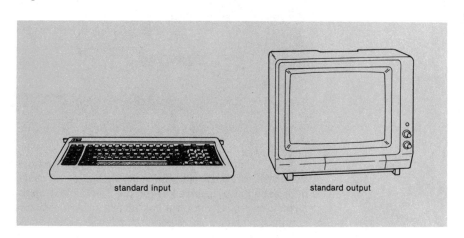

standard input   standard output

DOS sees things in black and white. There is a standard input device and a standard output device. By default these are the keyboard and display screen. But DOS doesn't really care what provides the input and output as long as you label them as the standard input and output devices when issuing commands. When you designate files, programs, or other devices as the means of input and/or output, you are using the concept of redirection.

REDIRECTING STANDARD OUTPUT

The output generated by a command, which normally is displayed on the screen of your computer's monitor, can be redirected to another device, such as a file on a disk or the printer. The > character, when used with a command, always means "redirect output to the following device."

The reasons why you might want to redirect output are numerous. Perhaps a specific program or command results in a new version of your data; you would like to keep this information in a separate file. Or you may want to have data automatically output to the printer. Perhaps you want to add output information to an already existing file.

No doubt you recognize the symbol > from your high school math classes. It means "greater than." But in MS-DOS this symbol indicates the redirection of output. Think of it as standing for "send to this place," with the arrow pointing the way to the file, program, or device to receive the information. Here is how you might redirect the output of a DIR command:

    A> dir > listing < ENTER>

As a result of this command, the directory of the diskette in the current drive is sent to a newly created disk file called "listing." The > character before the filename reassigns this file as the standard output device. Because the disk file is now the standard output device, you will not see the information on the screen (it hasn't been sent there). This process is reviewed in *Figure 10-2*.

Figure 10-2.
Redirection of Output

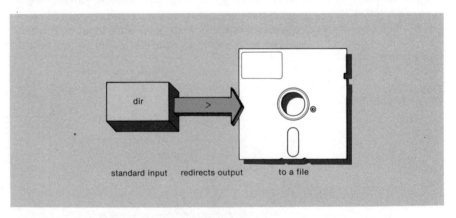

When you execute the command, the screen will show nothing, but the drives will whirr and the indicator lights will come on. After the information is transferred to the file, the standard output reverts to the display screen. If you want to change the destination of the next command, you must include a reassign marker in the command.

You haven't actually seen anything on the screen to tell you that the operation has been completed but you can check the new file by using the TYPE command.

A > type listing < ENTER >

The contents of the file "listing" will appear on the screen.

You can use directories and subdirectories in redirecting output.

A > dir \ fruits \ cherries > fruitdir < ENTER >

This puts the directory listing of the \ FRUITS \ CHERRIES subdirectory into a file called "fruitdir."

When a single > character is used to redirect output to a file, a new file is always created, overwriting any file by the same name if it exists. When the > > symbol is used, MS-DOS is instructed to append an already existing file with the output data.

One thing to keep in mind as you redirect output to files. If you redirect to an already existing file, the contents of the file are wiped out. But there is a simple solution to this problem: when you want to append the new output to the end of an already existing file you include > > in the command.

A > dir > > fruitdir < ENTER >

With this command, the directory listing of the current directory is put into the "fruitdir" file at the end of the contents of the file as it currently exists.

Redirection using > > is a handy and very safe way of keeping updated listings of your directories all in one file or for updating any information in a file (e.g., a mailing list).

REDIRECTING STANDARD INPUT

The < character is used to redirect input to a command instead of accepting input from the keyboard. For example, a command that normally displays a series of prompts requesting your input on the keyboard could have all of its prompts automatically answered by redirecting as input to the command a text file containing all the answers.

As you might expect, the opposite of output redirection is input redirection. This operation is symbolized by the "less than" character, <. Think of this symbol as saying "take the contents from this file and use it as input." Using this option you can make the standard input device a file instead of the keyboard. The uses for input redirection are more obscure than for output redirection. One very common use is to relieve yourself of the repetitious entries needed to start up a program. Simply include the responses necessary in a file named, for instance, "answers." Then redirect the input using this file.

But by far the most frequent use of redirected input is with the use of filters in piping information.

Piping

Although there are no real pipes involved, the analogy of a pipeline is a useful tool for understanding the flow of information from input to output devices.

When a water department constructs a pipeline, it lays sections of pipe in a line to form one long conduit. The pipeline takes water from its source and pipes it to a water-storage area. Along the way, there are reservoirs that store the water temporarily. The water is then sent to a purification plant, where it is filtered before it is piped to its final destination, your home.

A more sophisticated method of using the redirection of input and output is the use of filters in piping information. Piping is a method of chaining together a MS-DOS command with other special commands to modify the flow of input and output information.

When you construct an MS-DOS pipeline, you do very much the same thing. The data you are going to put into the pipeline are stored in a source file or program. You want to use the output of this program or file as the input to the next program or command. In this way you can hook commands, programs, and files together in a long chain, much as illustrated in *Figure 10-3*.

The data, however, do not go directly from the input file to the output file. If they did, you could accomplish the same goal by simply copying the file. Instead, in piping, the data are fed in from the input file, go through a filtering process where they are modified, and then go to their destination in the output file.

**Figure 10-3.
Piping**

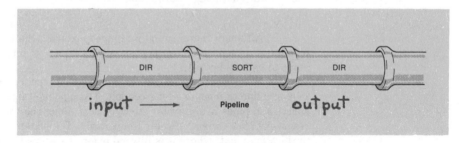

When you use piping, it appears to MS-DOS that the input is the same as if it were typed in from the keyboard. But in reality, MS-DOS creates internal temporary files, like reservoirs, to hold the data as they are being piped. You will encounter some of these temporary files as you work your way through the examples in this chapter. They appear in your directory like this:

%PIPEx.$$$

where x is an interger to distinguish different PIPE files.

Within the pipeline data can be modified by the use of filters.

Filters

Filters are special commands or programs used to modify input data in some manner and then output it again to an output device or to another command.

Filters are DOS commands or programs that read in data from the designated standard input device, modify the data in some way, and then output the modified data to the designated standard output device. Thus, by its position in the middle of the process (as shown in *Figure 10-4*), this command works to filter the data.

Filters allow us to use a program, command, or file as the standard input device. Filters output to files. MS-DOS contains three filters: SORT, FIND, and MORE.

**Figure 10-4.
Filtering**

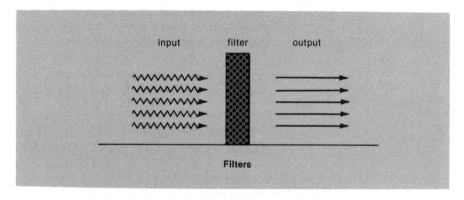

input   filter   output

Filters

The SORT Filter

The SORT command is a filter designed to sort text in a variety of ways. SORT can be executed as a normal command, or it can be piped with other commands.

This filter sorts file contents either alphabetically or by column number. Learning to use SORT is like learning how to drive. You know you existed without it, but it's hard to imagine how. To experience the real pleasure of using SORT, you have to try it on some actual data. So we are going to create a file to play SORT with.

For our SORT adventure you will need a formatted diskette; if you can find it, use the diskette you formatted with the volume label "wine cellar" in the exercise in Chapter 7. If you don't have this diskette handy, just format another one.

A> format b:/v <ENTER>

Enter the volume name.

wine cellar <ENTER>

Put your system diskette, which contains the filters in the SORT.EXE, FIND.EXE, and MORE.COM files, in drive A and your formatted diskette in drive B.

Assume that you are a connoisseur of fine wines and have a respectable wine cellar. The only way to keep up with its contents is to catalog immediately all new purchases before you taste any of them.

The first thing you need is a list of your new bottles of wine. Create a file called "wines" on the diskette in drive B. The name starts in column 1, the year in column 23, the appellation in column 28, and the country in column 50.

You must create this file as an ASCII text file (see Chapter 6). That means you should use EDLIN or COPY CON: to enter the text. Also do not use the <TAB> key to space between columns because SORT cannot handle this character.

A> copy con: b:wines <ENTER>

```
Lafite                  45  Bordeaux            France
Phelps Insignia         74  Cabernet Sauvignon  U.S.A.
Ridge Gyserville        73  Zinfandel           U.S.A.
La Mission Haut Brion   64  Bordeaux            France
Y'Quem                  58  Sauterne            France
^Z <ENTER>
```

You can use the TYPE command to check the contents of your list.

A> type b:wines <ENTER>

The first thing you want is an alphabetical listing of the names of the new bottles to make it easier to enter them into your master file. This means that you want to SORT on the first column. (An alphabetical sort on the first column is the default condition of SORT.)

SORT accepts input from another program, command, or file. But you must include the reassignment character as part of the statement.

A> sort <b:wines <ENTER>

With this command you have told MS-DOS to sort the contents of the file "wines." Now watch the screen.

```
La Mission Haut Brion   64  Bordeaux            France
Lafite                  45  Bordeaux            France
Phelps Insignia         74  Cabernet Sauvignon  U.S.A.
Ridge Gyserville        73  Zinfandel           U.S.A.
Y'Quem                  58  Sauterne            France
```

SORT will also sort by reverse alphabetical order. To perform a sort so that the end of the alphabet tops the list, you use the /r option.

A> sort/r <b:wines <ENTER>

MS-DOS responds with your list in reverse order.

Y'Quem	58	Sauterne	France
Ridge Gyserville	73	Zinfandel	U.S.A.
Phelps Insignia	74	Cabernet Sauvignon	U.S.A.
Lafite	45	Bordeaux	France
La Mission Haut Brion	64	Bordeaux	France

But SORT can do more. Suppose you want to list your acquisitions by year, from the oldest to the newest. This helps in planning storage. To do this use the /+n option. This switch allows you to sort by any column (indicated by the n in the command). You want to sort by year, which begins in column 23.

A> sort/+23 <b:wines <ENTER>

Immediately you have your new listing.

Lafite	45	Bordeaux	France
Y'Quem	58	Sauterne	France
La Mission Haut Brion	64	Bordeaux	France
Ridge Gyserville	73	Zinfandel	U.S.A.
Phelps Insignia	74	Cabernet Sauvignon	U.S.A.

You may also want to keep a listing of your wines by appellation. That's the information that begins in column 28. Again, you use the /+n switch.

A> sort/+28 <b:wines <ENTER>

Lafite	45	Bordeaux	France
La Mission Haut Brion	64	Bordeaux	France
Phelps Insignia	74	Cabernet Sauvignon	U.S.A.
Y'Quem	58	Sauterne	France
Ridge Gyserville	73	Zinfandel	U.S.A.

Would you like a list by countries?

A> sort/+50 <b:wines <ENTER>

Lafite	45	Bordeaux	France
La Mission Haut Brion	64	Bordeaux	France
Y'Quem	58	Sauterne	France
Phelps Insignia	74	Cabernet Sauvignon	U.S.A.
Ridge Gyserville	73	Zinfandel	U.S.A.

Just as you can use a file as the input for the SORT command, you can also redirect the output to a file. For clarity's sake you would like to keep each sort in a separate file. This makes referencing your collection much quicker. To output the results of a sort to a file, just include the output reassignment character > in the command.

A>

This command tells DOS to sort on column 1 the information in the "wines" file and put the output in a file called "vintners." When you perform a sort that redirects the output, you have assigned a new standard output device. Therefore, it follows that you will no longer see the sort on your standard output device, the screen. When SORT has transferred the results to a file, it returns you to the prompt.

A>

You can verify the new file by using DIR.

A> dir b:vintners <ENTER>

```
Volume in drive B is WINE CELLAR
Directory of B:\

VINTNERS      290  12-17-84  2:15p
              1 File(s)      360448 bytes free
```

Remember, the next time you want to add information to this "vintners" file you would need to use > > so that the output of the new SORT is appended to the contents of the "vintners" file.

A> sort <b:wines > >b:vintners <ENTER>

Using redirection, you can also create individual files to hold your other sorts.

A> sort/+23 <b:wines >b:years <ENTER>
A> sort/+28 <b:wines >b:type <ENTER>
A> sort/+52 <b:wines >b:country <ENTER>

When you have done all this your directory will look like this:

A> dir B:<ENTER>

```
Volume in drive B is WINE CELLAR
Directory of B:\

WINES         290   12-17-84   2:07p
VINTNERS      580   12-17-84   2:16p
YEARS         290   12-17-84   2:16p
TYPE          290   12-17-84   2:16p
COUNTRY       290   12-17-84   2:17p
              5 File(s)     357376 bytes free
```

SORT not only rearranges your data quickly but in conjunction with input and output redirection, becomes a powerful tool as well. You don't have to limit the use of SORT to files. Like all filters, it is really the most useful in piping. You can use the output of a command as input into the SORT filter. You create a piping sequence by separating the various commands, filters, and files with the vertical bar character (¦).

dir ¦ sort >b:alphadir

When piping several commands together, the ¦ character is always used to separate the commands on one line.

When using piping you leave a space before and after each vertical bar. The above command goes to the current directory, sorts the directory on the first column (because no options are included in the SORT command), and then puts the sorted directory into a file called "alphadir" on the diskette in drive B.

Let's try using your system diskette.

A>dir ¦ sort >b:alphadir <ENTER>

The directory won't be listed on the screen, but you will hear the drive working, and the indicator light will be on. This is PIPE creating the temporary file that holds the output of DIR and the output of SORT. When the sorted directory is completed, it will be redirected to the file "alphadir." If you want to see the sorted display, enter the command without output redirection.

A>dir ¦ sort <ENTER>

In a few seconds the sorted listing will appear on the screen.

                    25 File[s]   29696 bytes free

        Directory of A: \
        Volume in drive A has no label
        %PIPE1 $$$ 0   12-17-84   2:36p
        %PIPE2 $$$ 0   12-17-84   2:36p
        ANSI   SYS   1664   3-08-83   12:00p
        ASSIGN   COM   896   3-08-83   12:00p
        BACKUP   COM   3687   3-08-83   12:00p
        BASIC   COM   16256   3-08-83   12:00p
        BASICA   COM   25984   3-08-83   12:00p
        CHKDSK   COM   6400   3-08-83   12:00p
        COMMAND   COM   17664   3-08-83   12:00p
        COMP   COM   2523   3-08-83   12:00p
        DISKCOMP   COM   2074   3-08-83   12:00p
        DISKCOPY   COM   2444   3-08-83   12:00p
        EDLIN   COM   4608   3-08-83   12:00p
        FDISK   COM   6177   3-08-83   12:00p
        FIND   EXE   5888   3-08-83   12:00p
        FORMAT   COM   6106   3-08-83   12:00p
        GRAPHICS   COM   789   3-08-83   12:00p
        MODE   COM   3139   3-08-83   12:00p
        MORE   COM   384   3-08-83   12:00p
        PRINT   COM   4608   3-08-83   12:00p
        RECOVER   COM   2304   3-08-83   12:00p
        RESTORE   COM   4003   3-08-83   12:00p
        SORT   EXE   1280   3-08-83   12:00p
        SYS   COM   1408   3-08-83   12:00p
        TREE   COM   1513   3-08-83   12:00p

Notice the first two files in the listing. These are the temporary piping files created during the SORT procedure. It is important to remember that when you SORT a file it does not change the contents of the file. The file remains in the same order as it was before the sort. For instance, if you performed the above sort on your system diskette, the sorted listing would not appear the next time you entered DIR. Instead, you would get the normal directory listing. This is why it is valuable to redirect the output of a SORT to a file if you want to use the sorted information again.

The FIND Filter

FIND is a fast and easy way to locate specific items in a file. FIND works by finding strings. A string is simply a group of characters enclosed in quotation marks. Like the SORT filter, FIND can receive input from a file or command and send it to any designated standard output device, such as the screen, another file or program, or the printer. FIND's functions are illustrated in *Figure 10-5*.

Figure 10-5.
The Find Command

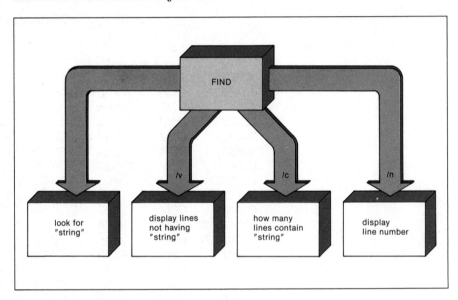

One note of caution about the use of strings. Strings within a file will be found only when they exactly match the enclosed string in the command. This includes the use of upper- and lowercase letters and all punctuation marks.

The FIND command is a filter that is used to search for and output specified text. It can be used as a standard command, or it can be piped with other commands and filters.

Suppose we want to find out which of our recent purchases were from France.

A>find "France" b:wines <ENTER>

Notice that you enter the command first, followed by the string, which must be enclosed in quotation marks. The name of the file to search is entered last. Every line containing the string will appear on the screen.

```
- - - - - - - - - - - - - b:wines
Lafite                   45  Bordeaux            France
La Mission Haut Brion    64  Boudeaux            France
Y'Quem                   58  Sauterne            France
```

Suppose you want a list of French wines, but you want it in alphabetical order. Then simply combine FIND in a pipeline with SORT.

A>find "France" b:wines ¦ sort <ENTER>

```
- - - - - - - - - - - - - b:wines
La Mission Haut Brion    64  Bordeaux            France
Lafite                   45  Bordeaux            France
Y'Quem                   58  Sauterne            France
```

If you want to, you can put this sorted French list into its own file for later reference.

A>find "France" b:wines ¦ sort >b:French <ENTER>

The last command would not produce any display, of course, because you reassigned the output to be sent to the file "French."

There may be times when you want to FIND lines in a file that do not contain a specified string. FIND allows you to do this with the /v option. You want to list your American purchase.

A>find/v "France" b:wines <ENTER>

FIND works for a few seconds.

```
- - - - - - - - - - - - - b:wines
Phelps Insignia          74  Cabernet Sauvignon  U.S.A.
Ridge Gyserville         73  Zinfandel           U.S.A.
```

Now you want all non-French wines, and you want them in alphabetical order.

A>sort <b:wines ¦ find/v "France" <ENTER>

Don't let the length of this command confuse you. Just take it one step at a time. It tells DOS to sort the items in the "wines" file (on the first column because no column is listed) and then to find all lines that do not display the string "France."

Now let's suppose you are not particularly interested in the names of the French wines, you just want to know how many are in the file. Then you would use FIND with the /c switch. The /c switch returns a count of the lines containing the string.

A>find/c "France" b:wines <ENTER>

The response is the name of the file, followed by a number.

- - - - - - - - - - - - - b:wines: 3

The final FIND option allows you to locate occurrences of the string very precisely. The /n switch displays the line number followed by the line itself, for every instance of the indicated string.

A>find/n "France" b:wines <ENTER>

- - - - - - - - - - - - - b:wines

[1]Lafite	45	Bordeaux	France
[4]La Mission Haut Brion	64	Bordeaux	France
[5]Y'Quem	58	Sauterne	France

The line numbers indicate the position of the entries in the original file. For example, there are only three items in our display. Yet Y'Quem is assigned a line number of 5. This is because Y'Quem was the fifth entry in our original "b:wines" file. Locating a string by line number can be useful in large files. It is a fast and easy way to locate any type of string.

You don't need to limit the use of FIND to a display on the screen or a redirection to a file. You can also use it with commands. Try this combination on your system diskette.

A>dir ¦ find "EXE" <ENTER>

MS-DOS responds.

SORT	EXE	1280	3-08-83	12:00p
FIND	EXE	5888	3-08-83	12:00p

Neither the SORT nor FIND command filter may be used with global characters (wildcards)—they require very specific input.

FIND will take your request literally. It will list not only the files with the extension EXE, but also any files that contain the string "EXE" within their filenames (e.g., AUTOEXEC.BAT).

Neither the SORT nor the FIND filter allows the use of global characters. In addition, in FIND, a quotation mark (") is interpreted as a search for an apostrophe (').

Now that you've practiced with the FIND filter, we will go on to another useful filter, MORE.

The MORE Filter

The MORE command is a filter that can be used as a command or piped with other commands. It causes a pause in the display of text when the screen is filled. Much like the TYPE command, MORE can be used as a command to display the contents of a file, but with the screen-pause function. When MORE is used as a filter to another command, it adds the pause function to any output generated by the command.

The idea of stopping a scroll at the bottom of a filled screen is not unfamiliar. You saw this action when you used the /p (pause) switch with the DIR command (only in that case the message from MS-DOS was "Strike any key when ready").

MORE does the same thing in a filter form: when the screen is full, MORE pauses at the bottom of the screen to make reading displays easier. This is how MORE would apply to our "wines" file.

A>more <b:wines <ENTER>

But it's not really worthwhile to enter this command because our "wines" file is less than one screen long in its entirety. Let's use MORE in a more realistic situation. Switch back to your system diskette drive (unless you're there now) and try this command.

A>dir ¦ more <ENTER>

This directory contains twenty-five files, so it will take MS-DOS a few seconds to construct the temporary pipe files. When it's finished, you should see the contents of your system diskette displayed until the screen is filled. The last line reads —More—. To get the remainder of the directory just press any key.

Combining FIND, SORT, and MORE

By combining the FIND, SORT, and MORE filters on a single command line, you can enhance the operation of standard MS-DOS commands.

Now that you've learned about the FIND, SORT, and MORE filters and have examples on how they are used in piping and redirection, let's use them as building blocks to show how they can interact. You have come to the conclusion that it would really be easier to read your system diskette directory if the files were listed alphabetically and the display stopped scrolling automatically when the page was full. This is a reasonable request.

When the piping of MS-DOS commands and filters is used, temporary files are created on the current disk that contain information needed by the various commands and filters. While a piping operation is in effect, you may see these files in a directory listing. However, these files are automatically deleted when the piping operation is completed.

A>dir ¦ sort ¦ more <ENTER>

```
                          25 File[s]      29696 bytes free
         Directory of A: \
         Volume in drive A has no label
         %PIPE1      $$$         0    12-17-84    2:45p
         %PIPE2      $$$         0    12-17-84    2:45p
         ANSI        SYS      1664     3-08-83   12:00p
         ASSIGN      COM       896     3-08-83   12:00p
         BACKUP      COM      3687     3-08-83   12:00p
         BASIC       COM     16256     3-08-83   12:00p
         BASICA      COM     25984     3-08-83   12:00p
         CHKDSK      COM      6400     3-08-83   12:00p
         COMMAND     COM     17664     3-08-83   12:00p
         COMP        COM      2523     3-08-83   12:00p
         DISKCOMP    COM      2074     3-08-83   12:00p
```

DISKCOPY	COM	2444	3-08-83	12:00p
EDLIN	COM	4608	3-08-83	12:00p
FDISK	COM	6177	3-08-83	12:00p
FIND	EXE	5888	3-08-83	12:00p
FORMAT	COM	6106	3-08-83	12:00p
GRAPHICS	COM	789	3-08-83	12:00p
MODE	COM	3139	3-08-83	12:00p

- - MORE - -

You press a key.

MORE	COM	384	3-08-83	12:00p
PRINT	COM	4608	3-08-83	12:00p
RECOVER	COM	2304	3-08-83	12:00p
RESTORE	COM	4003	3-08-83	12:00p
SORT	EXE	1280	3-08-83	12:00p
SYS	COM	1408	3-08-83	12:00p
TREE	COM	1513	3-08-83	12:00p

Another way to redesign the directory is to group all the same files together and then list them with the extensions in alphabetical order. To do this you need to know that the extension designation begins in column 10.

A>dir ¦ sort/+10 ¦ more <ENTER>

		25 File[s]	29696 bytes free	
%PIPE1	$$$	0	12-17-84	2:52p
%PIPE2	$$$	0	12-17-84	2:52p
MORE	COM	384	3-08-83	12:00p
GRAPHICS	COM	789	3-08-83	12:00p
ASSIGN	COM	896	3-08-83	12:00p
SYS	COM	1408	3-08-83	12:00p
TREE	COM	1513	3-08-83	12:00p
DISKCOMP	COM	2074	3-08-83	12:00p
RECOVER	COM	2304	3-08-83	12:00p
DISKCOPY	COM	2444	3-08-83	12:00p
COMP	COM	2523	3-08-83	12:00p
MODE	COM	3139	3-08-83	12:00p
BACKUP	COM	3687	3-08-83	12:00p
RESTORE	COM	4003	3-08-83	12:00p
EDLIN	COM	4608	3-08-83	12:00p
PRINT	COM	4608	3-08-83	12:00p
FORMAT	COM	6106	3-08-83	12:00p
FDISK	COM	6177	3-08-83	12:00p
CHKDSK	COM	6400	3-08-83	12:00p
BASIC	COM	16256	3-08-83	12:00p

- - More - -

You press a key.

COMMAND	COM	17664	3-08-83	12:00p
BASICA	COM	25984	3-08-83	12:00p

SORT	EXE	1280	3-08-83	12:00p
FIND	EXE	5888	3-08-83	12:00p
ANSI	SYS	1664	3-08-83	12:00p

Volume in drive A has no label
Directory of A: \

You could SORT by date and/or time, but this is useless. Because SORT is very literal, if it is presented with these three dates:

9-05-80   5-02-83   7-16-82

it would SORT them like this:

5-02-83   7-16-82   9-05-80

In other words, SORT interprets 9-05-80 as greater than 5-02-83, so it puts it at the bottom of the list. As we demonstrated in our "wines" file when we sorted by year, you can successfully use numbers to SORT, but they must run consecutively. You could sort the system diskette by file size.

A>dir ¦ sort/+17 ¦ more <ENTER>

And that concludes our discussion of these useful pipes and filters.

SUMMARY

In this chapter you learned about the various ways to use the redirection, piping, and sort features of MS-DOS. These are skills that will stand you in good stead as you use MS-DOS more and more. The SORT, FIND, and MORE filters are very useful in reorganizing and using your data. The next chapter is for those of you who have a hard disk.

WHAT HAVE WE LEARNED?

1. The keyboard is the standard input device; the screen is the standard output device.
2. The "greater than" and "less than" symbols (> <) are redirect commands; use them to redirect the output of MS-DOS commands to files.
3. The SORT filter sorts the contents of a file in alphabetical or reverse alphabetical order.
4. The FIND filter locates strings of alphanumeric characters within a file.
5. The MORE filter displays the contents of a file, pausing between each screenful.

Quiz for Chapter 10

1. The redirection of output to a device other than the monitor screen is accomplished by following an MS-DOS command with:
   a. the > character followed by a device name or filename.
   b. the >> character followed by a filename that is to be appended with the output information.
   c. either a or b.
   d. none of the above.

2. The redirection of input to an MS-DOS command other than the keyboard is accomplished by following the command with:
   a. the * character.
   b. the < character and a device name or filename.
   c. the \ character.
   d. the ? character.

3. Can both input and output redirection be used at the same time with a command?
   a. Always.
   b. Yes, but an input device or file cannot be the same as the output device or file.
   c. Never.

4. An MS-DOS pipeline is:
   a. an interface between computer and monitor.
   b. a tool used to modify the flow of input and output information to and from MS-DOS commands.
   c. a method of sequencing filenames.

5. An MS-DOS filter is a:
   a. device for filtering "bugs" from your system.
   b. program used to design special filters.
   c. special command designed to modify the input and output generated by other MS-DOS commands.
   d. none of the above.

6. Filters are used in the following ways.
   a. As a filter to another MS-DOS command.
   b. Some filters can be used as regular commands.
   c. As a filter to another MS-DOS command, combined with the use of other filters.
   d. Any of the above.
   e. None of the above.

7. The SORT filter can sort text in a variety of ways from:
   a. a file.
   b. output from another command.
   c. output from another filter.
   d. any of the above.

8. When an MS-DOS command is piped with one or more filters, each command or filter must be separated from another by what character?
   a. |
   b. *
   c. ?
   d. \

9. The | piping separator and the < and > redirection symbols can be used within the same pipe:
   a. always.
   b. if needed, but only if there are no conflicts.
   c. sometimes.
   d. never.

10. The FIND filter is used to search for and display specified text:
  a. found in a file.
  b. found in output from another command.
  c. found in output from another filter.
  d. any of the above.
  e. none of the above.

11. The MORE filter can be used:
  a. as a command to display the contents of a file and pause when the each screen is full.
  b. as a filter to cause displayed text output by another command to pause when the screen is full.
  c. as a filter to cause displayed text output by another filter to pause when the screen is full.
  d. any of the above.
  e. none of the above.

12. The SORT, FIND, and MORE filters can be used together within a single piping operation.
  a. No.
  b. Yes.

For Hard-Disk Users

ABOUT THIS CHAPTER

With the increased use of a computer, the need to expand disk storage space often arises. Hard disks are often considered to be the next logical step to expanding your system's on-line storage capability. Hard disks are particularly useful in cases where large amounts of data are being handled, making the constant changing of floppy diskettes bothersome and time-consuming.

This final chapter is for those of you who have a system with a built-in hard disk. It will give you some helpful pointers on using the commands associated with hard disks, BACKUP and RESTORE. Those of you who are not owners of a hard disk but who are interested in finding out some of its advantages and disadvantages will also benefit from this chapter.

Although you can buy a hard-disk drive as an add-on peripheral to your computer, the installation and operation of these types of units will not be covered in this chapter.

DISK DRIVES

No matter how many books you've read on how to purchase a system or how many articles you've read on why software should dictate your computer type, once you get inside a computer store you may be overwhelmed. The determining factor in your computer selection may come down to which machine is faster, cheaper, has the nicest monitor, the most built-in RAM, or the convenience of a built-in printer. But one thing you may not pay too much attention to is how much storage capacity it has—and storage may be the most important factor in your computer use.

You may have bought a system with only one disk drive. If so, you probably have already discovered that with only one drive, and access to only one floppy at a time, the time spent in storing and retrieving data is a large part of your total time on the system. Most likely, however, you have a system with two floppy disk drives. But whether you have one drive or two, you have come to rely on the 5¼-inch floppy diskette as your storage medium.

FLOPPY DISKETTES

Floppy diskettes are certainly a vast improvement over the tape cartridges used for storage in the early hobbyist computers. Because of their small size, floppies are easy to use, convenient to store, and simple to mail. And because most computer systems use standard-size floppies, they can be used on many types of machines (subject to formatting restrictions, of course). This means that there is a huge market for floppies; consequently, they are relatively inexpensive. But there are a few disadvantages to floppies.

Disadvantages

Because they are often inserted and removed from the drives—and sometimes left around carelessly—they can be easily damaged. And occasionally they do get lost. But with careful handling, floppies perform for us. The two big disadvantages of floppies are that they have a rather limited capacity and they are slow.

Floppy diskettes hold about 200K to 400K bytes of information. That's pretty impressive for a 5¼-inch circle of plastic, but unfortunately, it is nowhere near the amount of storage capacity you need. Early in your computer use you are probably amazed at the number of floppies that you accumulate. As bigger and better programs are put on the market, using many diskettes, they add to your storage problems. And as you fill up diskettes or dedicate certain diskettes to specific programs or data, the problem increases.

Even with their disadvantages, floppy diskettes are still necessary in hard-disk–equipped systems for archiving and backing files and for exchanging data between computers.

For instance, if the word-processing program you use is contained on one diskette, it is usually in drive A. The diskette in drive B holds the text you are working on. This setup works well until you want to use MS-DOS commands or the EDLIN processor or a BASIC program to create specific text or examples. When this situation arises, you have to first exit from the word-processing program, put a system diskette in drive A, put a new "examples" diskette in drive B, perform the operation, get a printout of the results, then reinsert the word-processing and text diskettes and enter the new information. If you want to use a spelling checker contained on two separate diskettes, the process becomes even more complicated.

The second real disadvantage of floppies is that they are slow. You may have noticed, now that you are a more experienced computer user, that most of your computer time is taken up with storing and retrieving data. In fact, preparing and checking diskettes, transferring data between the machine and the diskettes, reading in programs, and copying and erasing files create a real bottleneck in the smooth running of the computer system. Just compare how fast a computer can calculate with how long it takes to format a disk.

Although floppies do serve us well, there is an alternative.

HARD DISKS

Computer designers delight in the challenge of taking things originally created for big machines and adapting them for small machines. This is how Microsoft's MS-DOS began, as an adaptation of an operating system running on a mainframe. This mainframe "environment" is where the concept of tree-structured directories was also born. It is no surprise that hard disks also have come to us via the big computer connection.

Hard disks have been in use in large computer systems for many years. But only with the adaptation of this technology to smaller units were they available as practical storage devices for personal computers. Many personal computer systems use a 10-megabyte hard disk. That means the disks can hold more than 10 million characters, or the equivalent of thirty floppy diskettes. Other comparisons of floppy and hard disks are shown in *Table 11-1.*

A 10-megabyte hard disk (one of the most common sizes) holds up to the equivalent of approximately 10 million characters, which is equivalent to about thirty floppy diskettes.

**Table 11-1.
Floppy Diskettes Versus
Hard Disks**

Floppy Diskette	Hard Disk
Portable	Non-removable
Moderate access speed (250,000 bits/sec)	Fast access speed (5,000,000 bits/sec)
Capacity of 368,640 bytes	Capacity of 10,679,808 bytes
Need many for file storage	All files in one place
Quick backup	Slow backup
Inexpensive	Relatively expensive

Hard disks are so named because they are solid disks, magnetically coated like floppies, and sealed in a container that is never opened. Hard disks are very sensitive to smoke and other forms of damage. Compared with hard disks, floppies are indestructible. For this reason, many hard-disk systems are sealed inside the computer unit where they can never get dirty, never get lost, and never need to reside in smoke-filled rooms. Even when hard disks are not actually located inside the computer, they are still permanently sealed in a protective case.

In some ways it is inconvenient not to be able to get the disk out of the drive. It means that information you want to share must be copied to floppies. And it does make backing up data more inconvenient. But because of its enormous storage capacity, the hard disk more than compensates for its disadvantages.

This capacity means that you can have all your programs and data on tap, almost all the time. Accessing programs and files becomes much simpler. No more inserting and removing diskettes, no more lost information because of unlabeled missing diskettes. This is a real savings in time and frustration.

You don't have to be concerned about running out of room. Even if you manage to fill up your hard disk to its maximum 10-megabyte capacity, you don't need to worry. You can transfer any information on a hard disk to a floppy, simply by using the COPY command. It's not as if you have to go out and buy a new hard disk when you reach 10 megabytes (hard disks are expensive). Information can be transferred from the hard disk to floppies for storage. Of course, you can also put the information from the storage floppies back on the hard disk. This chapter discusses the commands that accomplish these transfers.

The second great thing about hard disks is that they are fast, roughly five times as fast as floppy diskettes. This means that while floppy diskettes have a modern access speed of 250,000 bits/second, hard disks have an amazing access time of 5,000,000 bits/second.

Although hard disks are often considered the ultimate in data storage, many of them are fragile devices and vulnerable to certain environmental conditions. The risk of a hard disk malfunctioning is relatively high, and it is therefore important to regularly back up your data.

Before you start to think that hard disks are all you'll need, let's look at the major disadvantage of hard disks. Surprisingly, the same thing that makes the disk so convenient—all your files in one place—is also a hazard. With all your information stored in one place, you must be doubly diligent about making backups. And backing up files from hard disk files is time-consuming. It can take more than a half hour to copy all the files on a full hard disk to thirty floppies.

You may ask, What's the point in copying to floppies? The reasons why you need backups for files stored on a hard disk are even more compelling than those for floppies. Remember, all you files are in one place, and they are inside the machine. This means that they are vulnerable to power failures or recurring power surges. One of these, and you could lose some or all of the data stored on your hard disk.

The heads that read the information from the disk can cause damage to the disk's surface if dust or dirt gets into the system. Again, you are looking at potential catastrophe. So don't "put all your eggs in one basket"; make backups of your hard-disk files.

HARD-DISK INSURANCE

MS-DOS makes protecting your files easier with two commands, BACKUP and RESTORE. BACKUP is used to copy files from the hard disk to floppies. RESTORE is used to put the files back on the hard disk. Be sure your hard disk is ready to go before you begin using these commands.

Preparing Your Hard Disk

To ease the task of backing up a hard disk, the BACKUP command was included with the MS-DOS operating system.

Before you can actually use your hard disk, it must be installed. This is a complicated process that requires some skill and is best left to your dealer the first time. Part of the installation procedure involves the question of partitioning. Partitioning, as you may expect, means dividing up the hard disk into different areas. This is necessary because the hard disk has a very useful feature. It allows you to use more than one operating system on your system. But just as you can't mix apples and oranges, you can't mix operating systems. This means you can have UNIX or CP/M (two other operating systems) on your diskette. But the instructions for putting these systems on your diskette are specific to each operating system. The question of partitioning is really outside the scope of this book. Full instructions, however, can be found in your specific hard-disk manual or in the part of your user's manual that deals with hard disks. For the purposes of our discussion, we will assume that you or your computer store technician have installed your hard disk with the appropriate partitions. Our discussion will be limited to how to use the hard disk once it is up and running. It's easy to tell if your hard disk is ready. If you try to use it, and it is not operable, you will get this message:

    Invalid drive specification

The BACKUP Command

The BACKUP command provides various options in the way your hard disk is backed up. It can back up the entire hard disk, back up only certain subdirectories, or back up only files that have changed since the last backup operation took place.

The BACKUP program works a lot like the COPY command. That is, it copies the files from one device to the other; in this case, from the hard disk to a floppy. BACKUP has several useful switches that allow you to precisely define the files to be backed up.

You will notice the use of the drive designator C: in some of the examples that follow. This may confuse you. When you use a hard disk, it is generally referred to as the C drive. Most hard-disk systems also include one floppy-disk drive. This floppy is referred to as drive A. We will use these designations when talking about the hard-disk drive. For a further explanation of the use of drive designators with a hard disk see your operations manual.

Using BACKUP follows the same pattern as the COPY command. In response to the DOS prompt A> you first indicate the name of the file (with appropriate slashes if it is not part of the root directory) and then give the letter of the target diskette. You must use the FORMAT to prepare the target diskette before issuing the command. To copy all of the files in FRUITS but not its subdirectories, you enter:

A> backup fruits a: <ENTER>

You do not need to include the initial \ because FRUITS is part of the root directory. All the files in FRUITS are now copied to the floppy disk in drive A.

If you want to copy all the files in FRUITS and include its subdirectories, you must use the /s switch.

A> backup fruits a:/s <ENTER>

This command copies the files in FRUITS ("weather" and "soil") and the contents of the subdirectory CHERRIES (the "yields" file), which is the only subdirectory in FRUITS.

You can also use BACKUP to copy only the files in a subdirectory of a subdirectory. To copy only the contents of FRUITS \ CHERRIES you issue this command:

A> backup fruits \ cherries a: <ENTER>

This copies all of the files in the CHERRIES subdirectory.

Remember, if there are subdirectories in the specified subdirectory and you want them included, you must indicate this by including the /s switch.

This may sound confusing at first. But if you have a copy of the TREE output for your hard disk, it will quickly tell you what files and subdirectories are included in each section of your overall directory.

You may also use the BACKUP command to copy the entire contents of the hard disk (like using *.* to copy all the files on a diskette). When you want to copy all the files and their associated subdirectories on a hard disk you enter this command:

A> backup c: a:/s <ENTER>

With this command you are instructing MS-DOS to copy everything on the hard disk (indicated by the c: drive designator) to the floppy in drive A. Of course, if you have lots of files, you will have to keep inserting new floppies until the entire copying procedure is completed. DOS will prompt you when a new diskette is needed.

To figure out how many formatted diskettes you need to have ready in order to copy the entire hard disk, you can use CHKDSK to find the total number of bytes that you have used. You must then divide the number of bytes by 360,000 (the number of bytes that a floppy can hold) to find out how many floppies are needed. As mentioned earlier, backing up an entire hard disk can be very time-consuming. If you make periodic backups, it is only necessary to back up files you have created since the last backup. This is where the /m and /d switches come in handy.

The /m Switch

The /m option lets you backup only those files that you have modified since the last BACKUP session. This can save you lots of time. Luckily, you don't have to remember the last time you used a file (although you could get this information from the DIR command, but that could take a long time). Built right into the BACKUP program is an internal marker that tells DOS if you have modified a file since your last BACKUP.

This command copies only those files in the \CHERRIES directory and its subdirectories that have been changed since the last BACKUP:

A>backup \cherries a:/s/m <ENTER>

The /d Switch

Another way to back up new and modified files is to use the /d switch. This copies only files that were modified after a certain date. For example, you last backed up your files on August 1, 1984. It is now August 15, 1984. You want to back up any files in the FRUITS directory that were created or modified since that date.

A>backup fruits a:/d:08-01-84 <ENTER>

The /s Switch

If you wanted to back up files created after a specific date and any files that have been modified in any way (not necessarily related to any particular time), you would add the /s switch:

A>fruits a:/d:08-01-84/s <ENTER>

Of course, you can use these switches to copy all modified files on the entire hard disk by using the C: drive designator. But in practice it is probably better to copy modified files in smaller increments, such as subdirectories, so that you can assign certain subdirectories to specific floppies. If you just back up all your files in one move, it may be difficult to find specific files when you want to use the backup for some operation.

The /a Switch

The /a switch tells MS-DOS to add the backup files to any files already on the diskette in the designated drive.

A>backup fruits \ cherries a:/a <ENTER>

If you issue this command, all the files in FRUITS \ CHERRIES will be added to the files on the diskette in drive A. Of course, you need to include this switch only if you want to save the files on the diskette.

If you do not specify this /a switch in the command, MS-DOS will prompt you to insert a formatted diskette. When you do not include /a in the command, all the files on the diskette in the designated drive are erased before any new files are written.

BACKUP conveniently displays the name of the files it is copying. You can get a printout of the files you are backing up by using the control key combination ^P. This is a handy way to document the backup session. If you write the number of the floppy that contains the files on the printout, it can provide a quick reference as to the location of your backup files. A review of the BACKUP command and its switches is provided in *Figure 11-1.*

Figure 11-1.
The BACKUP Command

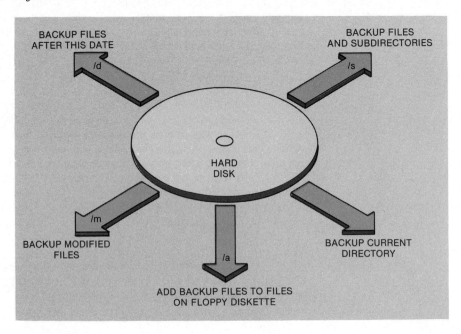

Using Batch Files to Simplify Backup

Your regular backup operation can be greatly enhanced by using a batch file containing the BACKUP command to check for such things as error conditions or to select backup options.

Batch files, which were discussed in Chapter 8, can make the backup procedure easier for you. You will remember that batch files contain MS-DOS commands, and these include the commands used with the hard disk. One of the features of BACKUP is that it sets up an exit code value (a numerical marker that is MS-DOS's version of tying a string to its finger) when it is finished copying. This code ranges from 0 to 4:

0   Indicates that everything was completed normally.
1   Indicates that DOS found no files to backup.
2   For some reason this value is not used.
3   Indicates that the user terminated the backup procedure.
4   Indicates that the backup was terminated by an error.

Glance back to the IF command that was discussed in the batch files section. You will see that IF can be used with ERRORLEVEL to cause a certain action to occur. By using IF in a batch file, you can automate the backup procedure and reduce the chance of making errors when performing backups. Using IF with BACKUP in a batch file is a good example of how useful and rewarding batch files can be. Here is how using ERRORLEVEL might clarify the operations going on in a batch file.

```
copy con: backall.bat
backup c: a/s
if errorlevel 0 echo backall completed
if errorlevel 1 echo backall failure
if errorlevel 3 echo you've terminated backall
if errorlevel 4 echo an error has terminated backall
```

This discussion on backing up your hard disk has accomplished two things: it has impressed upon you the importance of backing up your hard-disk files frequently, and it has demonstrated the ins and outs of the BACKUP command.

Sometimes, when you first read about a command that is unfamiliar to you and has several switches, it may seem like a lot of work. But BACKUP is really nothing more than COPY with a few added flourishes.

The rationale behind backup files is to prepare for the worst, the loss of a file. After you have all your files safely stored away, the next question is how to get them back on the hard disk from the floppies. The answer is the RESTORE command.

The RESTORE command

As a complement to the BACKUP command, the RESTORE command is provided to restore, or retrieve, backed up files from the backup diskettes and store them back on the hard disk.

When you restore something you return it to its original condition, such as restoring furniture (or attempting to restore hair). But "restore" might also mean "store again." Both of these meanings tell you what this command does: it copies back your files from the diskette to the hard disk in the same form as they were when you last backed them up.

You can use RESTORE only with files that have been copied with the BACKUP command. Files that were copied using COPY won't work with this command. You provide the same information in the RESTORE command as you do in BACKUP: the source diskette, the target disk, and the name of the files to be copied. To restore all of the files in the FRUITS directory, you enter this command:

A>restore a: c:fruits <ENTER>

Once again, if you want to copy all the files and any subdirectories in the directory, you must include the /s switch.

A>restore a: c:fruits/s <ENTER>

The RESTORE command can be used in a variety of ways, such as restoring all subdirectories and files, only the current directory, or only certain files.

RESTORE also has another switch, /p. You include /p when you want to see if the files you are restoring have changed since they were last backed up. This prevents you from restoring a copy of the files that does not include recent modifications. (Of course, if you have not made a backup since modifying the file, you are out of luck. This is another good reason to make frequent backups.) Including /p verifies the files to be sure they are the latest version.

A>restore a: c:fruits \ cherries/p <ENTER>

Like the BACKUP command, the RESTORE command can also be placed in a batch file to check for error conditions and to help with the selection of options.

RESTORE can also be used with the IF command and the ERRORLEVEL option when the command is to be included in a batch file. The uses of RESTORE are summarized in *Figure 11-2*.

BACKUP and RESTORE are the only two commands in MS-DOS that are reserved for hard-disk use. You can use all the other MS-DOS commands with your hard disk.

**Figure 11-2.
The RESTORE
Command**

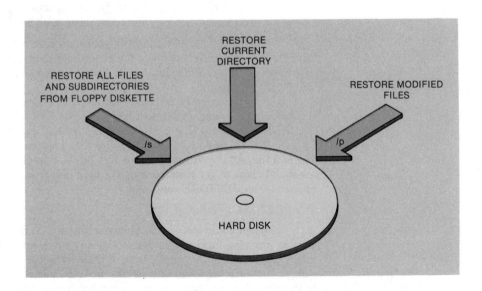

SUMMARY

This chapter presented some of the advantages and disadvantages of hard disks (the former outweigh the latter). You learned how to use the BACKUP and RESTORE commands to transfer files from hard disks to floppies and vice versa.

But once you have mastered the commands and operations presented in this book you will be ready for more advanced books that take you deeper into MS-DOS and build on the information you have learned from this book. One book that explains features and operations that make MS-DOS an even more rewarding tool for managing your files is Sams' *MS-DOS Bible.*

WHAT HAVE WE LEARNED?

1. Hard disk drives include a sealed, built-in disk that holds at least 30 times the information of a floppy disk and allows much faster access.
2. It is very important to back up your hard-disk files onto floppy disks; power failures, power surges, and misalignment can destroy your files or your ability to access them.
3. The BACKUP command copies files from a hard disk to floppy diskettes.
4. Use the /s switch to back up all files and subdirectories.
5. Use the /m switch to back up all files modified since the last backup.
6. Use the /d switch to back up all files modified since a specific date.
7. Use the /a switch to back up files onto a floppy diskette and save any existing files on that floppy diskette.
8. You can create a batch file to automate your backup process.
9. The RESTORE command copies one or more files from floppy diskettes to a hard disk.
10. The RESTORE command has two switches; the /s switch includes all subdirectories in the restoration; the /p switch checks to see if files being restored have been modified since they were last backed up.

Quiz for Chapter 11

1. The advantages of using a hard disk instead of floppy diskettes are that it:
   a. has a higher storage capacity.
   b. stores data faster.
   c. retrieves data faster.
   d. all of the above.

2. A 10-megabyte hard disk is capable of storing:
   a. 500,000 bytes.
   b. 5 million words.
   c. approximately 10 million characters worth of data or the equivalent of about thirty floppy diskettes.
   d. none of the above.

3. Are hard disks more sturdy than floppy diskette drives?
   a. Always.
   b. Never.
   c. Sometimes, depending on type of hard disk and the environmental conditions it is subjected to.
   d. None of the above.

4. Some of the disadvantages of a hard disk are that:
   a. it is relatively expensive.
   b. the more common "fixed" versions are not removable.
   c. it is slow to back up.
   d. all of the above.

5. Compared with the moderate 250,000 bits-per-second access speed of floppy disks, the access speed of hard disks is incredibly fast. What is the average access speed of a hard disk?
   a. 500,000 bits per second.
   b. 1 million bits per second.
   c. 5 million bits per second.
   d. 10 million bits per second.

6. The regular backing up of a hard disk is important because:
   a. the high amount of stored data represents a considerable investment of your time.
   b. many types of hard disks are prone to damage under certain conditions.
   c. the collective amount of time taken to back up a hard disk regularly can be insignificant compared with what can be required to reconstruct the files on a damaged hard disk.
   d. all of the above.

7. The command provided with MS-DOS with the specific purpose of backing up a hard disk is called:
   a. DIR.
   b. BACKUP.
   c. COPY.
   d. TYPE.

8. The BACKUP command can be used in a variety of ways to back up a hard disk, including:
   a. backing up the entire hard disk.
   b. backing up only certain subdirectories.
   c. backing up only files that have changed since the last backup.
   d. backing up only files created or modified after a certain date.
   e. any of the above.
   f. none of the above.

9. To retrieve backed up files from the backup floppy diskettes, what MS-DOS command should be used?
   a. COPY.
   b. CHKDSK.
   c. RESTORE.
   d. DIR.

10. The RESTORE command can be used in various ways, including:
a. restoring all subdirectories and files.
b. restoring only the current directory.
c. restoring only files that haven't been modified since the last backup.
d. any of the above.
e. none of the above.

11. The operation of the BACKUP and RESTORE commands can be enhanced by placing them in batch files that:
a. check for error conditions and act accordingly.
b. provide an easier method of selecting backup or restore options.
c. execute other MS-DOS commands to display information about files and disks.
d. all of the above.
e. none of the above.

Appendix: Error Messages

As with all things you do, you learn to use MS-DOS by doing, by trial and error. No matter how conscientious you are, you will make mistakes. Making mistakes and correcting your mistakes is an effective means of learning.

The designers of MS-DOS make mistakes sometimes. To make things easier, they have documented many of the most common errors. That is why MS-DOS has error messages—to help you correct your mistakes.

There are many types of error messages. Those most frequently encountered are covered in this appendix. There are some messages that are not included. See your user's manual for a complete list of the messages to be found on your computer system.

This appendix divides error messages into two categories. The first covers error messages that refer to devices. The second lists messages that may or may not apply to a device but which refer to MS-DOS commands or MS-DOS itself. The messages are listed in alphabetical order.

DEVICE ERROR MESSAGES

Device error messages are displayed if MS-DOS finds an error when it tries to use a device attached to the computer. These messages have a common format. It's easy to understand the message when you understand the format.

This format has two variations. The first is displayed when MS-DOS has a problem reading (trying to get information from) a device.

> *type* **error reading** *device*
> **Abort, Retry, Ignore?**

The second variation is displayed when MS-DOS has a problem writing (trying to put information on) a device.

> *type* **error writing** *device*
> **Abort, Retry, Ignore?**

Type defines the nature of this specific error and will vary with each instance. *Device* refers to the piece of hardware involved in the error, such as a disk drive or a printer.

The second line of our format offers you three options to recover from the error: abort, retry, ignore. MS-DOS is waiting for you to enter one of these options from the keyboard.

Before responding, check the obvious causes for the error. For instance, if the error concerns a disk drive, you may have left the door open or failed to insert the correct diskette. If the error indicates trouble with the printer, you may need to turn on the power or insert paper.

When you have checked all obvious causes, enter one of the three options:

R (Retry)   Causes MS-DOS to try to perform the command or message again. This sometimes works even if you have not adjusted anything because the error might be minor and may not recur on the next try.

A (Abort)   Causes MS-DOS to stop the operation in progress. You should enter this response if **R** fails to correct the error.

I (Ignore)   Causes MS-DOS to retry the operation but ignore any errors it may encounter. It is not recommended that you use this response because it can result in losing data being read or written.

The following messages are those that might appear in the *type* section of the error message.

Bad call format: A driver is a part of the operating system that controls a specific input/output device, for instance, a modem or printer. Each driver has specific codes in MS-DOS. One such identifier is a length request header. This message means an incorrect length request header was sent to the driver for the specified drive. Consult your dealer.

Bad command: The command issued to a device is invalid.

Bad unit: An incorrect sub-unit number (driver code) was sent to the driver for the specified drive. Consult your dealer (See "Bad call format.")

Data: An error was detected while reading or writing data. Use CHKDSK to see if your diskette has a defective area.

Disk: After three tries, a disk read or write error is still occurring. You may have inserted the wrong type of diskette (single-sided diskette in a double-sided drive) or your diskette may be inserted incorrectly. If neither is true, you may have a bad diskette. If you receive this message, try the standard corrective procedures before removing the diskette. You may be able to salvage the data on the diskette.

File allocation table bad, drive d: This message always refers to a specific disk drive. It tells you that the file allocation table (FAT) on the indicated drive is faulty. If you receive this error frequently, the diskette is probably defective.

No paper: This is an easy one to solve. There isn't any paper in your printer or the printer is not turned on. Correct the problem and press R.

Non-DOS disk: There is invalid data on the allocation table of the specified diskette in the indicated device. The diskette needs to be reformatted or the entire diskette may be wiped out.

Not ready: The device is not ready to read or write data. This may mean that the power is not turned on, the drive door is not closed, or there is no diskette in the indicated drive.

Read fault: For some reason the device cannot receive or transmit data. The power may not be on, the drive may not contain a diskette, or the device is not properly configured for MS-DOS use.

Sector not found: The sector holding the data you want cannot be located. The diskette may be defective, or you may be using a single-sided diskette in a double-sided drive.

Seek error: MS-DOS cannot locate the proper track on the diskette in the indicated drive.

Write fault: For some reason the device cannot receive or transmit data. The power may not be on, the drive may not contain a diskette, or the device is not properly configured for MS-DOS use.

Write protect: You have instructed MS-DOS to write to a diskette that is write-protected (either temporarily by you or permanently by the manufacturer). Either insert a new diskette or remove the write-protect tab from this diskette (be sure you want to write to it first). If there is no write-protect notch, you are out of luck.

ADDITIONAL ERROR MESSAGES

This is not a complete listing of all other error messages that may be received from MS-DOS. Check your system manual if you cannot locate the message among the device error messages or in this section.

Some error messages are associated with a specific command. When this is the case, the command has been written following the error message.

All specified file(s) are contiguous: CHKDSK. All the files that you requested to write are on the diskette sequentially.

Allocation error, size adjusted: CHKDSK. There was an invalid sector number in the file allocation table. The indicated filename was truncated at the end of the previous good sector.

Attempted write-protect violation: FORMAT. You attempted to FORMAT a write-protected diskette. Remove the diskette and insert a new one.

Bad command or filename: You entered the command or filename incorrectly. Check the spelling and punctuation and make sure the command or file you specified is on the diskette in the indicated drive. You may be calling an external command from a diskette that does not contain the command.

Cannot edit .BAK file—rename file: To protect your data, you cannot access a backup file that has a .BAK extension. Rename the file using REN, or copy the file, giving it a new name.

Cannot load COMMAND, system halted: While attempting to load the command processor, MS-DOS found that the area in which it keeps track of available memory is destroyed. Try booting MS-DOS again.

Contains XXX non-contiguous blocks: CHKDSK. The indicated file has been written in sections on different areas on the diskette (rather than in sequential blocks). Since fragmented files take longer to read, it is probably best to copy the file sequentially.

Disk boot failure: While trying to load MS-DOS, an error was encountered. If this continues, use a backup MS-DOS diskette.

Disk error writing FAT x: CHKDSK. There was a disk error while CHKDSK was trying to update the FAT on the indicated drive. X will be a 1 or a 2, depending on which of the allocation tables could not be written. If both allocation tables are indicated, the diskette is unusable.

Duplicate filename or file not found: RENAME. The name you indicated in a RENAME command already exists on the diskette, or the file to be renamed is not on the diskette in the specified drive.

Entry error: EDLIN. Your last command contains a syntax error.

Error loading operating system: An error was encountered while MS-DOS was trying to load from the fixed (hard) disk. If the problem persists, load MS-DOS from a diskette and use SYS to copy MS-DOS to the fixed disk.

File cannot be copied onto itself: You tried to give an already existing filename to a new file in the same directory.

File not found: The file named in a command parameter could not be found, or the command could not be found on the specified drive.

Incorrect DOS version: You attempted to run an MS-DOS command that requires a different version of MS-DOS. This should occur only when you are using MS-DOS Version 1.0 or 1.1 and attempt to use a command found only in MS-DOS Version 2.0 or later.

Insufficient disk space: There is not enough free space on the diskette to hold the file you are writing. If you think there should be enough space, use CHKDSK to get a diskette status report.

Intermediate file error during pipe: This message may mean that the intermediate files created during a piping procedure cannot be accommodated on the diskette because the default drive's root directory is full. Your diskette may also be too full to hold the data being piped, or the piping files cannot be located on the diskette.

Invalid COMMAND.COM in drive d: While trying to reload the command processor, MS-DOS found that the copy of COMMAND.COM on the diskette is a different version. Insert a diskette containing the correct version of MS-DOS.

Invalid directory: One of the directories in the specified pathname does not exist.

Invalid number of parameters: The specified number of parameters does not agree with the number required by the command.

Label not found: GOTO #. You have named a label in a GOTO command that does not exist in the batch file. Use EDLIN to review GOTO and make sure all GOTO statements contain valid labels.

No room for system on diskette: SYS. The specified diskette does not contain the required reserved space for the system. (Is the system already on the diskette?) You can solve this problem by using FORMAT/s to format a new diskette and then copying your files to this diskette.

Syntax error: The command was entered incorrectly. Check the format.

Terminate batch job (Y/N)?: You have pressed <Ctrl> <Break> or <Ctrl> C during the processing of a batch file. Press Y to end processing. Press N to stop the command that was executing when you pressed <Ctrl> <Break> or <Ctrl> C; processing will continue with the next command.

Glossary

86-DOS: The name of the operating system developed by Seattle Computer Products on which MS-DOS is based.

ANSI: An abbreviation for American National Standards Institute, an organization that has developed many standards for computer programming languages. Aspects of an ANSI screen-control standard were introduced in MS-DOS Version 2.00.

ASCII: An abbreviation for American Standard Code for Information Interchange, used to define the characters that are input (typed) and output (displayed) on most computers, including those with MS-DOS.

Allocation Space: The smallest number of magnetic disk sectors a file or a part of a file can occupy.

BIOS: An acronym for Basic Input/Output System, a component of the MS-DOS operating system that handles all input and output of devices attached to the computer.

Backing Up: A term used to denote the archiving or duplication of computer data stored on various types of storage media.

Batch: A computer process that automatically feeds commands to the computer one at time from a file created by the user (called a batch file.).

Binary Code: A pattern of binary digits (0 and 1) used to represent information such as numbers or instructions to a computer.

Bit: An abbreviation for binary digit; the smallest piece of binary information; a specification of one of two possible alternatives.

Boot: The process of loading the operating system software after the computer has been powered up or reset.

Byte: A group of 8 bits treated as a unit. Often equivalent to one alphabetic or numeric character.

CRT: An acronym for cathode-ray tube, the primary element in a computer monitor, which projects information on the screen.

Character: Any alphabetic, numeric, or symbolic character capable of being typed into or displayed by a computer.

Chip: A common word used to mean integrated circuit. The term was introduced because the first integrated circuits were fabricated using silicon chips.

Command Processor: The part of an operating system that processes commands entered by the user. The command processor in MS-DOS is contained in a file called COMMAND.COM.

CPU: An acronym for central processing unit, the brain of a computer.

Cursor: The blinking or solid object displayed on monitors to denote the position on screen where the next character will appear when typed by the user or output by the computer.

DOS: An acronym for disk operating system, the term given to any operating system designed for use in microcomputers equipped with magnetic storage disks.

Data Base: A collection of data elements stored in a file and organized in such a way so as to facilitate the retrieval and update of data.

Directory: A list of files stored on a magnetic disk.

External Command: A term specific to DOS operating systems to denote a command stored in a file. In MS-DOS, external commands are stored in files, whereas built-in commands are stored within the operating system itself.

FAT: An acronym for file allocation table, a portion of a magnetic disk used by MS-DOS to store a file-storage map showing which parts of a disk are allocated to what file or part of a file.

File: A collection of data stored under a given name on a magnetic disk; a means of separating collections of data from each other on a disk.

Filter: A mechanism in MS-DOS that is used in conjunction with a command to change the characteristics of data being processed.

Fixed Disk: A hard disk that is not removable.

Format: A term used to denote how data are arranged. Most commonly, it refers to how the characteristics of a magnetic storage disk are arranged, such as tracks, sectors, file allocation table, and directory.

I/O: An abbreviation for input/output.

Input: The act of delivering information to a computer, such as typing on a keyboard.

Integrated Circuit: A circuit whose connections and components are fabricated into one structure on a certain material, such as silicon.

Interface: The link between two components of a computer, such as a disk drive and the computer, or a printer and the computer. Often used to denote the means by which the user and the computer communicate (called the user interface).

Internal Command: A command that is contained within the operating system itself. In MS-DOS, all built-in commands are actually stored in the file called COMMAND.COM.

Kilobyte: 1024 bytes. Often expressed as K (2048 bytes = 2K, or 2 kilobytes).

MS-DOS: An acronym for Microsoft Disk Operating System.

Memory: The part of the computer other than disk storage media that is used for the temporary or permanent storage of data that are to be retrieved or manipulated by the computer.

Microcomputer: A computer that has its central processor unit (CPU) contained in a microprocessor integrated circuit.

Microprocessor: An integrated circuit that contains a complete central processing unit (CPU).

Modem: An abbreviation for modulator/demodulator; used for the transmission and reception of computer data over telephone lines.

Monitor: A computer display device, with or without a keyboard, monochrome or color, capable either of displaying only characters or of displaying graphics and characters.

Nibble: Half a byte or four bits. Used in computer programming to separate the upper four bits of a byte from the lower four bits.

Non-Volatile Memory: Memory that is not erased when power is turned off.

Output: Information that is generated by a computer, such as information displayed on a monitor.

Parallel: A term commonly used to denote the sending, receiving, or processing of data bits in parallel. For example, a "parallel interface" contains eight wires enabling the transmission of eight bits simultaneously.

Path: Indicates the series of subdirectories (route) needed to reach a given subdirectory or file. Used in MS-DOS Version 2.00 and higher versions only.

Piping: The process of channeling data input or output by command when used in conjunction with a filter.

Port: A part of a computer used to communicate with another device; usually contains a special interface and can handle input only, output only, or both input and output data according to the nature of the interface.

RAM: An acronym for random-access memory, a series of integrated-circuit memory devices used by a computer to temporarily store information that is to be processed. RAM is fully erased when power is removed from the system, except in some systems that contain RAM powered by batteries.

ROM: An acronym for read-only memory, an integrated circuit that contains permanent data that can be retrieved at any time by the computer. ROM is not erased when the computer's power is turned off.

RS-232: A serial communications interface standard commonly used to send and receive data to and from other devices such as other computers, modems, and printers.

Redirection: The process of directing output generated by a command to a file or device instead of the normal output destination. Input to a command (normally the keyboard) can also be redirected so that it comes from a file or another command.

Root: The main, or master, directory on a disk, from which all subdirectories originate.

Sector: A division along a track of a magnetic storage disk. According to how floppy diskettes are formatted under MS-DOS, each track of a diskette can contain eight, nine, or fifteen sectors, or divisions, per track.

Serial: A term commonly used to denote the sending, receiving, or processing of data bits successively, one bit at a time.

String: A collective stream of consecutive bits, bytes, characters, or words.

Subdirectory: A directory that originates from another directory (the root directory or another subdirectory). Subdirectories branch out from other directories much like the branches of a tree.

Track: A circular one-bit-wide path on a magnetic storage disk on which data are stored. A magnetic disk contains a series of concentric tracks between the outer and inner edges. Floppy diskettes used with MS-DOS can have either forty or eighty tracks.

Volatile Memory: Memory that is erased when power is turned off.

Write-Protection: A method of preventing the storing of new data on a magnetic storage disk, thereby preventing the erasure of existing data. Under MS-DOS, specific files or entire floppy diskettes can be write-protected.

Index

Answers to Quizzes

Chapter 1

1. a
2. d
3. a
4. e
5. b
6. c
7. a
8. c
9. a
10. d
11. d
12. e
13. e
14. b
15. a and b
16. d
17. a and b
18. d

Chapter 2

1. e
2. d
3. a
4. b
5. c
6. a
7. c
8. a
9. a
10. a
11. d

Chapter 3

1. b
2. b
3. e
4. g
5. b
6. c
7. c
8. e
9. a
10. c

11. c
12. b
13. c
14. b
15. e

Chapter 4

1. a
2. b
3. a
4. d
5. a
6. e
7. b
8. b
9. e
10. d

Chapter 5

1. b
2. c
3. a
4. b
5. b
6. c
7. a
8. b
9. d
10. a
11. c
12. d
13. e
14. a
15. b
16. a
17. b
18. a
19. b

Chapter 6

1. e
2. b
3. e
4. c

5. a
6. b
7. a
8. d
9. d
10. b
11. a

Chapter 7

1. f
2. d
3. a
4. b
5. a
6. f
7. e
8. c
9. a or b
10. b
11. a
12. c
13. d
14. a
15. a and b
16. d

Chapter 8

1. d
2. b
3. d
4. a
5. b
6. b
7. c
8. d
9. c
10. b
11. c
12. d
13. a and b
14. c
15. c

Chapter 9

1. d
2. b
3. a
4. b
5. c
6. a
7. d
8. c
9. b
10. a
11. c
12. b
13. b
14. c

Chapter 10

1. c
2. b
3. b
4. b
5. c
6. d
7. d
8. a
9. b
10. d
11. d
12. b

Chapter 11

1. d
2. c
3. c
4. d
5. c
6. d
7. b
8. e
9. c
10. d
11. d

HOWARD W. SAMS & COMPANY
HAYDEN BOOKS

Related Titles

The Waite Group's MS-DOS® Bible, Second Edition
Steven Simrin

The Waite Group's MS-DOS® Developer's Guide, Revised Edition
John Angermeyer and Kevin Jaeger

The Waite Group's Tricks of the MS-DOS® Masters
John Angermeyer, Rich Fahringer, Kevin Jaeger, and Dan Shafer

The Waite Group's Discovering MS-DOS®
Kate O'Day

The Waite Group's MS-DOS® Papers
The Waite Group

Understanding Expert Systems
Louis E. Frenzel, Jr.

Understanding Artificial Intelligence, Second Edition
Dan Shafer

Understanding C
Carl Townsend

Understanding Communications Systems, Second Edition
Don L. Cannon and Gerald Luecke

Understanding Computer Science Applications
Roger S. Walker

Understanding Data Communications, Second Edition
Revised by Gil Held

Understanding HyperTalk™
Dan Shafer

Understanding Local Area Networks
Stan Schatt

Understanding Microprocessors, Second Edition
Don L. Cannon and Gerald Luecke

Understanding Microsoft® Windows 2.0
Katherine Stuart Ewing

Understanding WordPerfect®, Version 5.0
Vincent Alfieri

For the retailer nearest you, or to order directly from the publisher, call 800-428-SAMS. In Indiana, Alaska, and Hawaii call 317-298-5699.

MORE
FROM
SAMS

☐ The Best Book of: dBASE II®/III®

Ken Knecht
Written in an enjoyable, conversational style, this book
describes how to detect and correct errors, sort files,
create new and useful programs, and manipulate data.
A time-saving guide for getting the most out of dBASE
II and dBASE III and applying these systems to specific
business needs.
ISBN: 0-672-22349-X, $21.95

☐ The Best Book of: Framework™

Alan Simpson
Practical examples and applications help you get the
most from Framework's frames, word processor,
spreadsheet, and other features. Learn how to access
national information systems; how to interface with
WordStar®, dBASE II®/III®, and Lotus® 1-2-3®; how to
use Framework macros; and how to program with
Fred™, Framework's programming language.
ISBN: 0-672-22421-6, $21.95

☐ Discovering MS-DOS®

Kate O'Day, The Waite Group
A comprehensive study of MS-DOS commands such as
DEBUG, LINK, and EDLIN is given the unique Waite
touch. The author begins with general information
about operating systems, then shows you how to use
MS-DOS to produce letters and documents; create,
name, and manipulate files; use the keyboard and
function keys to perform jobs faster; and direct, sort,
and find data quickly.
ISBN: 0-672-22407-0, $19.95

☐ MS-DOS® Developer's Guide

John Angermeyer and Kevin Jaeger, The Waite Group
This useful guide is written expressly for programmers
who want to learn tricks for getting their software
running in the MS-DOS environment. Included are
assembly coding tips, explanations of the differences
among MS-DOS versions 1.1, 2.1, and 3.1, and between
MS-DOS and IBM® PC-DOS™.
ISBN: 0-672-22409-7, $24.95

☐ CP/M® Bible: The Authoritative Reference Guide to CP/M

Mitchell Waite and John Angermeyer, The Waite Group
Already a classic, this highly detailed reference manual
puts CP/M's commands and syntax at your fingertips.
Instant one-stop access to all CP/M keywords,
commands, utilities, and conventions are found in this
easy-to-use format.
ISBN: 0-672-22015-6, $19.95

☐ CP/M® Primer (2nd Edition)

Mitchell Waite and Stephen Murtha, The Waite Group
This tutorial companion to the *CP/M Bible* includes the
details of CP/M terminology, operation, capabilities, and
internal structure, plus a convenient tear-out reference
card with CP/M commands. This revised edition allows
you to begin using new or old CP/M versions
immediately in any application.
ISBN: 0-672-22170-5, $16.95

☐ Soul of CP/M®: How to Use the Hidden Power of Your CP/M System

Mitchell Waite and Robert Lafore, The Waite Group
Recommended for those who have read the *CP/M
Primer* or who are otherwise familiar with CP/M's outer
layer utilities. This companion volume teaches you how
to use and modify CP/M's internal features, including
how to modify BIOS and use CP/M system calls in your
own programs.
ISBN: 0-672-22030-X, $19.95

☐ Modem Connections Bible
Carolyn Curtis and Daniel L. Majhor, The Waite Group
Describes modems, how they work, and how to hook 10 well-known modems to 9 name-brand microcomputers. A handy Jump Table shows where to find the connection diagram you need and applies the illustrations to 11 more computers and 7 additional modems. Also features an overview of communications software, a glossary of communications terms, an explanation of the RS-232C interface, and a section on troubleshooting.
ISBN: 0-672-22446-1, $16.95

☐ Printer Connections Bible
Kim G. House and Jeff Marble, The Waite Group
At last, a book that includes extensive diagrams specifying exact wiring, DIP-switch settings and external printer details; a Jump Table of assorted printer/computer combinations; instructions on how to make your own cables; and reviews of various printers and how they function.
ISBN: 0-672-22406-2, $16.95

☐ Using Your IBM® Personal Computer
Lon Poole
From system setup, through the use of commercial software, to writing your own programs, this book teaches you graphic screen displays, music, sound effects, and how to store and use them. Extensive tables, illustrations, sample programs, and appendices round out this essential tool for the PC user.
ISBN: 0-672-22000-8, $16.95

☐ Microsoft® Word for the IBM PC
Philip Lieberman and Phillip Gioe
This easy-to-follow text, containing hundreds of screen illustrations, provides a thorough, hands-on exploration of this word-processing package. It even includes a disk that saves typing time and lets you work through specific examples. The book shows you how to enter, revise, format, and print text and gives all the shortcuts and advanced techniques for print merging, speed formatting, style sheets, and multiple windows. Based on Version 2.0.
ISBN: 0-672-22348-1, $29.95

☐ Managing with dBASE III®
Michael J. Clifford
Learn to use such dBASE III features as memo and date fields, filters, and paths, the new PICTURE and RANGE statements, and the SET RELATION TO method of linking files. The book also gives programming strategies for using dBASE III to control inventory, manage accounts payable and receivable, update client files, and produce business graphics.
ISBN: 0-672-22455-0, $22.95

☐ C Primer Plus, Revised Edition
Mitchell Waite, Stephen Prata, and Donald Martin, The Waite Group
It's Waite at his best. Provides a clear and complete introduction to the C programming language. Interfacing C with assembly language is included, as well as many sample programs usable with any standard C compiler.
ISBN: 0-672-22582-4, $24.95

☐ MS-DOS® Bible, Second Edition
Steven Simrin
The second in the Waite Group's MS-DOS series helps intermediate users explore this operating system's capabilities from system start-up to creating, editing and managing files, handling data, and customizing the keyboard. Includes detailed coverage of the tree-structured directories, DOS filters, and the DEBUG, LINK, and EDLIN commands.
ISBN: 0-672-22617-0, $22.95

☐ IBM® PC Troubleshooting & Repair Guide   *Robert C. Brenner*
Repair your IBM PC yourself, simply and inexpensively. Troubleshooting flowcharts help you diagnose and remedy the probable cause of failure. A final chapter on advanced troubleshooting shows the more adventuresome how to perform complex repairs. Some knowledge of electronics required.
ISBN: 0-672-22358-9, $19.95

☐ 8088 Assembler Language Programming: The IBM® PC   *David C. Willen and Jeffrey I. Krantz*
This book is your comprehensive introduction to writing machine language software for the IBM PC. It functionally describes the 8088 microprocessor and furnishes detailed information about the PC's internal structure. Some programming experience is required.
ISBN: 0-672-22400-3, $16.95

MORE
FROM
SAMS

☐ **Interfacing to the IBM® Personal Computer** *Lewis C. Eggebrecht*
The IBM PC's open architecture lends itself to external device interfacing. Learn from the lead designer and architect of the IBM PC how to exploit this capability. Includes design tips and examples, many subroutines for interfacing, and BASIC programs to explain interfacing functions.
ISBN: 0-672-22027-X, $16.95

☐ **Understanding Artificial Intelligence**
Henry C. Mishkoff
This book provides an introduction and basic understanding of this new technology. The book covers definitions, history, expert systems, natural language processing, and LISP machines.
ISBN: 0-672-27021-8, $17.95

☐ **Understanding Automation Systems (2nd Edition)**
Robert F. Farwell and Neil M. Schmitt
For the newcomer, here is an in-depth look at the functions that make up automation systems—open loop, closed loop, continuous and semi-continuous process, and discrete parts. This book explains programmable systems and how to use micro-computers and programmable controllers.
ISBN: 0-672-27014-5, $17.95

☐ **Understanding Automotive Electronics (2nd Edition)**
William B. Ribbens and Norman P. Mansour
This book begins with automotive and electronic fundamentals—prior knowledge is not necessary. It explains how the basic electronic functions, including programmable microprocessors and microcomputers, are applied for drive train control, motion control and instrumentation. Illustrations clarify mechanical and electrical principles.
ISBN: 0-672-27017-X, $17.95

☐ **Understanding Computer Science Applications** *Roger S. Walker*
This book discusses basic computer concepts and how computers communicate with their input/output units and with each other by using parallel communications, serial communications, and computer networking.
ISBN: 0-672-27020-X, $17.95

☐ **Understanding Communications Systems (2nd Edition)**
Don L. Cannon and Gerald Luecke
This book explores many of the systems that are used every day—AM/FM radio, telephone, TV, data communications by computer, facsimile, and satellite. It explains how information is converted into electrical signals, transmitted to distant locations, and converted back to the original information.
ISBN: 0-672-27270-9, $17.95

☐ **Understanding Computer Science (2nd Edition)** *Roger S. Walker*
Here is an in-depth look at how people use computers to solve problems. This book covers the fundamentals of hardware and software, programs and languages, input and output, data structures and resource management.
ISBN: 0-672-27011-0, $17.95

☐ **Understanding Data Communications (2nd Edition)** *John L. Fike et al.*
Understand the codes used for data communications, the types of messages, and the transmissions channels—including fiber optics and satellites. Learn how asynchronous modems work and how they interface to the terminal equipment. Find out about protocols, error control, local area and packet networks.
ISBN: 0-672-27019-6, $17.95

☐ **Understanding Digital Electronics (2nd Edition)** *Gene W. McWhorter*
Learn why digital circuits are used. Discover how AND, OR, and NOT digital circuits make decisions, store information, and convert information into electronic language. Find out how digital integrated circuits are made and how they are used in microwave ovens, gasoline pumps, video games, and cash registers.
ISBN: 0-672-27013-7, $17.95

☐ Understanding Digital Troubleshooting
(2nd Edition) *Don L. Cannon*
This book presents the basic principles and
troubleshooting techniques required to begin digital
equipment repair and maintenance. The book begins
with overviews of digital system fundamentals, digital
system functions, and troubleshooting fundamentals. It
continues with detecting problems in combinational
logic, sequential logic, memory, and I/O.
ISBN: 0-672-27015-3, $17.95

☐ Understanding Microprocessors
(2nd Edition) *Don L. Cannon and Gerald Luecke*
This book provides insight into basic concepts and
fundamentals. It explains actual applications of 4-bit,
8-bit and 16-bit microcomputers, software, programs,
programming concepts, and assembly language. The
book provides an individualized learning format for the
newcomer who wants to know what microprocessors
are, what they do, and how they work.
ISBN: 0-672-27010-2, $17.95

☐ Understanding Solid State Electronics
(4th Edition)
William E. Hafford and Gene W. McWhorter
This book explains complex concepts such as
electricity, semiconductor theory, how electronic
circuits make decisions, and how integrated circuits are
made. It helps you develop a basic knowledge of
semiconductors and solid-state electronics. A glossary
simplifies technical terms.
ISBN: 0-672-27012-9, $17.95

☐ Understanding Telephone Electronics
(2nd Edition) *John L. Fike and George E. Friend*
This book explains how the conventional telephone
system works and how parts of the system are
gradually being replaced by state-of-the-art electronics.
Subjects include speech circuits, dialing, ringing,
central office electronics, microcomputers, digital
transmission, network transmission, modems, and new
cellular phones.
ISBN: 0-672-27018-8, $17.95

Look for these Sams Books at your local bookstore.

To order direct, call 800-428-SAMS or fill out the form below.

- -

Please send me the books whose titles and numbers I have listed below.

_____   Name *(please print)* _____

_____   Address _____

_____   City _____

_____   State/Zip _____

_____   Signature _____
                                                (required for credit card purchases)

Enclosed is a check or money order for $ _____
Include $2.50 postage and handling.

All states add local sales tax.   Mail to: Howard W. Sams & Co.

Charge my: ☐ VISA ☐ MC ☐ AE
Account No. _____ Expiration Date _____

☐☐☐☐ ☐☐☐☐ ☐☐☐☐ ☐☐☐☐   ☐☐☐☐

DC074